JEAN BAUDRILLARD

THE THINKERS, Volume 1

Andrew Parry

Published by Andrew Parry, 2024.

While every precaution has been taken in the preparation of this book, the publisher assumes no responsibility for errors or omissions, or for damages resulting from the use of the information contained herein.

JEAN BAUDRILLARD

First edition. September 16, 2024.

ISBN: 979-8224175895

Written by Andrew Parry.

Table of Contents

The Life and Times of Jean Baudrillard

Jean Baudrillard, born on July 27, 1929, in the French town of Reims, was one of the most influential intellectuals of the 20th century. His work challenged conventional understandings of reality, media, and society, inspiring deep contemplation about the world we inhabit and how we perceive it. Baudrillard was more than a philosopher; he was a cultural critic who dared to push the boundaries of thought, merging sociology, philosophy, and media theory into a radical analysis of the modern world. His journey from a modest background to becoming one of postmodernism's central figures is as fascinating as the ideas he championed.

Baudrillard's early life was shaped by his experience growing up in a relatively poor family. His parents were civil servants, and his upbringing was far removed from the intellectual circles he would later enter. He was the first in his family to attend university, studying German at the Sorbonne, a decision that exposed him to critical and philosophical thought. After a brief period teaching German in high school, Baudrillard transitioned into sociology, where he began his academic career that would forever change his intellectual trajectory. His exposure to existentialists like Jean-Paul Sartre and structuralists like Roland Barthes helped shape his early thinking, but he would soon distance himself from these frameworks to carve out his own path.

Baudrillard's early academic work was deeply engaged with Marxist theory, particularly the ways in which capitalist societies function. However, as he continued his intellectual journey, he became increasingly disillusioned with traditional Marxism, which he felt was inadequate to explain the rapidly changing dynamics of media and consumerism. The industrial age, dominated by the production of goods, had given way to a post-industrial society where images and symbols became the primary commodities. This shift from production to simulation, from the real to the hyperreal, became a central theme in Baudrillard's work. He argued that in contemporary society, the lines between reality and fiction had blurred to the point where they were indistinguishable. In this hyperreal world, simulations replaced the real, and media became the dominant force shaping our perceptions.

By the 1970s, Baudrillard was moving away from traditional sociological analysis and developing his own conceptual framework. It was during this period that he wrote some of his most influential works, including *Simulacra and Simulation* (1981). This text remains one of his most famous contributions, exploring how society has moved beyond the real into a world of signs and simulations. Baudrillard described how images, initially based on reality, began to replace and ultimately outdo reality itself. He famously used the concept of the simulacrum, which is a copy without an original. In the age of media saturation, Baudrillard argued, reality was no longer distinguishable from its representation. This provocative idea, that the representation could eclipse the real, would become a cornerstone of his critique of contemporary society.

Baudrillard's philosophy wasn't only theoretical; it had tangible connections to cultural phenomena. His work gained mainstream recognition when the Wachowskis referenced *Simulacra and Simulation* in their ground-breaking film *The Matrix* (1999). The movie's exploration of a simulated reality, where individuals are trapped in a virtual world without knowing it, was a direct nod to Baudrillard's ideas.

In fact, a scene in the film shows a character hiding a computer disk in a hollowed-out copy of Baudrillard's book. Though Baudrillard himself later remarked that the film misrepresented his ideas, the connection helped introduce his work to a broader audience, sparking interest in his complex theories of media, technology, and reality.

Despite his increasing fame, Baudrillard remained skeptical of the very media attention he received. He criticized how intellectuals, including himself, were often co-opted by the same media machines they sought to critique. He believed that the media didn't convey ideas but rather reduced them to soundbites, simplifying complex philosophical thoughts into digestible pieces. This critique of media extended to his views on politics, especially how modern politics had become a spectacle, where images of power mattered more than the power itself. He described events like the Gulf War and later conflicts as "virtual wars," staged for public consumption, where the reality of suffering and destruction was mediated and thus distorted by the television screen.

Baudrillard's later life saw him delving deeper into the themes of technology and globalization. He wrote extensively about how the digital age was accelerating the process of simulation, as social media and digital communication became new layers of hyper reality. His work continued to evolve, but he remained consistent in his skepticism of progress narratives. For Baudrillard, the modern world's obsession with advancement was not necessarily a path toward enlightenment but a further descent into artificiality.

His work often led to him being misunderstood as nihilistic or overly pessimistic, yet Baudrillard did not simply believe in the hopelessness of the human condition. Instead, he sought to expose the illusions we construct and the systems we take for granted. By deconstructing these illusions, Baudrillard encouraged a more reflective and critical engagement with the world. His writing, though complex, aimed to provoke thought and challenge the status quo, urging readers to see beyond the surface of things.

Jean Baudrillard passed away on March 6, 2007, leaving behind a body of work that continues to provoke, inspire, and challenge thinkers across various disciplines. His ideas remain relevant in an age dominated by media, technology, and simulations. Whether one agrees with his conclusions or not, Baudrillard's contribution to the intellectual landscape is undeniable. He raised profound questions about reality, culture, and the ways we understand the world around us. Through his work, Baudrillard invited us to question the fabric of our reality and, in doing so, changed the way we think about society, media, and ourselves.

In the end, Baudrillard's life and ideas present a compelling narrative of intellectual exploration. His journey from a small-town upbringing to becoming one of the most significant postmodern thinkers is a testament to his relentless curiosity and critical engagement with the world. His legacy endures, encouraging future generations to question what is real and what is merely a simulation.

The Evolution of Baudrillard's Thought

Jean Baudrillard's intellectual journey can be traced through the evolution of his thought, which reflects his continuous re-evaluation of the world around him. What makes Baudrillard's ideas so distinctive is his ability to critique society through various lenses—beginning with a Marxist framework, then moving toward a more radical exploration of media, technology, and reality itself. His theories are not just academic exercises but also cultural critiques that challenge us to think more deeply about how we construct and experience reality. To understand Baudrillard's intellectual evolution, it's essential to explore the different phases of his thinking, each representing a deepening complexity in his views on society, technology, and the human experience.

Baudrillard began his career with a strong foundation in sociology, drawing heavily on Marxist theory. In the 1960s, his work was influenced by Marx's critique of capitalism and its effects on human life. Like many intellectuals of his time, Baudrillard was concerned with the alienation of the individual within a capitalist system that prioritized profit and production over human well-being. However, unlike traditional Marxists who focused on labor and class struggle, Baudrillard's attention was already shifting toward the world of symbols, commodities, and consumer culture. His early works, such as *The System of Objects* (1968) and *The Consumer Society* (1970), analyze how consumerism and the rise of mass-produced goods began to shape not only economic systems but also culture and identity.

In these early texts, Baudrillard examined how objects in modern society were no longer valued for their utility but for their ability to signify status, lifestyle, and identity. For Baudrillard, this represented a significant shift from the Marxist understanding of commodities. Rather than focusing on how goods are produced, Baudrillard was more interested in how they were consumed, not just materially but symbolically. He argued that consumption had become a central feature of contemporary life, where individuals were not merely purchasing goods for their functional value but were participating in a system of signs, where objects signified something beyond themselves. This marked the beginning of his move away from Marxism toward a more semiotic and cultural approach.

As Baudrillard's thought developed, his critique of consumer society became more radical. He saw consumption not as a choice made by individuals but as a form of social control, where people were trapped in a web of signs and symbols that dictated their desires and identities. By the mid-1970s, Baudrillard's work began to take a more critical stance on the role of media and technology in society. This period marked a turning point in his thought as he moved beyond traditional sociological analysis and into the realm of postmodernism, where he explored the idea of simulation and hyper reality.

In his seminal work *Simulacra and Simulation* (1981), Baudrillard introduced the concept of the simulacrum, a representation of something that no longer has an original. This is where Baudrillard's thought evolved into one of his most well-known and influential ideas: the notion that we live in a world where the distinction between reality and representation has collapsed. For Baudrillard, modern society was no longer concerned with what was real but with what appeared real through media, advertising, and other forms of representation. In his view, the proliferation of images, symbols, and simulations had created a hyper reality, where reality itself was overshadowed by its representations.

This shift in Baudrillard's thought signalled his departure from Marxism. Where Marx saw economic structures as the fundamental reality shaping human life, Baudrillard believed that in a post-industrial society, it was no longer production but the circulation of images and signs that determined reality. For him, the rise of mass media, technology, and digital communication had replaced the physical world with a symbolic one, where simulations of reality became more powerful than reality itself. Baudrillard argued that in this hyperreal world, people were no longer connected to the real but were instead interacting with representations—copies without originals.

One of the key moments in Baudrillard's intellectual evolution was his controversial essay *The Gulf War Did Not Take Place* (1991). In this text, Baudrillard examined how media coverage of the Gulf War in 1990-1991 transformed the conflict into a spectacle, where images of war were constructed and consumed in a way that detached viewers from the actual events. His claim was not that the war didn't occur but that its representation in the media had so thoroughly mediated the reality of the conflict that what was presented to the public bore little resemblance to the actual war. The war, in Baudrillard's terms, became a virtual event, carefully curated by the media for consumption, and this marked another phase in his critique of how the media manipulates our perception of reality.

As Baudrillard's thought continued to evolve, he turned his attention more explicitly to the effects of globalization and the digital age. In later works such as *The Transparency of Evil* (1993) and *The Illusion of the End* (1994), Baudrillard explored the consequences of living in a world dominated by technology, information, and the global flow of capital. He saw globalization not as a unifying force but as a process that accelerates the collapse of reality into hyper reality. In a globalized world, everything becomes commodified, including information, culture, and even human experiences. Baudrillard was deeply skeptical of this process, arguing that it reduced human life to a series of simulations, where the distinction between real and fake became impossible to discern.

At the heart of Baudrillard's evolving thought was his increasing pessimism about the possibility of reclaiming the real in an age dominated by simulations. While his earlier work still contained traces of critical optimism—believing that by understanding the mechanisms of consumer culture, we could resist its effects—his later writings reflect a more nihilistic stance. In Baudrillard's later years, he came to view the hyperreal as inescapable. The collapse of reality into simulation had, in his view, gone too far to be reversed. Despite this apparent nihilism, Baudrillard's thought remains highly influential because of the depth with which he engaged with the philosophical implications of living in a media-saturated, technologically driven world. His ideas have resonated with many thinkers across disciplines, particularly in media studies, philosophy, and cultural criticism. Baudrillard's legacy lies in his ability to diagnose the condition of contemporary society, pushing us to confront the uncomfortable truth that what we take to be real is often nothing more than a carefully constructed simulation. In the end, the evolution of Baudrillard's thought reflects an intellectual journey that moves from a critique of consumer culture to a profound meditation on the nature of reality itself. His work asks us to question the structures that define our world—whether they are economic, cultural, or technological—and to consider how these structures shape not only our understanding of reality but also our very experience of it. As the world continues to be transformed by digital technology, Baudrillard's thought remains as relevant as ever, offering a critical lens through which to understand the complexities of the 21st century.

Understanding Postmodernism through Baudrillard

To grasp Jean Baudrillard's influence and significance, one must first understand the intellectual landscape he inhabited—postmodernism. Baudrillard was one of the key figures associated with postmodern thought, and his contributions to the field are crucial in understanding how postmodernism challenges traditional notions of reality, truth, and meaning. While postmodernism as a movement encompasses a wide range of thinkers, Baudrillard's work offers a unique perspective on the subject, particularly in relation to media, technology, and the erosion of reality.

Postmodernism emerged as a response to modernism, which was characterized by the belief in progress, rationality, and the possibility of discovering universal truths. Modernism, influenced by Enlightenment ideals, sought to explain the world through reason and science, believing that human advancement was possible through these means. Postmodernism, on the other hand, is marked by skepticism towards these grand narratives. It rejects the idea that there is a single, objective truth or that history follows a linear trajectory of progress. Instead, postmodernism emphasizes the fragmentation of meaning, the fluidity of identity, and the role of culture and language in shaping our understanding of the world.

Baudrillard's work is foundational to postmodernism, particularly his concept of hyper reality. At the heart of Baudrillard's thought is the idea that, in the postmodern era, the distinction between reality and representation has collapsed. In earlier times, representations—whether they were images, stories, or signs—were understood as reflecting some kind of underlying reality. A map, for example, was a representation of a real territory. However, in Baudrillard's view, postmodern society has reached a point where representations no longer reflect reality; instead, they create it. This is what he calls hyper reality—a world where simulations and signs are more real than the reality they supposedly represent.

Hyper reality is a core concept in understanding Baudrillard's postmodernism. In this hyperreal world, people are bombarded with images, symbols, and representations that shape their perception of reality. Media plays a crucial role in this process. Television, advertising, film, and now the internet generate an endless stream of images and information, which Baudrillard argues does not inform but rather distorts. In his view, the real has been replaced by simulations, copies without originals, and we live in a society where meaning itself is constantly produced, consumed, and reproduced, often detached from any tangible reality. This breakdown of reality is a hallmark of postmodernism, and Baudrillard's analysis provides a lens to understand how media and technology have brought about this transformation.

One of Baudrillard's most famous examples of hyper reality is Disneyland. For him, Disneyland is the perfect model of a hyperreal space. It is a place that doesn't simply represent fantasy but creates a reality where visitors experience a simulated version of the world. It is a world that is more real than reality itself because it offers the illusion of perfection, safety, and happiness that reality cannot provide. According to Baudrillard, Disneyland's function is not to provide an escape from reality, but to mask the fact that the rest of society has also become a hyperreal simulation. The theme park doesn't just simulate fantasy; it symbolizes a world where the line between reality and fantasy is blurred.

Postmodernism, through Baudrillard's lens, also challenges traditional ideas of identity and subjectivity. In a world dominated by media and consumer culture, identities are no longer fixed or stable. Instead, they are fluid, constantly shifting in response to the images, products, and narratives that surround us. Baudrillard believed that in the postmodern world, the individual subject—the sense of a stable, autonomous self—was disappearing, replaced by a fragmented, decentered identity shaped by the endless flow of media and symbols. This postmodern self is not an individual in the traditional sense but a collection of images and signs, constructed by external forces rather than internal essence.

Baudrillard's critique of the postmodern condition is not limited to consumer culture and media; it also extends to politics and history. He argued that politics, like media, had become a spectacle, where the images and appearances of political events were more important than the actual substance. In a hyperreal society, political campaigns, public relations, and media spin become the main vehicles for political action. The spectacle of politics, according to Baudrillard, is not about governance or policy but about creating the appearance of governance. This idea is central to his famous declaration that "the Gulf War did not take place." His point was not that the war did not occur but that its representation in the media was so manipulated, so filtered through spectacle, that the public experienced a version of the war that was more fiction than reality.

Baudrillard's work also intersects with the broader postmodern rejection of grand narratives—those overarching explanations of history, society, and meaning that modernism relies on. For Baudrillard, one of the greatest illusions of modern society was the belief in progress, the idea that human history is moving towards some kind of improvement or enlightenment. In his view, postmodern society has revealed the emptiness of this narrative. History, like reality, has become a simulation—endlessly replayed, reinterpreted, and repackaged by the media. The past is no longer something to be learned from or understood in a linear fashion; it becomes a repository of images and symbols that can be endlessly recycled for contemporary consumption. This critique resonates deeply with postmodernism's skepticism toward the notion of objective truth and its insistence on the plurality of meaning.

Baudrillard's postmodernism also engages with the notion of power. Traditional forms of power, based on authority, force, or control over material resources, have, according to Baudrillard, been replaced by power over images, information, and culture. In the hyperreal world, power is not wielded through physical dominance or political force but through the control of symbols and the creation of narratives. The ability to shape how events are perceived—whether through media, advertising, or political spectacle—becomes the primary form of power in the postmodern world.

In many ways, Baudrillard's thought encapsulates the paradoxes of postmodernism. His work is both a critique and a product of the world it describes. Baudrillard himself was aware of this irony. He often played with the idea that his work, too, might be a simulation—a reflection of the world of symbols and images he critiqued. This self-awareness is typical of postmodernism, which thrives on irony, ambiguity, and contradiction. Baudrillard didn't offer solutions or prescriptions for how to deal with the hyperreal world; instead, he invited us to recognize the profound transformations that had taken place in how we understand reality, truth, and power.

Ultimately, understanding postmodernism through Baudrillard involves recognizing how deeply media and technology have altered our perceptions of the world. His ideas challenge us to question the very fabric of what we take to be real, asking us to look beyond appearances and to confront the unsettling possibility that what we experience as reality may be nothing more than a carefully constructed illusion. Baudrillard's work continues to provoke thought and debate, offering a powerful lens through which to view the complexities of the postmodern condition.

The Concept of Hyper Reality

At the heart of Jean Baudrillard's intellectual legacy lies his provocative and influential concept of hyper reality. This idea is one of the most distinctive contributions he made to postmodern thought, and it challenges how we understand the relationship between reality and representation. In a world that is increasingly mediated by technology, media, and consumer culture, Baudrillard argued that the line between what is real and what is imagined has blurred to the point of disappearance. Hyper reality, in his view, is the state in which simulations of reality become more real than reality itself, a state where signs and symbols dominate our experience, creating a world of illusions that we take to be real.

Hyper reality is not merely the reproduction of reality but a condition in which reality is replaced by its representations. Baudrillard famously described this phenomenon using the example of a map and its territory. In traditional understanding, a map is a representation of a real place, the territory. But in hyper reality, the map has become so detailed and expansive that it no longer represents the territory; it becomes the territory. In this sense, reality and its representation become indistinguishable. The simulation replaces the real, and we live in a world where the signs and images we encounter take on more significance than the material world they were once supposed to depict.

One of Baudrillard's key insights is that hyper reality is not a phenomenon limited to a particular aspect of society; it permeates everything. Media, advertising, consumerism, politics, and even relationships are all mediated through simulations. What this means is that we increasingly experience life not directly, but through representations of it. Television, films, social media, and advertisements all produce images that present us with versions of reality, but these versions are often filtered, manipulated, and constructed in ways that distort the truth. Baudrillard argued that in the hyperreal world, these distorted images and simulations replace the truth entirely, leaving us in a state where we no longer know what is real and what is fake.

An everyday example of hyper reality can be found in the world of advertising. When we see advertisements for products—whether they are for food, clothing, or luxury items—what we are shown is not the product itself, but an idealized version of it. The burger in the fast-food commercial is never as perfect as the one we actually receive. The car in the commercial is portrayed not just as a means of transportation but as a symbol of freedom, success, and happiness. In these cases, the advertisement creates a hyperreal version of reality, one where the product is elevated into something more than its actual function. We begin to desire not the real object, but the hyperreal version of it that exists only in the world of advertisements.

Baudrillard argued that this proliferation of hyperreal images leads to the "death of the real." In earlier times, reality was something concrete, something we could trust as being true. Representations, whether they were paintings, stories, or photographs, were understood as reflecting or distorting this reality. However, with the rise of modern technology and media, Baudrillard believed that reality had become so heavily mediated that it no longer existed independently of its representations. In the world of hyper reality, representations do not just distort the truth; they replace it. The result is that we live in a world where what is real is constantly overshadowed by simulations, and the real itself becomes irrelevant.

The concept of hyper reality is most vividly illustrated in Baudrillard's analysis of Disneyland. For Baudrillard, Disneyland is not just a theme park but a perfect example of how hyper reality operates. Disneyland presents itself as a world of fantasy, where visitors are encouraged to escape from the "real" world. However, Baudrillard argues that

Disneyland's function is actually to mask the fact that the rest of the world has already become hyperreal. In other words, Disneyland is a place where people go to experience a carefully crafted simulation of fun and fantasy, but in doing so, they ignore the fact that everyday life outside the park is also a simulation—a world dominated by media images, consumerism, and artificial realities.

Baudrillard also explored the implications of hyper reality in the realm of politics and war. One of his most controversial arguments was made in his essay *The Gulf War Did Not Take Place* (1991), where he claimed that the Gulf War was not experienced as a real event but as a hyperreal simulation. His point was not that the war did not happen but that its representation in the media had transformed it into something else entirely. The war was presented to the public through carefully curated images of precision bombing, technological superiority, and heroic narratives, all of which served to create a version of the war that was more about spectacle than the reality of destruction and suffering. In this way, Baudrillard argued, the Gulf War became a media event, a virtual war, where the images shown on television had more influence on the public's perception of the war than the actual events on the ground.

In the digital age, Baudrillard's concept of hyper reality has only become more relevant. Social media platforms like Instagram, Facebook, and Twitter are prime examples of hyperreal environments. On these platforms, individuals create carefully curated versions of their lives, presenting images of themselves that are often idealized, filtered, and edited. The result is a world where social interaction takes place in a hyperreal space, where people interact with versions of each other that are more polished and perfect than reality allows. The self itself becomes a simulation, and we engage not with real individuals but with hyperreal versions of them. This phenomenon has profound implications for identity, relationships, and the way we perceive our place in the world.

Hyper reality, according to Baudrillard, also extends into our understanding of history. In the hyperreal world, history is not something that we engage with as a set of facts or events that happened in the past; it becomes a collection of images and narratives that are constantly reinterpreted and recycled. Movies, documentaries, and television shows about historical events often present these events not as they happened, but as they have been dramatized and reshaped for public consumption. The result is that our understanding of history is increasingly mediated by hyperreal images, where the distinction between historical fact and historical representation becomes increasingly difficult to discern.

Baudrillard's critique of hyper reality is not simply an observation about the state of modern society; it is also a warning. For Baudrillard, the rise of hyper reality signals the collapse of meaning itself. When simulations and representations replace the real, we lose the ability to engage with the world in a meaningful way. The endless production and consumption of images and signs lead to a state of inertia, where nothing is real, and everything is reduced to spectacle. In this hyperreal world, Baudrillard believed, we risk losing our ability to think critically, to understand the world beyond its surface, and to engage with deeper truths.

The concept of hyper reality continues to resonate in contemporary culture, particularly as technology continues to advance. Virtual reality, augmented reality, and artificial intelligence are all technologies that push the boundaries of what is real and what is simulated. Baudrillard's thought provides a framework for understanding these developments, offering us a critical lens through which to examine how technology and media shape our perceptions of reality.

In conclusion, hyper reality, as conceived by Baudrillard, is a radical critique of how modern society interacts with reality. It challenges us to question the images, signs, and simulations that surround us and to reflect on how these simulations shape our understanding of the world. Baudrillard's analysis of hyper reality invites us to confront the unsettling possibility that we live in a world where reality itself is no longer accessible, replaced instead by a never-ending series of simulations that obscure the truth and replace it with illusions.

Simulacra and Simulations: A New Reality

Jean Baudrillard's work *Simulacra and Simulation* is one of his most influential and widely discussed texts. Published in 1981, it presents a ground-breaking critique of modern society, exploring how the concepts of simulacra and simulation have redefined our understanding of reality. In this work, Baudrillard argues that we are living in an era where representations—simulacra—have replaced the real, and simulations have come to define our experience of the world. This new reality, according to Baudrillard, is one in which the boundary between the real and the simulated is not only blurred but, in many cases, entirely obliterated. The result is a world where simulations do not just imitate reality; they create a new form of reality—a hyper reality.

At the core of Baudrillard's theory is the distinction between simulacra and simulation. A simulacrum is a representation or imitation of something that was once real or had an original form. In the traditional sense, a simulacrum is a copy that is meant to resemble the original, such as a painting of a landscape or a photograph of a person. However, in Baudrillard's view, modern society has entered a phase where simulacra no longer represent something real. Instead, they have become detached from any original reference, existing as copies without a source. Simulations, on the other hand, refer to the process by which these simulacra create a reality of their own. In a simulated reality, the representations themselves become more significant than the real things they were supposed to depict.

Baudrillard outlines four stages in the development of simulacra. In the first stage, a simulacrum is a faithful copy of the original, where there is still a clear connection between the representation and the real. For example, a painting of a tree is meant to represent a real tree. In the second stage, the simulacrum becomes a perversion of reality, where the representation starts to distort or exaggerate the original. In the third stage, the simulacrum pretends to be a faithful copy but no longer has a direct relationship to the real. It becomes a sign that refers only to other signs, creating a self-referential system. Finally, in the fourth stage, the simulacrum becomes purely simulation—it no longer imitates anything real and exists independently of any original. It is in this final stage that we enter the realm of hyper reality.

In *Simulacra and Simulation*, Baudrillard argues that our world is increasingly dominated by these fourth-stage simulacra, where simulations have replaced reality entirely. This hyperreal world is one where the distinction between the real and the imaginary no longer holds. In the media-saturated societies of the late 20th and early 21st centuries, Baudrillard observed, we are constantly bombarded with images, signs, and representations that do not refer to anything real but are consumed as if they were. These images become the reality we experience, replacing the real with a simulation of reality that is more convincing, more seductive, and often more satisfying than the real world ever could be.

A powerful example of Baudrillard's concept of simulacra and simulations can be found in modern media and entertainment. Take, for instance, reality television. Shows like *Survivor* or *Big Brother* are designed to create the illusion that the participants are experiencing something authentic. These shows are presented as "real," unscripted events, but they are meticulously crafted simulations of reality.

The participants are placed in artificial environments, given scripted situations to navigate, and edited in ways that distort their behavior. What the audience sees is not reality but a highly mediated version of it—a simulation that pretends to be real. Baudrillard would argue that for the audience, the simulated reality of these shows becomes more real than the actual events they depict.

Similarly, social media platforms like Instagram or Facebook are spaces where people construct hyperreal versions of their lives. The images people post—often filtered, staged, and curated—are simulacra. They are representations of lives that may not actually exist in the form they are presented. The perfect vacation, the flawless meal, or the idealized version of the self on social media does not correspond to an authentic reality but to a simulation of life. This hyperreal version of life, however, is often more compelling and desirable than the real one. For many, the simulation becomes a more powerful reality than the actual experiences they live.

Baudrillard's theory of simulacra and simulation also extends to politics and the news media. In his essay *The Gulf War Did Not Take Place*, Baudrillard provocatively argued that the Gulf War was not a real war in the traditional sense. He claimed that the media's representation of the war, with its carefully curated images of precision bombing and sanitized footage, created a hyperreal version of the conflict. The war, as experienced by most people, was not the actual war happening on the ground, with all its violence and chaos, but a simulation of war—one that was easier to consume and understand. In this sense, the Gulf War became a media event, where the images and narratives constructed by news networks became the reality that people experienced, rather than the brutal and often confusing truth of the actual conflict.

The hyperreal nature of modern politics goes beyond media coverage of wars. Political campaigns themselves, particularly in the age of social media and 24-hour news cycles, often resemble simulations more than real debates about policies or ideologies. Politicians are frequently reduced to images, soundbites, and slogans, all of which are carefully crafted to create an idealized version of the candidate—a simulacrum. The substance of political discourse is overshadowed by the spectacle of representation, where the simulation of political engagement becomes more real than the actual issues being discussed.

Baudrillard's concept of simulacra and simulation also has profound implications for how we understand history. In the hyperreal world, history itself becomes a simulacrum, endlessly replayed, reinterpreted, and reimagined through movies, documentaries, and television shows. Historical events are no longer seen as facts or truths but as narratives that can be reshaped for contemporary consumption. The past, in Baudrillard's view, becomes a simulation—a collection of images and stories that serve more as entertainment or spectacle than as a way to understand the real forces that shaped the world. This process, Baudrillard argues, leads to the "death of history," where the past is no longer something to be remembered or understood but something to be consumed and forgotten.

In the digital age, Baudrillard's ideas about simulacra and simulations have become even more relevant. Virtual reality, augmented reality, and artificial intelligence are technologies that create entirely new forms of simulation, further eroding the distinction between the real and the artificial. In virtual reality, for instance, users can experience worlds that are entirely simulated, yet feel real to the senses. These hyperreal environments can offer experiences that are as meaningful—if not more so—than anything encountered in the real world. As these technologies continue to evolve, Baudrillard's warning about the dangers of living in a simulated reality becomes ever more pressing.

One of the most striking cultural reflections of Baudrillard's theory can be found in the film *The Matrix* (1999). Although Baudrillard himself claimed that the movie misunderstood his ideas, *The Matrix* provides a vivid illustration of the world of simulation Baudrillard described. In the film, humanity is trapped in a simulated reality created by machines, unaware that their experiences are not real. This concept of being trapped in a simulation mirrors Baudrillard's argument that in the modern world, we are surrounded by simulations that obscure the real, and that we have become so accustomed to these simulations that we can no longer distinguish them from reality.

In *Simulacra and Simulation*, Baudrillard challenges us to question the nature of the world we inhabit. Are we living in a reality defined by truth, or are we living in a hyperreal world where simulations have replaced the real? For Baudrillard, the answer is unsettling: we are surrounded by simulacra, and we live in a state of hyper reality where the boundary between the real and the simulated no longer exists. This new reality, where simulations dominate our experience, raises profound questions about the nature of truth, identity, and existence in the modern world.

The Precession of Simulacra

One of Jean Baudrillard's most intriguing and complex ideas is the concept of the *precession of simulacra*, which he introduces in *Simulacra and Simulation*. The term refers to the way in which representations—simulacra—no longer merely mirror or distort reality but actually precede and shape it. In Baudrillard's analysis, this precession signals a shift in the relationship between reality and its representations, as society moves from a world where representations are rooted in the real to one where representations themselves come to define and replace the real. This marks the movement toward hyper reality, a central theme in Baudrillard's work, where the line between the real and the simulated blurs to the point of nonexistence.

To understand the precession of simulacra, we must first explore the nature of simulacra themselves. Simulacra are representations or imitations of reality, but as Baudrillard points out, they are not simple copies. Traditionally, a simulacrum might refer to a work of art—a painting, for instance—that represents a real object, person, or landscape. However, in the modern era, Baudrillard argues that simulacra no longer function merely as representations of the real. Instead, they become independent of reality, creating a world where copies exist without originals. This leads to a situation where representations are no longer bound by the need to reference something real; they can exist purely as signs within a self-contained system of meaning.

The term "precession" typically refers to the movement of something ahead of another, as in the case of celestial bodies where one object moves in advance of another in orbit. Baudrillard uses this concept metaphorically to describe the way simulacra move ahead of reality—they come first and set the stage for what we perceive as real. In other words, instead of reality being the foundation upon which representations are built, representations—simulacra—take the lead and shape our perception of reality. The real becomes secondary, following behind the simulacra, which precede it and create the conditions for what we take to be reality.

Baudrillard illustrates this concept through several powerful examples. One of his most famous examples is the story of the map and the territory, borrowed from Jorge Luis Borges. In this story, Baudrillard imagines a kingdom where a map is created so precisely and accurately that it perfectly corresponds to the territory it represents. Over time, the map becomes so detailed that it covers the entire territory. Eventually, the map itself starts to decay, and all that remains is the map, with no trace of the original territory. The map, in this scenario, has become more real than the land it once represented. This allegory encapsulates the idea of precession: the map (the simulacrum) precedes the territory (the real), and reality itself becomes lost in the simulation.

Baudrillard argues that this precession of simulacra can be seen in many aspects of contemporary society, particularly in media, advertising, and technology. Take, for instance, the world of fashion. Clothing brands create images of beauty, style, and identity that consumers are invited to adopt.

These images are not necessarily based on any "real" sense of beauty or personal identity; instead, they create a new reality, where consumers shape their sense of self and worth according to the simulacra provided by the fashion industry. In this way, the representations (the marketing images and trends) precede and shape the reality (how people perceive themselves and others). The fashion industry is not responding to an already existing sense of identity; it is creating identities through its representations.

Another example is the world of advertising, where products are often marketed through images and narratives that bear little resemblance to the actual product's use or value. The advertisement becomes more real than the product itself. Take, for example, the advertising of luxury goods like perfume or cars. A perfume commercial might not focus on the scent itself but instead portray an idealized lifestyle—luxury, romance, adventure—that consumers are invited to buy into. The precession of simulacra here means that the lifestyle, which is a simulacrum, precedes and shapes the reality of the product, making the representation more significant than the product's actual qualities.

In Baudrillard's view, the precession of simulacra extends even further into the realm of politics and public life. Political campaigns, particularly in the age of mass media, are often built on images, slogans, and soundbites that have little to do with the reality of governance or policy. Politicians are constructed as media figures, and their success often depends on their ability to perform within the spectacle of media representation. Their policies, ideas, and actions become secondary to their image, and the image itself creates the public perception of reality. In this sense, the politician's media persona (a simulacrum) precedes and shapes the reality of their leadership.

The precession of simulacra also manifests in how we experience history. Baudrillard argues that in a world dominated by media and technology, history itself becomes a simulation. Events are represented and reinterpreted so often through media narratives, documentaries, and dramatizations that the representation becomes more significant than the historical event itself. For instance, historical films or television series might depict historical events with such emotional intensity or dramatic flair that they reshape how we understand those events. The representation, in this case, preempts the real historical facts, creating a version of history that is more accessible, more engaging, and more "real" to audiences than the actual history ever was.

In the realm of technology, the precession of simulacra is even more pronounced. Virtual reality and augmented reality technologies allow users to immerse themselves in environments that are completely simulated yet experienced as real. In these cases, the simulation precedes the experience of reality. Users in virtual reality are not engaging with a reflection of the real world but with a simulation that creates its own reality. The boundaries between the simulated and the real dissolve as users navigate spaces that exist entirely as representations but feel real to the senses. This, too, is an example of how simulacra precede and define reality.

Baudrillard's theory of the precession of simulacra speaks to a profound shift in how we understand and experience the world. In pre-modern times, representations—whether they were religious icons, paintings, or maps—were understood as reflections or interpretations of a deeper reality.

These representations had a secondary status, subordinate to the real world they depicted. However, in the postmodern era, Baudrillard argues that representations have come to dominate the real. The simulacra no longer refer to something real; they exist in their own right, creating new realities that shape how we experience the world.

This idea is particularly relevant in the context of mass media, where the images we see on television, in movies, or online often shape our perceptions of reality more than our direct experiences do. The media does not just report on reality; it constructs it. Whether we are watching news coverage, advertisements, or entertainment, we are constantly interacting with representations that influence how we think, feel, and act in the world. In this way, the precession of simulacra has profound implications for how we navigate contemporary society.

Baudrillard's concept of the precession of simulacra challenges us to question what we take to be real. Are the things we encounter—whether in media, politics, or even our personal identities—based on some underlying reality, or are they simulacra, representations that have come to shape and define our understanding of the world? For Baudrillard, the unsettling truth is that we are living in a world where the simulacra have won. They have moved ahead of the real, creating a new kind of reality—one that is not based on truth or authenticity but on images, signs, and simulations that precede and define the real world.

The precession of simulacra, then, is not just a theoretical concept but a lens through which we can understand the shifting nature of reality in the postmodern world. It invites us to think critically about the images, narratives, and representations that surround us and to question the extent to which they shape our understanding of what is real. In a world dominated by simulations, Baudrillard warns, we risk losing touch with the real altogether, living in a reality constructed entirely by simulacra that have no original.

The Death of the Real

Jean Baudrillard's concept of *the death of the real* is one of the most radical and challenging aspects of his philosophy, encapsulating his critique of modern media, technology, and culture. This idea represents a profound shift in how we understand the nature of reality in a world where representations and simulations have overtaken the real. Baudrillard argued that in contemporary society, particularly in the age of mass media and digital technology, reality itself has been eclipsed by images, signs, and simulations to the point where it no longer exists as an independent, objective truth. Instead, we live in a world dominated by hyper reality, where the real is replaced by a series of artificial constructs that are consumed as if they were more real than reality itself.

To grasp Baudrillard's notion of the death of the real, it is essential to understand how he viewed the relationship between reality and its representations. Traditionally, representations—whether they are paintings, photographs, or stories—were seen as reflections of a reality that existed independently of them. A painting of a landscape, for instance, was understood as an artistic interpretation of a real place. Reality was something that existed outside of these representations, and representations were simply ways of communicating or depicting the real.

However, Baudrillard argued that in the modern world, particularly in advanced capitalist societies, this relationship between reality and representation has fundamentally changed. With the rise of media, advertising, and digital technology, representations have become so pervasive and powerful that they no longer reflect reality—they create it. This process, which he calls *simulation*, means that we now live in a world where representations no longer refer to something real but instead generate their own form of reality, a hyper reality. The result, according to Baudrillard, is the death of the real: reality no longer exists as something separate from or prior to its representation; it has been entirely subsumed by the endless proliferation of images and signs.

A striking example of the death of the real can be seen in the world of news media. News reports are traditionally supposed to convey the truth about events in the world—whether political, social, or natural. However, Baudrillard would argue that the modern news media no longer reports on reality; instead, it creates a version of reality that is shaped by the needs of the media itself. News stories are often framed, edited, and constructed in ways that prioritize sensationalism, entertainment, or ideological agendas over the objective truth of the events being reported. The result is that what we experience as "news" is often a carefully curated simulation of reality, designed to evoke certain emotions, reactions, or beliefs, rather than a faithful reflection of the truth.

This process extends beyond the news to all forms of media. Television shows, films, advertisements, and social media all contribute to the creation of a hyperreal world, where images and signs dominate our experience. The boundaries between what is real and what is artificial are increasingly blurred, as we consume representations that no longer refer to anything outside themselves.

For instance, reality television, which purports to show "real" people in "real" situations, is often heavily scripted, staged, and edited to create a more compelling narrative than reality could provide. The participants themselves become characters in a story, shaped by the needs of entertainment, and the "reality" presented to viewers is not an unfiltered glimpse into real life but a simulation designed to look real.

Baudrillard extends this critique to the realm of politics and warfare. In his essay *The Gulf War Did Not Take Place*, Baudrillard provocatively argued that the Gulf War, as experienced by most people, was not a real war but a simulated event. This does not mean that the war did not happen or that there was no violence or destruction. Instead,

Baudrillard's point was that the representation of the war in the media, particularly through sanitized images of precision bombing and military technology, created a hyperreal version of the conflict that obscured the brutal reality of the war itself. The images and narratives constructed by the media became the reality that people experienced, even though these representations bore little resemblance to the actual events on the ground. In this sense, the real war was overshadowed by its simulated counterpart, and for most people, the war became a virtual event rather than a concrete reality.

The death of the real is also evident in the realm of consumer culture. Baudrillard argued that in advanced capitalist societies, commodities are no longer valued for their material function or utility but for their symbolic value. Products are sold not based on what they do but on what they represent. A luxury car, for instance, is marketed not as a means of transportation but as a symbol of status, success, and wealth. The real object becomes secondary to its representation, and consumers are encouraged to buy not the product itself but the lifestyle or image it represents. In this way, consumer culture is driven by the production and consumption of signs and symbols rather than real goods or services. The result is that reality, in the economic sense, is replaced by a system of simulation where signs refer only to other signs, creating a self-contained loop of meaning that has no connection to anything real.

The death of the real has profound implications for our understanding of identity. In a world dominated by simulations, identity itself becomes a performance, shaped by the representations we consume and project. Social media platforms like Instagram, Facebook, and Twitter encourage users to curate and construct idealized versions of their lives, often using filters, editing tools, and selective sharing to create a more appealing image. The result is a hyperreal version of the self—a simulacrum that exists in the digital world but bears little resemblance to the complexities of real life. This simulated self is consumed by others as if it were real, and in turn, the person behind the screen may come to identify more with their hyperreal persona than with their real identity. The line between the real self and the simulated self becomes increasingly blurred, leading to a fragmentation of identity and a loss of authenticity.

Baudrillard's concept of the death of the real challenges us to question the nature of truth and reality in a world where simulations dominate our experience. In the pre-modern world, reality was understood as something solid, something that could be known and represented through art, literature, or other forms of communication.

Representations, while important, were secondary to the real world they depicted. In the modern and postmodern world, however, Baudrillard argues that this relationship has been inverted. Representations have become primary, and reality has been subsumed into the world of signs and simulations. The real no longer exists independently of its representation, and what we take to be real is often nothing more than a carefully constructed simulation.

The death of the real is not merely a theoretical concept but a reflection of the profound changes brought about by technology, media, and consumer culture. In the digital age, the proliferation of images, information, and simulations has accelerated this process, creating a world where we are increasingly disconnected from the real. Virtual reality, artificial intelligence, and augmented reality technologies all contribute to the erosion of the real, as they offer experiences that feel real but are entirely artificial. In this sense, the death of the real is not just a critique of modern media but a commentary on the future of human experience itself.

Baudrillard's analysis is both a warning and a challenge. He invites us to reflect on the extent to which our understanding of the world is shaped by simulations, and to consider what it means to live in a world where the real has been eclipsed by the hyperreal. The death of the real forces us to confront uncomfortable questions about the nature of truth, meaning, and existence in a society that prioritizes representation over reality. For Baudrillard, the collapse of the real is not something to be lamented but something to be critically examined, as it reveals the underlying structures of power, control, and illusion that govern modern life.

In the end, Baudrillard's concept of the death of the real offers a powerful critique of contemporary society, challenging us to reconsider how we understand reality in an age of simulations. It forces us to question the authenticity of the world we inhabit and to reflect on how we navigate a reality that is increasingly defined by images, signs, and artificial constructs.

Signs, Symbols, and Their Illusions

In the realm of Jean Baudrillard's thought, one of the most compelling and foundational aspects of his philosophy revolves around the role of signs and symbols in modern society. Baudrillard's work is deeply rooted in semiotics, the study of signs and how they produce meaning, but he takes this exploration into uncharted territory by showing how signs and symbols have detached themselves from reality, creating a world of illusions. The interplay between signs, symbols, and the illusions they generate is central to Baudrillard's critique of postmodern culture, particularly in how these representations no longer reflect reality but, instead, create a new hyper reality.

Baudrillard's analysis begins with the concept of the sign, which, in traditional semiotics, consists of two parts: the *signifier* and the *signified*. The signifier is the physical form of the sign—such as a word, an image, or a sound—while the signified is the concept or idea that the signifier represents. For instance, the word "tree" is a signifier, and the mental image or concept of an actual tree is the signified. In classical terms, signs are supposed to represent or refer to real objects, ideas, or experiences. However, Baudrillard's critique is that, in contemporary society, this relationship between signifier and signified has broken down. Signs no longer refer to anything real; they exist within a closed system of meanings, where they only refer to other signs. The result is a world where meaning itself is floating, unmoored from reality, creating layers of illusion.

Baudrillard argues that modern capitalist society, driven by media, technology, and consumerism, produces an endless proliferation of signs that serve to mask the absence of reality. In his view, signs once had a direct connection to the real world, but as society has evolved, signs have become more detached from the objects they were supposed to represent. This leads to the creation of *simulacra*—signs that imitate or simulate reality but are entirely divorced from any actual referent. In other words, simulacra are copies without originals, and they populate the modern world, giving rise to a hyper reality where illusions dominate our perception of the world.

One of Baudrillard's most striking examples of this phenomenon is found in the world of advertising. Advertisements do not simply promote products; they create symbolic associations between the products and abstract ideals like happiness, success, and desire. A car commercial, for instance, might show a sleek vehicle speeding through a picturesque landscape, evoking feelings of freedom and adventure. The car itself, the product being sold, becomes secondary to the symbolic meaning it carries. The signifier (the car) is no longer just a mode of transportation; it has been transformed into a symbol of success, power, and personal identity. Baudrillard would argue that the reality of the car is irrelevant to the consumer, who is drawn not to the product but to the illusion created by the advertisement.

This detachment of signs from reality is central to Baudrillard's idea of *symbolic exchange*. In earlier societies, symbols had a clear, direct relationship to the real world and were often used in rituals or practices that reinforced social cohesion and meaning.

However, in modern society, symbols have become commodified, circulated, and consumed in ways that obscure their original meaning. Instead of facilitating genuine human connection or understanding, symbols are now exchanged like any other commodity, stripped of their authentic value. The illusion here is that these signs still carry meaning, when, in fact, they have been hollowed out, leaving behind only a façade.

Baudrillard also explores how signs and symbols are used to create illusions of power and authority in politics. In modern political systems, leaders and governments rely heavily on signs—images, speeches, and symbols of power—to maintain control and legitimacy. However, Baudrillard argues that these signs often mask the absence of real power or effective governance. For example, political leaders might project an image of strength and decisiveness through media appearances, carefully choreographed speeches, and symbolic actions, but this image may have little to do with their actual ability to govern or solve complex problems. In this sense, the signs of power create an illusion of control, where the reality of political effectiveness is irrelevant. What matters is the perception of power, which is constructed and maintained through the manipulation of symbols.

This critique is perhaps most evident in Baudrillard's analysis of the media's role in constructing reality. In the age of television, film, and now social media, signs and symbols are constantly produced, circulated, and consumed at an unprecedented rate. These media forms create a world of signs that presents itself as reality but is, in fact, a carefully crafted illusion. The news, for instance, does not simply report on events; it frames them, selects them, and packages them in ways that align with specific narratives or agendas. The result is not an objective reflection of the world but a mediated reality that serves the interests of those in power or caters to the desires of the audience.

The same process can be seen in entertainment media, where films and television shows create fictional worlds that are often more compelling and immersive than reality itself. Baudrillard argues that this constant consumption of signs—whether through news, advertisements, or entertainment—has created a world where the line between reality and fiction is no longer discernible. We become so accustomed to consuming signs that we forget they are just that: representations, not the real thing. This creates a culture of illusion, where what we take to be real is often nothing more than a series of signs that refer only to other signs, not to any underlying truth.

One of Baudrillard's most powerful examples of this process is Disneyland, which he sees as the epitome of hyper reality. Disneyland presents itself as a world of fantasy, a place where visitors can escape from the real world and enter a magical realm. However, Baudrillard argues that Disneyland's function is not to offer an escape from reality but to reinforce the illusion that there is a distinction between reality and fantasy in the first place. In his view, the rest of the world has become so saturated with simulations and illusions that Disneyland is no different from the world outside its gates. The theme park, therefore, serves to convince visitors that reality still exists outside, even though both inside and outside the park, the world is constructed from signs and symbols. In this way, Disneyland masks the fact that we are already living in a hyperreal world, where the boundary between the real and the simulated has dissolved.

In Baudrillard's theory, the illusion created by signs and symbols is not just a superficial problem; it has profound implications for how we understand and interact with the world. In the past, symbols were grounded in the real and served to communicate deeper truths about the human condition, society, or nature. In modern society, however, symbols have become detached from these roots, existing in a closed system of meaning where they only refer to other symbols. The result is a world where meaning itself has become hollow, where the signs we consume no longer connect us to reality but to a series of illusions.

This process of creating illusions through signs and symbols is most evident in the digital age, where social media, virtual reality, and digital communication allow for the constant production and consumption of images and symbols. Online, individuals create curated versions of their lives, presenting idealized images of themselves, their experiences, and their relationships. These representations, often carefully filtered and edited, create a hyperreal version of the self that bears little resemblance to the complexities of real life. In this sense, social media becomes a platform for the exchange of illusions, where users consume and create signs that reinforce an artificial version of reality.

Baudrillard's critique of signs, symbols, and their illusions forces us to confront the unsettling truth that much of what we take to be real is, in fact, an illusion. The signs and symbols that populate our world, from advertisements to social media profiles, create a reality that is disconnected from any underlying truth. This hyperreal world, where meaning is constructed through signs that refer only to other signs, challenges our ability to engage with the real and raises profound questions about the nature of truth, identity, and reality in the modern age.

Ultimately, Baudrillard's analysis invites us to look beyond the surface of signs and symbols and to question the illusions they create. In a world dominated by simulations, it becomes increasingly difficult to distinguish between what is real and what is merely an illusion, but Baudrillard's work challenges us to remain critical of the signs we consume and to seek a deeper understanding of the forces that shape our perception of reality.

The Society of the Spectacle: Baudrillard vs. Debord

When discussing Jean Baudrillard's ideas, it is impossible to overlook his intellectual connection and divergence from Guy Debord, the French Marxist theorist and author of *The Society of the Spectacle* (1967). Debord's work profoundly influenced how we understand modern culture and media, particularly how consumer society creates a "spectacle" that mediates human experience. Baudrillard, building on some of Debord's insights, would later push these ideas even further, developing his own theories around hyper reality and the precession of simulacra. While both thinkers analyze the pervasive influence of images, media, and consumerism, their views diverge significantly in how they interpret the consequences of these phenomena. To understand Baudrillard fully, it is useful to place his ideas in conversation with Debord, as this comparison illuminates their shared concerns as well as the philosophical and theoretical differences between them.

Guy Debord's *The Society of the Spectacle* offers a powerful critique of how capitalist society transforms life into a series of images and representations. For Debord, the "spectacle" is a form of social control, where real social relations and authentic human experiences are replaced by representations mediated through images, media, and commodities. The spectacle, in Debord's analysis, is not merely about entertainment or distraction; it is the central organizing principle of contemporary capitalist society. The spectacle creates a world where people relate to each other, not directly, but through images and representations. These images are shaped by the interests of capitalism, which commodifies every aspect of life, reducing social relations to transactions and human experiences to consumer goods.

For Debord, the spectacle functions as a tool of alienation. He argues that in pre-capitalist societies, humans interacted with each other and their environment in more direct, authentic ways. In modern capitalism, however, these direct interactions are replaced by a world of appearances, where people are alienated from both the means of production and from each other. The spectacle serves to maintain this alienation by creating a world where everything is commodified and consumed through representations—whether it is products, politics, or even personal relationships. In this way, the spectacle is both a symptom and a mechanism of control, reinforcing the power structures of capitalism by keeping people focused on appearances rather than realities.

While Baudrillard's critique of modern society is indebted to Debord, he takes a different path, particularly when it comes to understanding the role of media and images. Like Debord, Baudrillard believed that modern society is dominated by representations and images that mediate our experience of the world. However, Baudrillard argues that by the time we reach the late 20th century, the spectacle has evolved into something even more insidious: hyper reality. While Debord's spectacle still implies a reality behind the images—a reality that can be recovered or reclaimed—Baudrillard claims that in hyper reality, the distinction between the real and the simulated has collapsed entirely.

In *The Society of the Spectacle*, Debord laments how images and representations have obscured the real, but he still holds onto the hope that through revolutionary action, people might return to a more authentic relationship with reality and with each other.

His Marxist outlook sees the spectacle as a function of capitalism, one that can potentially be dismantled if the underlying economic structures are transformed. For Debord, behind the spectacle lies a real world of human labor, production, and social relations that capitalism distorts but does not entirely erase. If capitalism were to be overthrown, the spectacle could be dissolved, and authentic social relations could be restored.

Baudrillard, on the other hand, argues that such a return to reality is no longer possible. In *Simulacra and Simulation*, he introduces the concept of hyper reality, where signs and images have become so dominant that they no longer reflect any underlying reality. Instead, they create their own reality, one that is entirely detached from any "real" world. For Baudrillard, the spectacle has not just obscured reality; it has replaced it. In hyper reality, the images and simulations that we encounter in media, advertising, and consumer culture are not simply distortions of the real—they are the real. There is no reality to return to, because what we perceive as reality is now entirely constructed by these representations.

This is a fundamental point of departure between Debord and Baudrillard. Where Debord sees the spectacle as a tool of capitalist alienation, Baudrillard sees hyper reality as a more profound ontological shift. Debord's spectacle is a veil over reality, while Baudrillard's hyper reality is a new kind of reality altogether. In Baudrillard's view, we no longer live in a world where images reflect or distort reality; we live in a world where images *are* reality. This is what he calls the "precession of simulacra," where simulations precede and define the real rather than the other way around.

Another significant difference between the two thinkers lies in their attitudes toward resistance. For Debord, resistance to the spectacle is possible. His Marxist framework suggests that if people become aware of their alienation and the way the spectacle distorts reality, they can organize and resist, potentially overthrowing the capitalist system that generates the spectacle. There is a utopian dimension to Debord's thought, rooted in the belief that revolutionary action can restore a more authentic way of living, free from the distortions of commodification and spectacle.

Baudrillard, however, is far more pessimistic. In his view, there is no outside to hyper reality, no way to break free from the endless cycle of images and simulations that define contemporary life. For Baudrillard, even resistance becomes part of the system. Acts of rebellion, protests, and attempts to expose the truth are themselves absorbed into the logic of hyper reality, becoming just another set of images to be consumed. Baudrillard points out how media coverage of protests or revolutionary movements often reduces these events to spectacles, transforming genuine dissent into entertainment or symbolic gestures with little real impact. In this sense, Baudrillard is skeptical of the possibility of escaping hyper reality, as every attempt to do so is immediately co-opted and rendered harmless by the very system it seeks to challenge.

A clear illustration of this difference can be seen in how both thinkers analyze the role of media in politics. For Debord, the spectacle is used by those in power to control and manipulate the masses, but the underlying political reality—the struggles over power, class, and economics—remains. The spectacle distracts people from these real struggles, but it does not eliminate them. In contrast, Baudrillard argues that politics itself has become a simulation. Political campaigns, media coverage of elections, and even the acts of governing have been reduced to performances, where the image is all that matters. Politicians are no longer engaged in real struggles over policy or power; instead, they are engaged in the performance of power, where the spectacle of politics replaces the reality of governance.

Baudrillard's analysis of the Gulf War in *The Gulf War Did Not Take Place* exemplifies his departure from Debord. While Debord would argue that media coverage of war transforms it into a spectacle, obscuring the real violence and destruction, Baudrillard claims that the war itself has become a simulation. The media's portrayal of the war—its focus on technology, precision bombing, and sanitized images—creates a version of the war that bears little resemblance to the actual events on the ground. For Baudrillard, the Gulf War is not merely a spectacle that distorts the truth; it is a hyperreal event, where the simulation of war replaces the reality of conflict. The war, as it was experienced by most people, did not take place in any meaningful sense—it existed only as a media event, a series of images and narratives constructed for consumption.

In conclusion, while both Baudrillard and Debord offer powerful critiques of modern capitalist society and the role of media in shaping human experience, their theories diverge significantly in how they interpret the consequences of the spectacle. Debord's spectacle is a tool of alienation that can be resisted, while Baudrillard's hyper reality is a new form of reality that offers no escape. For Debord, there is still a hope that reality can be recovered through revolutionary action, but for Baudrillard, the real has already disappeared, replaced by a world of simulations and signs that precede and define what we take to be reality. This distinction highlights the shift from Debord's Marxist critique of capitalism to Baudrillard's more radical postmodern theory of hyper reality, where the death of the real leaves us in a world where only the spectacle remains.

The Role of Media in Simulated Reality

Jean Baudrillard's critique of modern society is inseparable from his exploration of the media's role in creating and perpetuating simulated realities. For Baudrillard, media is not simply a neutral tool that transmits information or reflects reality; it is a powerful force that constructs reality itself, shaping our perceptions, thoughts, and experiences. In Baudrillard's theory, the media plays a central role in the creation of hyper reality—a condition in which simulations and representations become more real than the reality they supposedly reflect. The media, through its constant production and circulation of images and narratives, has become the dominant force in creating the hyperreal world we now inhabit.

To understand the media's role in simulated reality, it's essential to begin with Baudrillard's concept of simulation. In his view, simulations are not just false representations or imitations of the real world; they are models of reality that replace the real entirely. This occurs through the proliferation of signs and images that no longer have any connection to an original or authentic reality. Instead, they form a self-contained system of meaning where signs refer only to other signs, creating a world that is entirely constructed by representations. In this system, the media becomes a primary agent in producing and disseminating these signs, thus playing a crucial role in shaping the simulated reality we experience.

One of the most striking ways the media constructs simulated reality is through its selective framing of events and information. News media, for instance, does not simply present an objective account of events; it filters, edits, and frames stories in ways that often reflect specific political, economic, or ideological interests. The result is a version of reality that has been carefully constructed for consumption, rather than a faithful representation of actual events. Baudrillard would argue that the media's portrayal of war is a clear example of this process. In his essay *The Gulf War Did Not Take Place*, Baudrillard critiques how the media's coverage of the Gulf War in 1990–1991 transformed the conflict into a sanitized, hyperreal event, where images of precision bombing and technological superiority overshadowed the brutal reality of violence and suffering. The media didn't simply distort the war; it created a version of the war that became more real for the public than the war itself.

This process of mediation extends beyond news and politics to entertainment, advertising, and even social media. In each of these spheres, the media produces endless streams of images and narratives that shape how we perceive the world and our place within it. For Baudrillard, this constant production of images leads to a state of hyper reality, where the line between the real and the simulated becomes indistinguishable. Consider the world of reality television, where the media creates highly controlled, edited versions of supposedly "real" events. Shows like *Keeping Up with the Kardashians* or *The Bachelor* present themselves as unscripted glimpses into the lives of real people, but in reality, they are carefully crafted simulations. The participants often play exaggerated versions of themselves, and the scenarios they navigate are constructed for dramatic effect. The audience, however, consumes these simulations as if they were real, blurring the boundary between fiction and reality.

Social media is another powerful example of how the media constructs simulated realities. Platforms like Instagram, Facebook, and Twitter encourage users to curate and present idealized versions of their lives. People selectively post images and updates that project a certain image of themselves—often one that is more polished, successful, or happy than their actual experience. These curated profiles become simulacra, representations of the self that bear little resemblance to the complexities of real life. For the audience, these simulacra are consumed as if they were real, creating a hyperreal world where people interact not with real individuals but with their simulated selves. The self, in this sense, becomes a media construct, shaped by the signs and symbols circulating on social platforms.

Advertising, too, plays a significant role in the media's construction of simulated reality. Advertisements are not just about promoting products; they create symbolic associations between commodities and abstract ideals like happiness, success, love, or freedom. A perfume commercial, for instance, does not simply promote a scent; it constructs a narrative about beauty, desire, and luxury, encouraging consumers to buy into a simulated version of identity and lifestyle. The product becomes secondary to the image it represents, and consumers are drawn not to the real object but to the simulation of the ideal life it promises. Baudrillard would argue that in this process, advertising creates a hyperreal world where the signs of consumer goods have replaced any authentic experience of life. The illusion becomes more desirable than the reality, and the real world is subsumed by a series of media-generated fantasies.

For Baudrillard, the media's role in creating simulated reality has profound implications for how we understand truth and meaning. In a hyperreal world, traditional distinctions between true and false, real and imaginary, lose their significance. The media doesn't just report on reality; it actively produces it. This production of reality happens through what Baudrillard calls the "implosion of meaning," where the sheer volume of signs and images overwhelms any attempt to distinguish between what is real and what is not. In this media-saturated environment, meaning becomes fragmented and dislocated, as signs circulate without any grounding in a stable or coherent reality. The result is a world where truth itself becomes a simulation, produced and consumed in the same way as entertainment or commodities.

The role of media in creating simulated reality is perhaps most visible in the phenomenon of "fake news" and the broader manipulation of information. In recent years, the rise of misinformation, propaganda, and disinformation has further blurred the lines between reality and simulation. News stories, images, and videos can be easily fabricated or manipulated, creating convincing simulations of events that never happened. These fake narratives often spread rapidly through social media and other media platforms, where they are consumed and believed by large audiences. In this context, Baudrillard's idea of the "death of the real" becomes alarmingly relevant. When simulations of reality are indistinguishable from reality itself, the real loses its power and meaning, leaving us in a world where truth is constantly constructed and reconstructed by the media.

Baudrillard's analysis also suggests that in a world dominated by media simulations, resistance becomes increasingly difficult. In traditional political theory, resistance to power involves uncovering and exposing the truth, revealing the ways in which power operates behind the scenes. However, in Baudrillard's hyperreal world, where media produces endless simulations, there is no stable reality to return to. Resistance itself can be co-opted by the media, transformed into yet another spectacle or simulation to be consumed. Protests, revolutions, and acts of dissent are often mediated and represented in ways that neutralize their power, reducing them to symbolic gestures that fit neatly within the existing system of hyper reality.

For instance, media coverage of protests often focuses more on the spectacle of the event—the signs, the slogans, the clashes with police—than on the underlying issues or demands of the protestors. The protest, in this mediated form, becomes a performance, a simulation of resistance that can be consumed by the public without challenging the structures of power it seeks to oppose. In this way, the media can absorb and neutralize dissent, transforming it into a simulation that serves to reinforce the status quo rather than disrupt it.

Baudrillard's theory of the media's role in simulated reality also has implications for how we think about identity and subjectivity. In a hyperreal world, where media creates and circulates endless simulations, identity itself becomes fluid and fragmented. Traditional notions of the self, grounded in a stable sense of reality, give way to a postmodern subject that is constantly shaped and reshaped by the media. The self becomes a simulation, constructed from the images, narratives, and signs that circulate in the media landscape. In this sense, identity is no longer something that is discovered or realized; it is something that is produced, consumed, and performed within the context of media representations.

Ultimately, Baudrillard's analysis of the media's role in simulated reality challenges us to rethink our relationship with the images, signs, and narratives that surround us. In a world where the media constructs reality, we must question the authenticity of our experiences, the truth of what we see, and the ways in which our perceptions are shaped by simulations. Baudrillard invites us to critically examine the media's power to define reality, to recognize the ways in which it produces illusions that are consumed as truth, and to reflect on the implications of living in a world where the real has been eclipsed by the simulated.

Consumer Culture and the Masses

Jean Baudrillard's analysis of consumer culture provides a critical lens through which we can understand the profound shifts in how society, identity, and meaning are constructed in the postmodern era. Baudrillard believed that in advanced capitalist societies, consumerism is not just an economic activity but a system that shapes every aspect of social life. For Baudrillard, consumption is not merely about satisfying needs or acquiring goods; it is about creating meaning, identity, and social order through signs and symbols. His critique of consumer culture goes beyond traditional economic analysis and delves into how the masses are shaped, manipulated, and controlled by the system of consumption, where the act of consuming becomes central to modern life.

At the core of Baudrillard's critique is the idea that consumer goods are no longer valued for their utility or material function but for their symbolic value. In modern consumer culture, products are imbued with meanings and symbols that go far beyond their practical use. When people purchase a product, they are not just acquiring an object; they are buying into a set of values, a lifestyle, or an identity. This shift from use-value to symbolic value is fundamental to understanding how consumer culture operates. A luxury car, for example, is not merely a mode of transportation; it is a sign of success, status, and wealth. A designer handbag is not just a container for personal items; it represents fashion, taste, and social distinction. In this system, consumption is less about material necessity and more about constructing and displaying one's place in society through the use of symbols.

Baudrillard argues that this symbolic system of consumption is deeply tied to the production of social identity. In consumer culture, individuals are defined by what they consume. The clothes people wear, the cars they drive, the phones they use—all serve as signs that communicate their social status, personal identity, and values to others. Consumer goods become a language of sorts, a way for individuals to express themselves and navigate their social environments. This creates a society where the act of consuming becomes central to one's sense of self and place in the world. The masses, in Baudrillard's view, are drawn into this system, not merely as passive consumers but as active participants in the creation of meaning through consumption.

However, Baudrillard is critical of this process because it represents a form of social control. In a world where meaning is constructed through consumption, individuals are trapped in a system that dictates their desires, identities, and relationships. The masses are constantly bombarded with images, advertisements, and messages that tell them what to desire, how to behave, and who to be. In this way, consumer culture functions as a form of social regulation, where the masses are conditioned to find meaning and fulfillment in the act of consumption, rather than in more traditional or authentic forms of social engagement.

One of the key ways that consumer culture controls the masses, according to Baudrillard, is through the creation of needs. In modern capitalist societies, the economy no longer revolves around the production of goods to meet existing needs; instead, it operates by creating new needs. Advertising, marketing, and the media are all complicit in this process, constantly generating desires for new products, experiences, and lifestyles.

The masses are led to believe that their happiness, self-worth, and social status depend on acquiring these goods, even though these needs are artificially constructed. The result is a cycle of consumption where individuals are continually chasing after new products in an attempt to fill an ever-expanding void of desires.

This phenomenon is particularly evident in the world of fashion and technology, where trends and products are constantly being updated, replaced, and rebranded. A smartphone, for example, is marketed not just as a tool for communication but as a symbol of modernity, innovation, and social connectedness. Each new model is presented as a must-have item, even though the differences between models may be minor. The masses are encouraged to discard perfectly functional products in favor of the latest version, driven by the belief that staying up-to-date with the latest technology or fashion is essential to maintaining one's social identity. Baudrillard would argue that this creates a system of endless consumption, where individuals are constantly driven to consume more, not because they need more but because their sense of self is tied to the act of consuming.

Baudrillard's critique of consumer culture also extends to the ways in which the media plays a central role in shaping and maintaining this system. The media, through advertising, television, films, and now digital platforms, produces and circulates the signs and symbols that define consumer culture. Advertisements do not just sell products; they sell ideals, values, and identities. They create a world where happiness, success, and fulfillment are tied to the acquisition of goods, reinforcing the notion that consumption is the path to a meaningful life. The media, in this sense, functions as a tool of social control, perpetuating the illusion that consumerism offers the key to personal satisfaction and social harmony.

Baudrillard is particularly concerned with how this system of consumption reduces the masses to passive spectators, where their role in society is limited to that of consumers. In his analysis, the masses are no longer active participants in the political, social, or cultural life of society; instead, they are conditioned to consume the products, images, and experiences provided to them by the system. This passivity is encouraged by the media, which creates a spectacle of consumption that distracts the masses from more substantive forms of engagement. In this way, consumer culture becomes a means of controlling and pacifying the masses, keeping them focused on the pursuit of material goods rather than on political or social change.

This reduction of the masses to consumers also has implications for democracy and citizenship. In a society where consumption is the primary mode of engagement, traditional forms of political participation, such as voting, activism, or public debate, are sidelined. Instead, individuals express their identities and values through the products they buy, the brands they support, and the lifestyles they adopt. Baudrillard would argue that this shift undermines the foundations of democratic society, where citizens are supposed to engage in public life as active, informed participants. In consumer culture, the role of the citizen is replaced by that of the consumer, and the political sphere is increasingly dominated by media-driven spectacles rather than meaningful discourse.

Baudrillard's critique of consumer culture also touches on the idea of the "silent majority"—the masses who are neither politically active nor resistant but are instead absorbed into the system of consumption. The silent majority, in Baudrillard's view, are not passive because they are oppressed or unaware; they are passive because they have been fully integrated into the consumer system. They find meaning, pleasure, and identity in the act of consumption, and they are complicit in maintaining the system that shapes their desires and identities. In this sense, the masses are not victims of consumer culture; they are participants in it, willingly consuming the signs and symbols that define their lives.

Despite Baudrillard's critique, he does not offer a clear solution to the problem of consumer culture. In his view, the system is so pervasive and all-encompassing that it is difficult to imagine a way out. Resistance to consumer culture, he argues, is often co-opted by the system itself, transformed into another form of consumption. For example, the rise of "ethical" or "sustainable" consumerism—where individuals try to resist the excesses of capitalism by buying eco-friendly or fair-trade products—still operates within the logic of consumerism. Even acts of resistance are commodified and sold back to the masses as another form of consumption.

In the end, Baudrillard's analysis of consumer culture offers a powerful critique of how the masses are shaped and controlled by the system of consumption. In this world, the act of consuming is not just about acquiring goods; it is about creating meaning, identity, and social order. The masses are drawn into this system, not as passive victims but as active participants, conditioned to find fulfillment in the act of consuming. The media, advertising, and marketing all play central roles in perpetuating this system, creating a world where signs and symbols define reality, and where the real is subsumed by the endless pursuit of material goods. Baudrillard's critique forces us to confront the ways in which consumer culture shapes our lives, our identities, and our society, raising critical questions about the nature of freedom, control, and meaning in the modern world.

The Implosion of Meaning in the Media Age

Jean Baudrillard's concept of the *implosion of meaning* is one of his most provocative and critical insights into how modern media shapes our perception of reality. In the context of his broader critique of postmodern society, the idea of the implosion of meaning refers to the collapse of clear distinctions between truth and falsehood, reality and representation, and meaningful communication and empty noise. As media has become more pervasive, saturating every aspect of life with images, messages, and information, Baudrillard argues that meaning itself has been overwhelmed, fragmented, and ultimately rendered meaningless. In this media-saturated world, where we are constantly bombarded with signs and symbols, meaning no longer coheres in a stable or understandable way, leading to a collapse—or implosion—of meaning.

To understand Baudrillard's notion of the implosion of meaning, it's essential to consider his views on how media functions in contemporary society. For Baudrillard, media is not simply a vehicle for transmitting information or reflecting reality; it is a system that generates its own reality, a hyper reality. In this hyperreal world, media does not just communicate; it creates, transforms, and distorts. It produces a world where the boundaries between the real and the simulated dissolve, and where signs no longer point to any underlying reality. This constant flow of images, information, and representations results in a world where meaning becomes unstable, as the media endlessly recycles signs and symbols without any clear referent.

Baudrillard describes this process as an "implosion" because meaning does not simply disappear; it collapses in on itself. The more information we receive, the less we are able to make sense of it. The media bombards us with so many messages, images, and narratives that we are overwhelmed by the sheer volume. Instead of helping us understand the world, the media overloads us, saturating our senses to the point where distinctions between truth and fiction, important and trivial, meaningful and meaningless, become impossible to discern. The result is a condition where all meaning is flattened, leaving us in a state of disorientation, where nothing seems to matter or hold significance.

One of the key drivers of the implosion of meaning is what Baudrillard calls *the proliferation of signs*. In contemporary media culture, signs—images, words, symbols—are constantly produced and circulated at an unprecedented rate. In earlier societies, signs were tied to specific meanings and contexts; they represented something real or communicated a particular message. However, in the modern media age, signs have become detached from their original referents. They no longer point to a clear or stable meaning but instead circulate within a system of endless repetition and reproduction. In this process, signs lose their connection to reality, becoming floating symbols that refer only to each other in an infinite loop.

An example of this proliferation of signs can be seen in advertising. Advertisements do not just promote products; they create entire worlds of meaning, filled with images and narratives that promise happiness, success, and fulfillment. A perfume commercial, for instance, may show a glamorous celebrity in a luxurious setting, surrounded by beautiful people and exotic locations. The perfume is no longer just a scent; it becomes a symbol of desire, allure, and sophistication.

However, this meaning is not grounded in any real experience or truth; it is an illusion, constructed by the media to create a desire that can never be fully satisfied. The advertisement is filled with signs—images, music, slogans—but these signs do not point to anything real. Instead, they create a hyperreal world where meaning is continually produced and consumed, but never truly understood or realized.

The implosion of meaning is also evident in the way the media covers news and politics. In Baudrillard's view, the media's representation of events does not simply distort reality; it creates a hyper reality where the event itself becomes secondary to its media portrayal. News outlets, in their quest for attention and ratings, often prioritize sensationalism over substance, creating narratives that are designed to capture viewers' attention rather than provide meaningful insight. The result is that news becomes a spectacle, where events are reduced to soundbites, headlines, and images that evoke emotional reactions but do little to deepen understanding.

Take, for example, the media coverage of political campaigns. Baudrillard would argue that modern political campaigns are not about substantive debates over policies or ideologies but about image management and media spectacle. Politicians are reduced to media personalities, and their success often depends on how well they can perform within the confines of the media system. The media creates narratives about candidates, focusing on their appearance, their charisma, or their ability to generate controversy, rather than on their political platforms. In this way, political discourse is emptied of meaning, replaced by a simulated version of reality where the image is all that matters. The implosion of meaning in political media leaves the public in a state of confusion, where the line between performance and reality is blurred, and meaningful political engagement becomes increasingly difficult.

Baudrillard's concept of the implosion of meaning also extends to the realm of entertainment. In the world of reality television, for instance, the distinction between reality and fiction is deliberately blurred. Shows like *The Bachelor* or *Survivor* present themselves as unscripted glimpses into real people's lives, but in reality, they are carefully controlled simulations, designed to evoke specific emotions and reactions from the audience. The participants are often cast in archetypal roles, and the scenarios they face are crafted to create dramatic tension. The audience, however, consumes these simulations as if they were real, reinforcing the collapse of meaning between reality and its representation.

Social media further accelerates the implosion of meaning by encouraging users to curate and present idealized versions of their lives. Platforms like Instagram and Facebook are filled with images of perfection—beautiful vacations, happy families, successful careers—that often bear little resemblance to the complexities of real life. These images, while presented as authentic, are highly edited and filtered, creating a hyperreal version of reality where the line between truth and illusion is difficult to discern. In this environment, meaning becomes fragmented and shallow, as individuals are constantly bombarded with representations that encourage them to compare themselves to others, creating a cycle of desire and dissatisfaction.

The implosion of meaning in the media age is also closely tied to the phenomenon of *information overload*. In today's digital world, we have access to more information than ever before. News, entertainment, social media, and advertising all compete for our attention, creating a constant stream of content that we are expected to consume. However, the sheer volume of information we encounter makes it difficult to process or make sense of any of it. Instead of helping us understand the world, this flood of information overwhelms us, leading to a situation where nothing stands out as particularly meaningful or important. In this sense, more information does not lead to more understanding; it leads to confusion and disorientation.

Baudrillard's concept of the implosion of meaning is particularly relevant in the context of "fake news" and the broader manipulation of information in the digital age. As news sources, social media platforms, and political actors increasingly use misinformation and disinformation to shape public perception, it becomes even more difficult to distinguish between what is real and what is fabricated. The media produces endless narratives that compete for attention, but the truth becomes lost in the noise. In this environment, meaning collapses as individuals struggle to determine what is true, what is false, and what matters.

Baudrillard's critique of the media's role in the implosion of meaning is not just a theoretical observation; it is a challenge to how we understand and navigate the world. He invites us to recognize the ways in which the media, rather than clarifying or illuminating reality, often serves to obscure it. The endless production and consumption of signs and symbols, whether in advertising, news, entertainment, or social media, creates a world where meaning is constantly produced, but never fully realized. In this world, the real is subsumed by the simulated, and our ability to engage with reality in a meaningful way is diminished.

Ultimately, Baudrillard's concept of the implosion of meaning forces us to question the role of media in shaping our perceptions, desires, and identities. It challenges us to consider the consequences of living in a hyperreal world, where meaning is constantly fragmented and reconstituted, and where the distinction between truth and illusion becomes increasingly difficult to discern. In the media age, where we are surrounded by signs, images, and narratives that vie for our attention, Baudrillard's critique invites us to reflect on how we engage with the world, and whether we can find meaning in a landscape dominated by simulations and spectacle.

How Baudrillard Defined Reality's End

Jean Baudrillard's provocative claim that reality has come to an end is one of the most challenging and radical ideas in his body of work. Central to his philosophy is the notion that the very concept of reality has been fundamentally transformed, and in many cases, obliterated by the rise of media, technology, and the overwhelming proliferation of signs and symbols. Baudrillard didn't mean that physical existence has ceased but rather that our ability to experience and define reality as something separate from representation or simulation has disappeared. What he called the "end of reality" reflects a profound shift in how we engage with the world, where what we consider to be "real" is no longer grounded in material or experiential truth but in hyper reality—a world of simulations and representations that replace the real.

Baudrillard's analysis begins with his theory of *simulacra* and *simulation*. Simulacra are copies or representations of reality, and simulation refers to the process by which these copies create their own reality, one that supersedes or replaces the original. Traditionally, representations were understood as imitations of the real world. A painting might depict a landscape, a news report might describe an event, and a photograph might capture a moment in time. In each case, there was a clear distinction between the representation and the reality it was meant to reflect. However, Baudrillard argued that in the modern world, this distinction has collapsed. Representations no longer refer to a reality outside themselves; instead, they create a new form of reality—a hyper reality—where the real is indistinguishable from its simulations.

For Baudrillard, this process marks the "end of reality." In his view, reality has been replaced by an endless series of simulations that no longer point to anything real. This means that what we experience as "real" is no longer rooted in any material or objective truth but is constructed by the media, technology, and other systems of representation. In the hyperreal world, simulations precede and define the real, creating a reality that is entirely produced and controlled by the proliferation of signs and symbols. In this sense, Baudrillard suggests that reality as we once understood it—something external, stable, and independent—has ceased to exist.

One of the key examples Baudrillard uses to illustrate the end of reality is the world of mass media and entertainment. In his analysis, the media doesn't simply reflect the real world; it creates a new reality through the endless production of images, narratives, and simulations. Take, for example, the coverage of major political events or wars. Baudrillard argues that these events, as presented by the media, are not experienced as real occurrences but as carefully constructed spectacles. The media creates a version of reality that is designed for consumption—sensationalized, simplified, and packaged to capture attention. The result is that the event itself becomes secondary to its media representation. In this process, the line between the real event and its media simulation is blurred, and for most people, the media version becomes the only reality they know. This is what Baudrillard refers to as the *precession of simulacra*, where the representation comes before and defines the real.

A striking example of this phenomenon is Baudrillard's analysis of the Gulf War in his essay *The Gulf War Did Not Take Place*. Baudrillard did not mean that there was no military conflict but rather that the war, as experienced by the global public, was entirely mediated by the images and narratives constructed by the media. The reality of the war—its violence, destruction, and human suffering—was obscured by a hyperreal version of the conflict, where precision bombing and technological superiority were highlighted, and the human costs were minimized or ignored. In Baudrillard's view, the war, as presented to the public, was a simulation, a controlled and sanitized version of reality that bore little resemblance to the actual events on the ground. The media-created version of the war was so powerful that it replaced the real war in the public's consciousness, marking the end of reality as something distinct from its representation.

Another critical area where Baudrillard identified the end of reality is in the realm of consumer culture. In advanced capitalist societies, consumer goods are not just functional objects; they are symbols that carry meaning beyond their material use. A smartphone, for example, is not just a device for communication; it represents status, identity, and belonging in a digital world. Baudrillard argues that in consumer culture, we no longer engage with objects based on their utility but on the symbolic value they carry. This shift from use-value to symbolic value is a key aspect of hyper reality, where the signs and symbols associated with goods become more important than the goods themselves. The result is a world where reality is subsumed by a system of signs, and our experience of the real is mediated entirely by the symbolic meanings attached to consumer products.

In this context, Baudrillard suggests that reality has been replaced by a form of simulation, where signs and symbols define our understanding of the world. Advertising, for example, creates a simulated reality where happiness, success, and fulfillment are tied to the consumption of goods. A car commercial doesn't just sell a vehicle; it sells a lifestyle, a sense of identity, and a symbolic association with power, freedom, or luxury. The real object becomes secondary to the simulation it represents, and consumers are drawn not to the material good but to the hyperreal world created by advertising. In this way, consumer culture contributes to the end of reality by creating a system where the real is obscured and replaced by simulations that define our desires, identities, and relationships.

The end of reality is also evident in the rise of digital technology and virtual experiences. Virtual reality, social media, and digital communication have created new forms of interaction that blur the boundary between the real and the simulated. In virtual reality environments, users can immerse themselves in entirely simulated worlds that feel real to the senses, but are entirely artificial. These experiences challenge our understanding of what is real, as the line between physical reality and digital simulation becomes increasingly difficult to discern. Similarly, on social media, individuals create curated versions of their lives, presenting idealized images of themselves that are consumed by others as if they were real. These digital representations, however, are often highly edited and filtered, creating a hyperreal version of reality where the self is a simulation constructed for public consumption.

Baudrillard's analysis of the end of reality extends to the broader implications for identity, truth, and power. In a world where reality is replaced by simulations, traditional notions of truth and authenticity lose their meaning. If the real is no longer distinguishable from the simulated, then truth itself becomes fluid, constructed, and manipulated by those who control the systems of representation. Baudrillard suggests that in this hyperreal world, power is no longer exercised through direct control or coercion but through the management of images, signs, and simulations. Those who control the media, technology, and other systems of representation have the power to define reality, shaping public perception and constructing a version of the world that serves their interests.

This has profound implications for how we understand politics, culture, and social life in the postmodern era. In a hyperreal world, where simulations replace the real, traditional forms of resistance and critique become increasingly difficult. Baudrillard argues that even acts of rebellion, protest, or dissent are often co-opted by the system and transformed into simulations of resistance. For example, media coverage of protests may focus more on the spectacle of the event—the signs, the slogans, the clashes with police—than on the underlying political issues. In this way, protest itself becomes part of the hyperreal system, a performance consumed by the public rather than a genuine challenge to the structures of power.

In Baudrillard's view, the end of reality does not mean the end of existence, but it signals a profound shift in how we experience and understand the world. In the hyperreal world, reality is no longer something external or objective; it is something that is constantly produced, reproduced, and consumed through simulations. This shift challenges our ability to engage with the world in meaningful ways, as the distinction between truth and illusion becomes increasingly difficult to maintain.

Ultimately, Baudrillard's concept of the end of reality is a critique of the ways in which media, technology, and consumer culture have transformed our understanding of the world. He invites us to reflect on the implications of living in a world where reality is no longer a stable, independent category but a fluid construct shaped by the systems of representation that define modern life. In this hyperreal world, where simulations replace the real, Baudrillard asks us to consider what it means to live in a reality that has, in many ways, come to an end.

The Matrix and Baudrillard's Influence

The 1999 film *The Matrix* stands as one of the most iconic works of science fiction, and its themes of simulated reality, control, and the nature of existence have resonated deeply with audiences and scholars alike. Central to its conceptual framework is the influence of Jean Baudrillard's philosophy, particularly his ideas about simulation, hyper reality, and the end of reality. Although *The Matrix* directly references Baudrillard's seminal work *Simulacra and Simulation*, even showing a hollowed-out copy of the book in an early scene, the film uses his ideas in ways that both reflect and, in some respects, diverge from Baudrillard's original theories.

At its core, *The Matrix* explores the concept of simulated reality—an artificial world created to deceive and control the population, leading them to believe they are living in a real, physical world. This idea directly parallels Baudrillard's theory of hyper reality, where simulations replace reality and become indistinguishable from it. In the world of *The Matrix*, humans are unknowingly trapped in a virtual environment constructed by machines, believing they are living ordinary lives when, in fact, they are experiencing a simulation. This theme of questioning what is real, and whether the reality we perceive is authentic or manufactured, is central to Baudrillard's philosophy and runs throughout the film.

Baudrillard's notion of *simulacra*—copies or representations that have no original—also finds expression in *The Matrix*. In the film, the simulated world is not an imitation of a real world that exists somewhere else; rather, it is a completely fabricated reality, a simulacrum that has replaced the real. The Matrix itself is a perfect example of a simulacrum in Baudrillard's sense: it is a copy of a world that doesn't exist, yet it is accepted as real by those trapped within it. This mirrors Baudrillard's argument that in postmodern society, simulacra no longer refer to any original reality; they are self-sustaining, producing a reality that no longer needs to be anchored in the real world.

The film's philosophical question—"What is the Matrix?"—echoes Baudrillard's exploration of how reality is mediated and distorted by simulations. For Baudrillard, the distinction between reality and its representations has collapsed, leaving us in a state of hyper reality, where we can no longer tell the difference between what is real and what is simulated. This idea is central to *The Matrix*, where the protagonist, Neo, begins to realize that the world he has always known is a simulated construct, and the real world exists outside the Matrix. The famous "red pill" and "blue pill" choice offered to Neo symbolizes the decision to either remain in the illusion of the simulated world (the blue pill) or wake up to the harsh reality beyond the simulation (the red pill). This moment in the film encapsulates Baudrillard's argument that we are often complicit in maintaining the illusion of reality, preferring the comfort of simulation to the difficult truths of the real world.

Despite these clear resonances with Baudrillard's ideas, *The Matrix* also diverges from his philosophy in significant ways. While the film suggests that it is possible to escape the simulation and return to a "real" world outside of the Matrix, Baudrillard's philosophy offers no such possibility. For Baudrillard, there is no escape from hyper reality; the distinction between the real and the simulated has collapsed so completely that there is no longer a real world to return to.

In Baudrillard's view, even acts of rebellion or attempts to expose the truth are absorbed into the system of simulation, becoming part of the spectacle. Resistance, in Baudrillard's hyperreal world, is itself a simulation, co-opted by the system it seeks to challenge.

In *The Matrix*, however, Neo's journey is framed as one of liberation, where he wakes up to the truth and fights against the system that has enslaved humanity. The film offers a clear distinction between the Matrix (the simulation) and the real world (the realm of human resistance), and it suggests that by waking up from the illusion, one can return to an authentic reality. This binary distinction between the simulated and the real, as well as the possibility of escape, contrasts with Baudrillard's more pessimistic view that there is no longer any "outside" to the system of simulation. For Baudrillard, hyper reality is inescapable; it defines our existence, and any attempt to resist or return to a more authentic reality is futile, as the real has already been subsumed by the simulated.

Baudrillard himself was critical of *The Matrix* for this very reason. In interviews, he remarked that the film misunderstood his ideas, particularly the notion of hyper reality. He felt that the filmmakers had oversimplified his philosophy by suggesting that the real world could still be accessed and that the Matrix was a kind of external illusion that could be broken free from. For Baudrillard, hyper reality is not a separate, virtual world but a condition that permeates the entire social and cultural fabric. The real and the simulated are so intertwined that they cannot be disentangled, and the idea of waking up from the illusion to find a stable, real world waiting on the other side is, for him, a misunderstanding of how hyper reality works.

Despite Baudrillard's critique, *The Matrix* has undeniably popularized his ideas and brought them into mainstream consciousness. The film's exploration of simulated reality, control, and the nature of existence resonates deeply with Baudrillard's theory of simulation, even if it departs from his more radical conclusions. In many ways, *The Matrix* serves as a gateway for audiences to engage with Baudrillard's philosophy, encouraging viewers to question the nature of reality and the ways in which media, technology, and power shape our perceptions of the world.

One of the most compelling aspects of *The Matrix* is how it dramatizes Baudrillard's concept of *the precession of simulacra*, where simulations precede and define reality. In the film, the Matrix is a fully constructed reality that shapes the perceptions, thoughts, and experiences of those trapped within it. People accept the simulated world as real because it is the only reality they know, much like how, in Baudrillard's analysis, hyper reality becomes the dominant form of reality in postmodern society. The simulated world of the Matrix precedes and replaces the real, just as Baudrillard argues that in the hyperreal world, simulations replace the real to the point where the distinction between the two is erased.

In addition to exploring the philosophical implications of simulation, *The Matrix* also touches on Baudrillard's ideas about control and power in the postmodern world. The film portrays the Matrix as a system of control, designed to keep humanity enslaved by feeding people a simulated reality that pacifies them and prevents them from questioning the world around them. This mirrors Baudrillard's argument that in a hyperreal society, power operates not through direct coercion but through the management of signs, images, and simulations. In the hyperreal world, people are controlled not by force but by the subtle manipulation of reality, where simulations shape their desires, thoughts, and behaviors without them realizing it.

Baudrillard's influence on *The Matrix* also extends to the film's treatment of technology. The Matrix itself is a technological construct, a digital simulation created by machines to enslave humanity. This reflects Baudrillard's concerns about the role of technology in creating and perpetuating hyper reality. In his view, modern technology—particularly media, digital communication, and virtual reality—plays a central role in producing the simulations that define our experience of the world. In *The Matrix*, technology is both the means of enslavement and, paradoxically, the tool that enables Neo to escape and fight back against the system. This duality reflects Baudrillard's ambivalence about technology, which he saw as both a source of liberation and a mechanism of control.

In conclusion, *The Matrix* draws heavily on Jean Baudrillard's ideas about simulation, hyper reality, and the collapse of the real, even as it departs from some of his more radical conclusions. The film's exploration of a simulated reality that controls and deceives the population is deeply influenced by Baudrillard's critique of modern society, where the media, technology, and consumer culture create a world of simulations that replace the real. While Baudrillard rejected the film's portrayal of the possibility of escaping the simulation, *The Matrix* nonetheless serves as a powerful dramatization of his core ideas, encouraging viewers to question the nature of reality and the forces that shape their perceptions of the world. Through its blend of philosophy, science fiction, and action, *The Matrix* brings Baudrillard's concepts into mainstream culture, inviting audiences to engage with the complexities of simulation, control, and the end of reality.

Virtual Reality: Baudrillard's Perspective on the Digital Age

Jean Baudrillard's analysis of the digital age, particularly in relation to virtual reality, offers a profound critique of how technology reshapes our experience of the world, further blurring the boundaries between reality and simulation. Baudrillard's ideas about hyper reality, simulacra, and the collapse of the real take on new dimensions when applied to the rise of virtual reality (VR) and other digital technologies. While Baudrillard did not live to witness the full extent of today's digital revolution, his philosophical insights are remarkably prescient in predicting how virtual reality, augmented reality, and the broader digital environment would accelerate the "end of reality" and intensify our immersion in a world of simulations.

Baudrillard's concept of *hyper reality*—where the distinction between the real and the simulated disappears—directly applies to virtual reality, which creates fully immersive environments that feel real but are entirely fabricated. For Baudrillard, hyper reality is a condition in which simulations of reality become more real than reality itself, and in many ways, VR epitomizes this shift. In virtual environments, users can experience worlds that are designed to simulate reality so convincingly that they can evoke real emotions, reactions, and sensations, even though these environments have no physical or material existence. Virtual reality, then, is a clear embodiment of Baudrillard's theory, as it represents a space where the real and the simulated collapse into one.

What is striking about Baudrillard's perspective on virtual reality and the digital age is his understanding of how technology not only replicates reality but creates a *hyperreal* version of it—one that may be more appealing, more compelling, and in some cases, more desirable than the real world. In VR, users are not just escaping into fantasy worlds; they are entering environments that simulate real-world experiences, often with enhancements that make these experiences more perfect than reality itself. For instance, virtual worlds can offer idealized landscapes, perfect bodies, or situations free from the limitations of real life, such as pain, danger, or social constraints. In this sense, virtual reality becomes a space where the simulation is preferable to the real, reinforcing Baudrillard's claim that in the digital age, the simulated can replace the real entirely.

Baudrillard's critique of simulation goes beyond simple imitation or illusion. He argued that in the modern age, simulations no longer refer back to any original reality; instead, they create their own reality. This is especially true in the context of VR, where the virtual worlds are not copies of the physical world but entirely new constructs. Users of virtual reality aren't simply interacting with a digital reflection of the real world; they are engaging with environments that have no real-world counterpart, and yet these experiences are often experienced as deeply real. In this way, virtual reality represents a new stage in the development of hyper reality, where simulations are not just imitations but become their own reality—completely self-sustained and independent of any external truth.

Baudrillard's concept of *the precession of simulacra*—where simulations precede and create reality—also finds a clear application in virtual reality. In his view, modern media and technology produce simulations that no longer imitate reality but instead generate their own forms of truth.

This is particularly evident in VR environments where the experience of the virtual can shape how people think, feel, and behave in the real world. Virtual reality creates experiences that can precede and shape real-life interactions. For example, in military training, VR simulations are used to prepare soldiers for combat by creating realistic scenarios that help shape their reactions and decisions in actual warfare. In this way, the simulation (the VR training) comes before the real experience and shapes it, embodying Baudrillard's idea that simulations now precede reality.

The rise of digital avatars and online identities further complicates Baudrillard's analysis. In virtual environments and social media, individuals can create avatars or digital representations of themselves that may bear little resemblance to their real-world identities. These digital selves, often carefully curated and idealized, allow people to construct and project a version of themselves that exists only in the virtual realm. Baudrillard would argue that these digital identities are a form of *simulacra*—representations that have no real counterpart. In the virtual world, the avatar becomes more real than the person behind it, as it is the avatar that interacts with others, forms relationships, and experiences the virtual environment. This creates a condition where the line between the real self and the virtual self is blurred, leading to a situation where the simulated identity becomes more meaningful than the real one.

One of Baudrillard's most important concerns about the digital age, including virtual reality, is the *loss of the real*. He argued that the proliferation of media and technology had led to the disappearance of any stable or coherent sense of reality. In the hyperreal world, people no longer engage with reality directly; instead, they interact with simulations, representations, and images that mediate their experience of the world. Virtual reality, as the ultimate simulation, epitomizes this condition. It creates environments where users can lose themselves in a simulated world, disconnecting from the physical world around them. This detachment from the real, Baudrillard would argue, represents the culmination of a long process in which media and technology have gradually eroded our connection to the material world.

In virtual reality, the idea of *authentic experience* is fundamentally challenged. Baudrillard questioned whether authentic experiences were even possible in a world dominated by simulations, and this question becomes even more pertinent in the context of VR. When users experience emotions, sensations, or interactions in a virtual environment, these experiences may feel real, but they are entirely constructed. For Baudrillard, this raises the question of whether these experiences have any authenticity or whether they are simply the product of a carefully designed simulation that mimics reality without ever touching on anything true. In this sense, virtual reality represents a further step in the process of replacing the real with the simulated, leaving us in a state where we can no longer distinguish between the two.

The implications of virtual reality for Baudrillard's theory of power and control are also significant. He argued that in the postmodern world, power no longer operates through direct coercion or force but through the manipulation of signs, images, and simulations. Virtual reality, as a technology that can completely control and shape one's sensory experience, offers a new level of potential control. In a virtual environment, every aspect of the user's experience can be manipulated—from what they see and hear to how they move and interact.

In this sense, VR becomes a tool for controlling perception itself, creating a situation where those who control the simulation control reality. Baudrillard would see this as a further extension of the media's role in shaping hyper reality, where power is exercised not through overt domination but through the creation of a simulated reality that dictates how people understand and experience the world.

Despite Baudrillard's critical stance on the rise of simulations and hyper reality, his work also contains an ambivalence about the digital age. While he recognized the dangers of living in a world where simulations replace the real, he also acknowledged that these developments were inevitable in a world dominated by technology and media. Virtual reality, in Baudrillard's view, represents both the fulfillment of his theory of hyper reality and a reflection of the larger cultural shift toward simulation as the dominant mode of experience. In this sense, Baudrillard did not advocate for a return to a pre-digital, pre-simulation world but rather invited us to confront and understand the implications of living in a reality constructed by technology.

In conclusion, Baudrillard's perspective on the digital age, particularly in relation to virtual reality, provides a powerful critique of how technology reshapes our experience of the world, collapsing the distinction between the real and the simulated. For Baudrillard, virtual reality is not just a technological innovation; it is the embodiment of the hyperreal condition, where simulations create their own reality, and the real is replaced by the virtual. His analysis challenges us to think critically about the ways in which digital technologies, including VR, shape our identities, experiences, and perceptions, and it invites us to reflect on the broader cultural implications of living in a world where simulations have overtaken the real.

Seduction and Power in Baudrillard's Thought

Jean Baudrillard's exploration of seduction and power is one of the more nuanced and complex aspects of his philosophical work. While he is best known for his theories on simulation, hyper reality, and the collapse of the real, his ideas about seduction represent an important counterpoint to traditional notions of power and control. For Baudrillard, seduction is not merely a form of attraction or manipulation; it is a radical alternative to the logic of power, a form of resistance and subversion that undermines the very structures of domination that define modern society. In his thought, seduction operates on a symbolic level, where meaning, desire, and social relations are not dictated by force or coercion but through play, illusion, and the subtle reversal of power.

Baudrillard's concept of seduction contrasts sharply with traditional theories of power, which are often based on control, domination, and the exercise of force. Power, in most classical understandings, involves the ability to compel others to act in certain ways or to enforce compliance through authority or coercion. In this sense, power is a visible, active force, always seeking to assert itself, impose rules, and maintain control. Baudrillard, however, saw power as fundamentally fragile, subject to subversion and reversal through seduction. Seduction, for him, represents a force that operates not through direct confrontation or resistance but through the manipulation of appearances, signs, and desire.

In Baudrillard's view, seduction works by playing with the surface of things—symbols, gestures, and appearances—rather than engaging in the straightforward exercise of force. It is a form of symbolic exchange, where meanings are constantly shifting, and nothing is ever fully captured or controlled. Seduction, in this sense, is elusive; it evades the directness of power by creating a game of appearances, where what is real and what is simulated are constantly in flux. By refusing to be pinned down or dominated, seduction resists the demands of power, which seeks stability and order.

One of the key differences between power and seduction, according to Baudrillard, is that power is focused on achieving clear, tangible outcomes, whereas seduction is about maintaining a sense of mystery, uncertainty, and play. Power operates by establishing rules and enforcing obedience, while seduction works through subtlety, illusion, and the suspension of certainty. In seduction, there is no final victory or resolution, only the constant play of appearances and the allure of the unknown. This makes seduction a fundamentally disruptive force, one that challenges the rigid structures of power by refusing to play by its rules.

For Baudrillard, seduction is also linked to the idea of symbolic exchange. In a world dominated by the logic of production, consumption, and accumulation, seduction offers an alternative way of relating to others and the world. Instead of being driven by the need to control or possess, seduction operates through the circulation of signs and symbols, where meaning is created through the act of exchange itself. In this sense, seduction is not about taking or holding power but about participating in a dynamic process of give and take, where control is always fleeting and provisional. This form of symbolic exchange, for Baudrillard, undermines the linear, goal-oriented logic of power, introducing a more fluid, open-ended way of relating to the world.

Baudrillard also connects seduction to the idea of reversibility, a key concept in his philosophy. In his view, seduction involves the possibility of reversing power, turning it back on itself in unexpected ways. Power, in its conventional sense, seeks to establish dominance and control, but seduction destabilizes this by introducing ambiguity and play. Through seduction, the power dynamic can be reversed, with the seducer becoming the seduced, and the dominant becoming the dominated. This reversibility makes seduction a powerful form of resistance, one that does not confront power head-on but instead subverts it from within by playing with its symbols and signs.

Baudrillard's fascination with seduction also stems from his critique of modern society's obsession with transparency, visibility, and truth. In a world where everything is expected to be revealed, exposed, and explained, seduction represents a form of resistance to this demand for total visibility. Seduction, for Baudrillard, thrives on the power of the hidden, the veiled, and the mysterious. It resists the drive to uncover and possess by maintaining an aura of secrecy and ambiguity. In this sense, seduction is aligned with illusion, which Baudrillard sees as a vital counterpoint to the hyperreal world of total transparency, where everything is visible and nothing is left to the imagination.

This emphasis on illusion and play is central to Baudrillard's critique of contemporary power structures, particularly in the context of media and technology. In a hyperreal world dominated by media images, simulations, and virtual realities, power is exercised through the control of signs and symbols. The media, for example, produces a constant flow of images and narratives that shape our perception of reality, creating a world where appearances and simulations are more real than the real. In this context, seduction offers a way of disrupting the media's control by playing with its symbols, introducing uncertainty, and subverting the logic of representation.

Baudrillard's idea of seduction as a form of resistance is perhaps most clearly illustrated in his critique of feminist movements that focus on empowerment through visibility and equal representation. He argued that while these movements seek to gain power by asserting themselves in the public sphere, they may be inadvertently reinforcing the logic of power by adopting its terms. In contrast, Baudrillard saw seduction as a more radical form of resistance, one that operates by refusing the logic of visibility and control. Seduction, in this sense, does not seek to gain power by entering the structures of domination; instead, it undermines those structures by refusing to play by their rules.

Baudrillard was not dismissive of power's influence in society, but he believed that power was fragile and vulnerable to seduction's reversals. He often described power as something that always wants to be seen, to be exercised openly, and to assert itself through the logic of domination. Seduction, however, operates in the shadows, using the power of absence, illusion, and the unseen to destabilize power's desire for visibility. In this sense, seduction is not just a game or a surface-level distraction; it is a profound strategy of resistance that operates at the symbolic level, challenging power's claim to authority by introducing the possibility of reversal and subversion.

For Baudrillard, seduction's refusal to be fixed or defined makes it an inherently political act. It is not about aligning with a particular ideology or seeking to gain power in the traditional sense; rather, it is about disrupting the systems of power by playing with their symbols and undermining their certainty. Seduction introduces a kind of symbolic warfare, where meaning and power are constantly in flux, and where control can never be fully asserted or maintained.

This understanding of seduction as a form of resistance is closely tied to Baudrillard's broader critique of modern society's emphasis on production, consumption, and control. In a world where everything is commodified, consumed, and controlled, seduction represents an alternative way of engaging with the world—one that is not based on accumulation or dominance but on the play of appearances and the reversibility of power. By embracing the logic of seduction, Baudrillard challenges the idea that power is inevitable or absolute, suggesting instead that it is always vulnerable to subversion through the symbolic games of desire and illusion.

In conclusion, Baudrillard's exploration of seduction offers a radical rethinking of power and resistance in the modern world. While traditional theories of power focus on control, domination, and visibility, Baudrillard's concept of seduction introduces a form of symbolic resistance that operates through play, illusion, and the manipulation of appearances. Seduction, for Baudrillard, is a way of subverting power without directly confronting it, by introducing uncertainty, ambiguity, and the possibility of reversal. In a world where power seeks to assert itself through control, seduction offers an alternative—a way of resisting domination through the subtle, elusive play of signs and symbols.

The Hyperreal in Art and Culture

Jean Baudrillard's concept of *hyper reality* has had a profound impact on how we understand the intersection of art, culture, and media in the modern world. In Baudrillard's thought, hyper reality refers to a state where the distinction between reality and its representations collapses, and the simulated becomes more real than reality itself. This concept has been particularly influential in discussions of contemporary art and culture, where the boundaries between reality, simulation, and representation have become increasingly blurred. As the world of media and technology has evolved, hyper reality has permeated not only the visual arts but also film, architecture, fashion, and other forms of cultural production, reshaping how we engage with and interpret the world around us.

For Baudrillard, hyper reality is a condition that arises in postmodern societies, where media and consumer culture dominate daily life. In this world, images and representations no longer reflect reality but create a new form of reality—a hyperreal world in which simulations take precedence over the real. This phenomenon is particularly evident in art, where the line between representation and reality is often deliberately challenged, questioned, or erased. Artists, filmmakers, and designers working in the postmodern era often engage with the idea of hyper reality by creating works that blur the boundary between the real and the simulated, inviting audiences to question what is real and what is constructed.

One of the most prominent ways hyper reality manifests in contemporary art is through the use of hyperrealism, a genre of art that seeks to create lifelike representations of reality that are so detailed and precise that they appear more real than the original subject. Hyperrealist painters, for example, produce works that mimic the appearance of photographs, often using extreme precision and attention to detail to create an image that feels more vivid and perfect than reality itself. This approach to art challenges traditional notions of representation by creating an image that does not simply depict reality but enhances it, pushing it beyond the limits of what is actually real. In this way, hyperrealism reflects Baudrillard's idea that simulations can become more real than the real, creating a world where the representation eclipses the original.

In the world of architecture, hyper reality is also present, particularly in the design of spaces that prioritize spectacle, simulation, and consumer experience over functionality. Shopping malls, theme parks, and casinos, for example, are often designed to create immersive environments that transport visitors into simulated worlds. Las Vegas, with its replicas of iconic landmarks such as the Eiffel Tower, the Venetian canals, and the pyramids of Egypt, is a quintessential example of a hyperreal environment. In these spaces, the architecture does not seek to reflect the reality of the original structures but instead offers an idealized, simulated version that feels more impressive, more perfect than the original. The experience of visiting these spaces is not one of engaging with reality but of being immersed in a simulation that is designed to be more spectacular and appealing than the real world.

Baudrillard would argue that these hyperreal environments are emblematic of a broader cultural shift, where the line between the real and the simulated is increasingly difficult to discern. In hyperreal spaces, visitors are not just consuming goods or experiences; they are consuming simulations of reality, participating in a world where the artificial is more desirable than the authentic. This blurring of boundaries extends beyond architecture into other areas of culture, including film, fashion, and advertising, where hyper reality plays a central role in shaping how we perceive and engage with the world.

In film, hyper reality is often used to create immersive, artificial worlds that feel real to the audience, even though they are entirely constructed. Movies such as *The Matrix* (1999) and *Inception* (2010) explicitly explore themes of simulated reality, inviting viewers to question the nature of the world they inhabit and whether it is real or a simulation. These films are influenced by Baudrillard's ideas, particularly his notion that in the hyperreal world, the simulation can become so convincing that it replaces the real. *The Matrix*, for example, depicts a world where humans live in a virtual simulation created by machines, and the simulated world is so convincing that most people do not realize they are living in a constructed reality. This theme directly echoes Baudrillard's argument that in postmodern society, reality has been replaced by simulations that are consumed as if they were real.

The influence of hyper reality extends to fashion and advertising as well, where images and representations are often used to create idealized versions of reality that are more appealing than the real world. In fashion, models are often airbrushed and digitally altered to create perfect bodies that do not exist in reality. These hyperreal images of beauty are consumed by audiences who aspire to the perfection they see in magazines and advertisements, even though this perfection is a simulation. Baudrillard would argue that these hyperreal images of beauty, wealth, and success have replaced the real, creating a world where people chase after simulations of life rather than engage with reality as it is.

In advertising, the concept of hyper reality is perhaps most evident in the way products are marketed as symbols of success, happiness, or identity. A car commercial, for instance, might show a luxurious lifestyle, where the product is not just a vehicle but a symbol of freedom, power, and success. The car becomes more than just a mode of transportation; it becomes a signifier of an idealized life that consumers are invited to buy into. The product itself becomes secondary to the hyperreal image it represents, and consumers are drawn not to the object but to the lifestyle and identity it promises. In this way, advertising creates a hyperreal world where goods and commodities are not valued for their material function but for the symbolic meaning they carry, leading to a situation where reality is replaced by a network of signs and images.

Baudrillard's concept of hyper reality also finds expression in digital culture, particularly in the world of social media and virtual reality. On platforms like Instagram, Facebook, and TikTok, individuals curate idealized versions of their lives, presenting images and videos that often bear little resemblance to their everyday experiences.

These curated identities create a hyperreal version of the self, where the line between the real person and the digital persona becomes blurred. Baudrillard would argue that in this hyperreal digital space, people are no longer engaging with each other as real individuals but as simulations of themselves, creating a world where identity is constructed through images, filters, and algorithms.

Virtual reality (VR) takes this concept even further by creating fully immersive digital environments that feel real to the senses but are entirely artificial. In VR, users can explore simulated worlds, interact with digital objects, and experience sensations that mimic real life. These virtual environments offer a form of hyper reality that challenges our understanding of what is real and what is simulated. Baudrillard's critique of hyper reality suggests that as virtual reality technologies become more advanced and widespread, we may increasingly live in a world where the simulated experiences provided by VR are more compelling, more desirable than the real world itself. This raises important questions about how we engage with reality and whether our experiences in virtual spaces will ultimately replace our connection to the physical world.

In contemporary art, hyper reality has also become a subject of exploration, with many artists using digital technologies, photography, and mixed media to create works that challenge our perceptions of reality. Artists such as Jeff Koons, for example, have created sculptures and installations that play with the idea of hyper reality by presenting objects that are simultaneously real and artificial. Koons' sculptures of balloon animals, for instance, are meticulously crafted to resemble real balloons but are made of stainless steel, creating a disorienting effect where the object feels both familiar and alien. This kind of artistic play with reality and simulation reflects Baudrillard's argument that in the hyperreal world, the boundaries between the real and the artificial are constantly shifting, leaving us in a state of uncertainty about what is real and what is not.

Baudrillard's concept of hyper reality has had a profound impact on how we understand art and culture in the digital age. As media, technology, and consumer culture continue to shape our perceptions of the world, the distinction between the real and the simulated becomes increasingly difficult to maintain. Hyper reality challenges traditional notions of representation and authenticity, inviting us to question how much of what we see, experience, and believe is real and how much is a construction designed to evoke certain emotions, desires, or behaviors.

In conclusion, hyper reality, as defined by Baudrillard, has become a central feature of contemporary art and culture, influencing how we create, consume, and interpret the world around us. Whether through hyperrealist paintings, immersive virtual environments, or the curated personas of social media, hyper reality blurs the line between the real and the simulated, leaving us in a world where images, signs, and symbols often feel more real than reality itself. Baudrillard's critique invites us to reflect on the ways in which hyper reality shapes our understanding of art, culture, and identity, challenging us to consider what is lost—and what is gained—when reality is replaced by its simulations.

From Critique to Nihilism: Baudrillard's Vision

Jean Baudrillard's philosophical journey moves from a sharp critique of contemporary society to what some have interpreted as a form of nihilism, a profound disillusionment with reality, truth, and meaning in the modern world. His work, especially in the later stages of his career, grapples with the implications of living in a world dominated by simulation, hyper reality, and the collapse of traditional values. Baudrillard's vision, as it evolves, can be seen as a response to the breakdown of meaning in postmodern culture, where the boundaries between reality and illusion, truth and falsehood, have disintegrated. For Baudrillard, this breakdown leads not just to a critique of society but to an acceptance of a kind of nihilism, where reality itself becomes irrelevant, and the search for meaning is abandoned.

At the core of Baudrillard's philosophy is his analysis of the *simulacra* and the transition from reality to *hyper reality*. Simulacra are representations that no longer correspond to any original reality; they are copies without an original. Baudrillard argues that in contemporary society, we have moved beyond the phase where images and signs represent the real. Instead, we now live in a world where these signs and images—whether in media, advertising, or consumer culture—create their own reality, a *hyperreal* world that replaces the real. The real is no longer something that can be accessed or understood in any meaningful way because it has been replaced by layers of simulation.

Baudrillard's shift toward nihilism is rooted in this realization that the real no longer exists as an independent or stable category. In earlier phases of his work, Baudrillard engaged in a critique of the forces—capitalism, media, technology—that had led to the dominance of hyper reality. His writings in the 1970s and 1980s focused on exposing how consumer culture, advertising, and mass media create a simulated world where meaning is produced, consumed, and manipulated by power structures. In these works, Baudrillard seems to hold onto the possibility of resistance, offering a critique that suggests there might be a way to recover some sense of authenticity or reality.

However, as Baudrillard's thinking developed, his philosophy took on a more nihilistic tone. By the time he published works like *The Gulf War Did Not Take Place* (1991) and *The Perfect Crime* (1995), Baudrillard had become increasingly pessimistic about the possibility of resisting or escaping the logic of hyper reality. In these later works, he argues that the real has been so thoroughly consumed by simulation that there is no longer any hope of returning to a more authentic or meaningful reality. Instead, we are trapped in a world where everything is a simulation, and where even the most basic distinctions—between reality and illusion, truth and falsehood—have collapsed.

Baudrillard's provocative claim in *The Gulf War Did Not Take Place* encapsulates this nihilistic vision. He did not mean that there was no conflict or that no bombs were dropped, but rather that the media's portrayal of the war created a version of reality that was so distorted and sanitized that it bore no resemblance to the actual events on the ground. For Baudrillard, the war, as experienced by the global public, was a media event, a simulation that obscured the violence and chaos of the real conflict. The images of precision bombing and technological superiority presented by the media created a hyperreal version of war, one that was consumed as entertainment rather than understood as a brutal, destructive reality. In this sense, the real war "did not take place" because it was replaced by its simulation.

This move from critique to nihilism is evident in Baudrillard's concept of the *precession of simulacra*, where simulations precede and create reality rather than the other way around. For Baudrillard, the world of hyper reality is one where the simulation no longer refers back to anything real; it becomes the real. In this world, everything becomes a simulation of something else, and the very idea of reality becomes meaningless. This is a nihilistic vision because it suggests that there is no longer any possibility of accessing the real or uncovering any deeper truths. All that remains are the simulations, endlessly replicating and circulating without reference to any underlying reality.

Baudrillard's turn toward nihilism is also reflected in his views on truth and meaning. In a hyperreal world, truth is no longer a stable or coherent concept; it is something that can be constructed, manipulated, and consumed like any other commodity. The collapse of the real leads to the collapse of truth, leaving us in a state where meaning is constantly produced and consumed but never fully realized. Baudrillard argues that in postmodern culture, we are inundated with information, images, and signs, all of which claim to convey meaning, but in reality, this flood of information leads to a breakdown of meaning. The more information we have, the less we are able to make sense of it, leading to what Baudrillard calls the "implosion of meaning."

This implosion of meaning is a key aspect of Baudrillard's nihilism. In a world where everything is mediated through simulations, where truth is indistinguishable from falsehood, and where signs no longer point to any underlying reality, the search for meaning becomes futile. For Baudrillard, this leads to a condition of radical indifference, where nothing matters because everything is equally real and unreal. In this sense, Baudrillard's vision of the hyperreal world is one of nihilism, where the collapse of meaning leaves us in a state of disorientation, unable to distinguish between what is real and what is simulated.

Baudrillard's nihilism also extends to his views on power and resistance. In his earlier works, he critiqued the ways in which power operates through the manipulation of signs, images, and simulations. He exposed how media, advertising, and consumer culture shape our desires, thoughts, and identities, creating a world where power is exercised not through direct control but through the production of meaning. However, in his later works, Baudrillard becomes increasingly skeptical about the possibility of resisting this system of power. He argues that even acts of resistance or rebellion are absorbed into the system of hyper reality, becoming part of the spectacle rather than challenging it. In this sense, resistance itself becomes a simulation, a performance that reinforces the very structures of power it seeks to oppose.

Baudrillard's vision of a world without reality, truth, or meaning can be seen as a form of nihilism, but it is also more than that. His philosophy invites us to confront the unsettling possibility that the world we inhabit is one where the real has been replaced by the simulated, where meaning is no longer stable, and where truth is a construct rather than an absolute. Baudrillard does not offer a solution to this condition, nor does he suggest that we can escape from the hyperreal world. Instead, he challenges us to recognize the radical implications of living in a world where the boundaries between the real and the simulated have collapsed.

In *The Perfect Crime*, Baudrillard takes this nihilistic vision even further by suggesting that the disappearance of reality is the "perfect crime"—one that has gone unnoticed because it has been so seamlessly carried out by the forces of media, technology, and simulation. The real has been murdered, but there is no body, no evidence, and no one to prosecute. The perfect crime is that we live in a world where the disappearance of reality has gone unrecognized, and we continue to participate in a system where simulations dominate our experience without questioning the loss of the real.

For Baudrillard, this disappearance of reality is not something to mourn or lament. Instead, he invites us to embrace the absurdity of living in a world where reality has been replaced by its simulations. His turn toward nihilism can be seen as an acceptance of the futility of seeking meaning in a world where meaning no longer exists. In this sense, Baudrillard's philosophy is not simply a critique of contemporary society but a radical vision of a world where the real, the true, and the meaningful have all disappeared, leaving us to navigate a world of simulations and illusions.

In conclusion, Baudrillard's philosophical trajectory from critique to nihilism reflects his growing disillusionment with the possibility of resisting the forces of simulation, hyper reality, and the collapse of meaning in postmodern society. His vision of a world where the real has disappeared, and where simulations dominate our experience, leads to a form of nihilism, where truth and meaning are no longer stable or accessible. Rather than offering a path back to reality, Baudrillard's later works challenge us to confront the radical implications of living in a world without reality, where simulations have replaced the real and meaning has imploded into nothingness. This nihilistic vision forces us to question our assumptions about truth, power, and meaning in a world where the boundaries between the real and the simulated have irrevocably collapsed.

The Concept of the 'Perfect Crime' in Reality

Jean Baudrillard's concept of the *perfect crime* is one of his most enigmatic and provocative ideas, central to his critique of contemporary society and its relationship with reality, truth, and simulation. The "perfect crime," as Baudrillard presents it, is not a conventional crime in the legal sense but a metaphor for the disappearance of reality itself—an act so flawlessly executed that it leaves no trace, no evidence, and no body. For Baudrillard, the "crime" is the eradication of the real, the murder of reality, perpetrated by the forces of media, technology, and simulation. The brilliance of this crime is that it has gone unnoticed; people continue to live in the illusion that reality persists, even as it has been entirely replaced by hyper reality, where simulations dominate.

Baudrillard's use of the term *perfect crime* underscores his view that the obliteration of reality is not recognized or acknowledged. In fact, it is celebrated by modern culture, which thrives on the production of images, signs, and simulations that supplant the real. This concept builds on Baudrillard's broader theories of hyper reality and the precession of simulacra, where the real has been gradually eroded and replaced by its representations—so much so that people no longer seek or expect reality in its traditional form. The "perfect crime" is the complete success of this process: the real has been murdered, yet no one is aware, and there is no evidence of the crime because the simulacra have entirely taken its place.

Baudrillard elaborates this idea in his 1995 book *The Perfect Crime*, where he explores how reality has been "disappeared" in much the same way that a criminal might commit a flawless act of violence without leaving a trace. In Baudrillard's vision, the forces responsible for this crime are the very institutions and technologies that claim to represent or protect reality—media, science, politics, and communication. These systems, rather than reflecting or revealing the real, obscure and erase it. They create a hyperreal world that presents itself as more real than reality, thus completing the "crime" of replacing the actual with the artificial.

One of the most potent examples of the perfect crime, according to Baudrillard, is the role of media in shaping reality. In contemporary society, the media does not simply report on or reflect events; it constructs a version of reality that often has little connection to the actual events it supposedly covers. This process of mediation creates a hyperreal version of the world—one that is more dramatic, sensational, and digestible than the complex, messy reality it replaces. Baudrillard argues that in the media age, people are no longer connected to reality but to a series of images and narratives that simulate reality. The "perfect crime" is that the media's representation has become the reality people accept, with no suspicion that the real has been erased.

Baudrillard's analysis extends beyond the media to encompass technology and digital communication, which he sees as key agents in the disappearance of reality. The rise of the internet, social media, virtual reality, and artificial intelligence are all examples of how technology creates layers of simulation that further distance individuals from any authentic experience of the real.

In Baudrillard's view, the virtual worlds created by these technologies are not simply alternatives to reality; they are new forms of reality that replace the real. In this digital age, where people spend much of their time interacting with screens, avatars, and digital personas, the experience of the real is increasingly mediated by simulations. The "crime" here is that individuals no longer seek the real, as their lives are fully immersed in a hyperreal environment that feels more compelling and immersive than reality ever could.

The *perfect crime* is also evident in Baudrillard's critique of science and the pursuit of knowledge. Traditionally, science has been viewed as a discipline that uncovers truth and reveals the reality of the natural world. However, Baudrillard argues that in the postmodern world, even science has become complicit in the murder of reality. Scientific models, theories, and simulations often create versions of reality that are more abstract and detached from the real world they are meant to explain. For instance, in fields like quantum mechanics or cosmology, scientific explanations often rely on models and representations that have little connection to the human experience of reality. While these models are useful in advancing scientific knowledge, they also contribute to the erasure of the real by constructing versions of reality that are inaccessible or irrelevant to everyday life. In this sense, science participates in the perfect crime by replacing the tangible, experiential world with abstract representations that remove individuals from any direct engagement with reality.

In Baudrillard's view, politics too has been swept up in the perfect crime. The political sphere, once grounded in real issues and ideologies, has become increasingly dominated by spectacle, image, and performance. Baudrillard's concept of the "hyperreal" political landscape refers to a situation in which politicians, elections, and policies are more about image management and media appearances than about substantive engagement with reality. In this context, political figures become simulacra—representations of leadership and authority without any connection to genuine governance or decision-making. The real concerns of citizens are often replaced by political spectacles designed to evoke emotional reactions rather than address real problems. The perfect crime, in this case, is the disappearance of authentic political engagement, replaced by a simulation of democracy that hides the absence of real power and choice.

Baudrillard's concept of the perfect crime also touches on the role of consumer culture in the disappearance of reality. In consumer societies, goods and commodities are not valued for their material function or utility but for the symbolic meaning they carry. Advertising, branding, and marketing create hyperreal worlds where products are sold not as objects but as experiences, lifestyles, and identities. The consumer is not buying a pair of shoes or a car; they are buying into a fantasy or an idealized version of themselves. In this sense, consumer culture plays a key role in the perfect crime by replacing the real world of objects and needs with a simulated world of desires and dreams. The perfect crime here is the erasure of the material reality of goods in favor of a symbolic economy where the representation of the product is more important than the product itself.

Baudrillard's analysis of the perfect crime is deeply tied to his broader critique of postmodern society, where meaning, truth, and reality are all subject to the forces of simulation and representation. For Baudrillard, the real crime is not just that reality has disappeared, but that no one has noticed or cared. The crime has been so perfect because it has been executed through the very systems—media, technology, politics, consumerism—that people rely on to understand and engage with the world. These systems create the illusion that reality persists even as it is replaced by simulations. The result is a world where people continue to live in the hyperreal without any awareness that the real has been erased.

One of the more unsettling aspects of Baudrillard's concept of the perfect crime is its suggestion that the disappearance of reality may be irreversible. Once the real has been replaced by simulations, it is difficult—if not impossible—to return to an authentic experience of the world. The systems of simulation are so pervasive and powerful that they shape every aspect of human life, from how we consume information to how we form relationships and engage with politics. In this sense, Baudrillard's perfect crime is not just a commentary on the present but a vision of the future, where the real is permanently replaced by its artificial double, and no one even remembers what was lost.

Baudrillard's concept of the perfect crime forces us to confront the unsettling possibility that we live in a world where reality no longer exists as an independent, objective truth. Instead, reality has been replaced by simulations that are consumed, produced, and manipulated by systems of power and representation. The perfect crime, as Baudrillard presents it, is not a conspiracy or a deliberate act of violence but a gradual, pervasive process that has unfolded through the rise of media, technology, and consumer culture. The brilliance of this crime lies in its invisibility; the real has been erased, but the world continues as if nothing has changed.

In conclusion, the concept of the perfect crime in Baudrillard's thought represents the culmination of his critique of hyper reality, simulation, and the disappearance of the real. It is a metaphor for the erasure of reality in a world dominated by media, technology, and consumerism, where simulations take the place of the real and no one notices the difference. The perfect crime is the flawless execution of this erasure, leaving no evidence or trace of what has been lost. Baudrillard's vision of the perfect crime challenges us to question the systems that shape our understanding of reality and invites us to reflect on the possibility that we are living in a world where the real has already disappeared, replaced by a network of simulations that define our existence.

The Gulf War Did Not Take Place: Baudrillard's Media Critique

Jean Baudrillard's provocative claim that "The Gulf War Did Not Take Place" serves as one of the most striking examples of his critique of media and the role it plays in shaping our perception of reality. Published as a series of essays in 1991 during and after the Gulf War, Baudrillard's argument was not that the military conflict between Iraq and a coalition led by the United States didn't occur. Instead, he was making a deeper philosophical point: the Gulf War, as it was experienced by the global public, was a simulation, a media event that bore little resemblance to the real human suffering and destruction happening on the ground. Baudrillard's critique exposes how modern media, by framing and mediating events, creates a hyperreal version of reality that replaces the actual experience of war, rendering the real conflict invisible and irrelevant to those consuming it.

In Baudrillard's analysis, the Gulf War as presented by the media was a highly controlled spectacle, an event shaped by the logic of media production rather than by the realities of war. The coverage of the conflict was dominated by images of precision bombing, clean technology, and clinical military operations, giving the impression of a sanitized, almost bloodless war. The chaos, violence, and death typically associated with war were largely absent from the screens of Western audiences. What viewers saw instead was a carefully crafted narrative that emphasized technological superiority, efficiency, and the righteousness of the coalition forces. For Baudrillard, this was not the reality of war but a hyperreal simulation that obscured the true horror of what was happening on the ground.

Baudrillard's central claim that "The Gulf War did not take place" hinges on his concept of *hyper reality*, a condition where representations of events become more real than the events themselves. In the case of the Gulf War, the media's portrayal of the conflict created a hyperreal version of war that existed only on television screens and in the minds of viewers. This hyperreal war, constructed through images, reports, and military briefings, became the dominant reality for those watching around the world, even though it bore little resemblance to the physical and human devastation occurring in Iraq. The real war, with its civilian casualties, destruction, and suffering, was hidden behind the spectacle of military technology and sanitized news coverage.

Baudrillard's critique also touches on the role of *simulacra*—copies without an original—in the media coverage of the Gulf War. The images and narratives broadcast to the public were not reflections of the actual events but simulations constructed by the media and military to control how the war was perceived. These simulations were designed to produce a specific version of reality that served political and military interests, reinforcing the idea that the war was just, efficient, and largely devoid of human cost. The public consumed these simulations as if they were real, but in Baudrillard's view, they were disconnected from the true reality of the conflict. The real war, with its messiness, unpredictability, and brutality, was replaced by a simulated war that was easier to digest, control, and support.

One of the key elements of Baudrillard's critique is his analysis of the role of technology in shaping the hyperreal experience of the Gulf War. The conflict was one of the first wars to be broadcast live to global audiences, with real-time images of missile strikes and military operations streamed into homes around the world. This technological mediation of the war created an illusion of transparency and immediacy, as if viewers were witnessing the conflict firsthand. However, Baudrillard argues that this technological mediation did not bring people closer to the reality of the war; it distanced them from it. The images of smart bombs hitting targets with precision, for example, gave the impression of a clean, controlled war, where violence was minimized and civilian casualties were avoided. In reality, the war was far more chaotic and destructive than the media portrayed, but the hyperreal version of the war, mediated through technology, became the dominant reality for global audiences.

Baudrillard also critiques the way in which the Gulf War was framed as a kind of spectacle or entertainment event. The war was presented to the public much like a sporting event, with live updates, expert commentary, and dramatic visuals. News networks competed for ratings by providing constant coverage, often focusing on the technological aspects of the war, such as the capabilities of stealth bombers and guided missiles. This focus on technology and military hardware turned the war into a spectacle of power and control, where the human cost of the conflict was hidden behind the spectacle of military precision. For Baudrillard, this transformation of war into entertainment is emblematic of the broader shift toward hyper reality, where even the most violent and tragic events are repackaged as consumable media products.

Another important aspect of Baudrillard's critique is his exploration of the relationship between war and politics in the hyperreal world. In traditional warfare, political goals and military strategies are closely intertwined, with war serving as a means of achieving specific political ends. However, Baudrillard argues that in the Gulf War, the political dimension of the conflict was obscured by the media spectacle. The war was presented as a purely technical exercise, focused on military objectives rather than political debate. The public was encouraged to focus on the efficiency of the military campaign, rather than on the broader political context or the morality of the war. In this sense, the war became depoliticized, reduced to a spectacle of military power divorced from the larger geopolitical issues at stake. This, for Baudrillard, is another form of the perfect crime, where the reality of the war's political motivations and consequences is erased by its simulation.

Baudrillard's critique also addresses the question of *truth* in the context of media coverage of the Gulf War. In his view, the media's portrayal of the war was not simply a distortion of reality; it was a simulation that replaced reality altogether. The constant flow of images, reports, and briefings created an overwhelming sense of immediacy and truth, but this truth was constructed and manipulated by those in power. Baudrillard argues that in the hyperreal world of media, truth itself becomes a commodity that can be produced, packaged, and consumed. The truth of the Gulf War, as presented by the media, was not the reality of the conflict but a carefully crafted version of events designed to serve political and military interests. In this sense, the Gulf War was not simply misrepresented; it was a media event that created its own reality, one that was accepted by the public as true despite being a simulation.

Baudrillard's claim that "The Gulf War Did Not Take Place" is also a commentary on the changing nature of warfare in the postmodern world. In previous wars, the violence, destruction, and human suffering were visible and undeniable, forcing people to confront the reality of conflict. However, in the Gulf War, the use of advanced military technology, combined with the media's selective coverage, created a war that was largely invisible to those not directly involved. The public saw images of missile strikes and military operations, but they did not see the human cost of the war— the civilian casualties, the destroyed infrastructure, and the long-term consequences for the people of Iraq. In this sense, the Gulf War was a postmodern war, one in which the violence was hidden behind the spectacle of technology, and the reality of the conflict was replaced by a hyperreal simulation.

In conclusion, Baudrillard's provocative assertion that "The Gulf War Did Not Take Place" is a powerful critique of how media and technology shape our perception of reality in the modern world. Through his analysis of the Gulf War, Baudrillard exposes how the media creates hyperreal simulations that replace the real, rendering the true nature of events invisible to the public. The Gulf War, as experienced by global audiences, was not the messy, violent reality of war but a carefully constructed simulation that served political and military interests. Baudrillard's critique challenges us to question the ways in which media shapes our understanding of the world, creating a hyperreal environment where simulations become more real than reality itself. In the context of the Gulf War, this hyperreal world turned a brutal conflict into a media spectacle, obscuring the true human cost and political implications of the war.

Baudrillard's Criticism of Marxism

Jean Baudrillard's intellectual journey began within a Marxist framework, but over time, he developed a profound critique of Marxism, ultimately moving beyond it to formulate his own distinct theories on society, culture, and power. Baudrillard's critique of Marxism focuses on its limitations in understanding the complexities of late capitalist society, particularly in an era dominated by media, technology, and simulation. While Marxism is primarily concerned with the economic structures that define class relations and the exploitation of labor, Baudrillard believed that Marxist theory failed to account for the symbolic and cultural dimensions of power and control in a world increasingly shaped by images, signs, and consumption. Baudrillard's rejection of Marxism marks a significant shift in his thought, as he moved from a materialist understanding of society to a postmodern critique centered on *simulation*, *hyper reality*, and the collapse of traditional categories like class, value, and labor.

Baudrillard's early works, particularly *The System of Objects* (1968) and *For a Critique of the Political Economy of the Sign* (1972), are heavily influenced by Marxist ideas, especially in their analysis of consumer society and the role of commodities. Like Marx, Baudrillard recognized that capitalism commodifies objects and relationships, transforming them into products that can be bought and sold. However, Baudrillard soon realized that Marxism's focus on use-value and exchange-value, rooted in labor and production, was insufficient for understanding the dynamics of post-industrial capitalism. In modern consumer society, Baudrillard argued, objects are no longer valued for their material use or the labor that produces them; instead, they are valued for their symbolic meaning, their ability to signify status, identity, and desire.

This shift from *use-value* to *sign-value* is central to Baudrillard's critique of Marxism. In traditional Marxist theory, commodities are understood as products of labor that possess a dual value: use-value, which is tied to the object's practical function, and exchange-value, which reflects its market price. Marx saw the exploitation of labor as the source of value in capitalist economies, with the surplus value generated by labor being appropriated by capitalists. Baudrillard, however, believed that this framework no longer applied to the late capitalist world of consumer culture. In this new context, commodities are primarily consumed for their sign-value, which refers to the social and cultural meanings that they convey. A luxury car, for example, is not just a mode of transportation or a product of labor; it is a sign of wealth, status, and prestige. The value of the car is no longer rooted in its material function or the labor that produced it but in the symbolic meaning it carries in the social sphere.

This focus on sign-value leads Baudrillard to critique Marxism's fixation on production as the primary site of exploitation and power. For Marx, the central struggle in capitalist society is between labor and capital, with workers being exploited by those who own the means of production. However, Baudrillard argues that in a society dominated by consumption and media, the traditional Marxist focus on labor relations and production becomes less relevant. Power is no longer exercised solely through the exploitation of labor but through the manipulation of signs, symbols, and desires. In this sense, Baudrillard moves away from Marx's materialist understanding of power and class struggle, emphasizing instead the ways in which power operates through culture, media, and consumption.

Baudrillard's critique of Marxism also extends to its emphasis on historical materialism, the belief that the development of society is driven by material conditions and economic relations. Marxist theory posits that history unfolds through a series of stages, with each stage defined by a particular mode of production (feudalism, capitalism, socialism), and that the contradictions within each mode lead to revolutionary change. Baudrillard, however, argues that in the postmodern world, history has come to an end. He does not mean this in the sense that events have ceased to occur, but rather that history, as a linear narrative of progress and revolution, has been replaced by a series of simulations and repetitions. In a hyperreal world dominated by media and technology, Baudrillard claims, the possibility of revolutionary change has disappeared. Instead of moving forward through history, society is caught in a perpetual present, where the same images, signs, and events are endlessly reproduced and consumed without any meaningful change.

This leads to Baudrillard's critique of the *proletariat*, a central concept in Marxist theory. For Marx, the proletariat, or working class, is the revolutionary subject capable of overthrowing capitalism and establishing a socialist society. The proletariat's alienation from the means of production, its exploitation by capitalists, and its collective power as a class give it the potential to initiate radical social change. Baudrillard, however, argues that the traditional working class has been dissolved in the consumer society, where individuals are no longer defined primarily by their role in production but by their role as consumers. In this sense, the proletariat as a revolutionary class no longer exists, because class identity has been replaced by the identities created through consumption. People are no longer united by their position in the economic structure but by the brands they wear, the products they buy, and the media they consume. This shift from production to consumption as the primary organizing principle of society renders Marxist class analysis increasingly irrelevant.

Baudrillard also criticizes Marxism's faith in the possibility of revolution and emancipation. For Marx, the contradictions of capitalism would eventually lead to its downfall, as the exploited proletariat rises up to overthrow the system and establish a more just, egalitarian society. Baudrillard, however, is deeply skeptical of this revolutionary promise. He argues that in the postmodern world, the very idea of revolution has been co-opted by the system of hyper reality. Acts of resistance, rebellion, or protest are no longer seen as genuine challenges to the system; instead, they are absorbed into the media spectacle, becoming just another form of entertainment or simulation. In this context, even revolution becomes a commodity, something to be consumed rather than enacted. Baudrillard's critique of revolution reflects his broader pessimism about the possibility of meaningful change in a world dominated by simulations and signs.

Baudrillard's break with Marxism becomes even more apparent in his analysis of *ideology*. Marxist theory is rooted in the idea that ideology functions as a tool of class domination, a set of beliefs and values imposed by the ruling class to maintain its power and control over the working class. According to Marx, ideology obscures the true nature of exploitation by making the capitalist system appear natural and inevitable. For Baudrillard, however, ideology has become irrelevant in the postmodern world. In a society dominated by media and hyper reality, there is no longer any need for ideology because there is no longer any reality to obscure. The media does not work to conceal the truth; it works by creating a world where truth and falsehood no longer matter.

Baudrillard argues that in a world of simulations, ideology is replaced by a system of signs and images that produce a superficial, empty version of reality. This is what Baudrillard refers to as the "end of ideology," where the traditional Marxist critique of ideology no longer applies because there is no longer any real content to critique.

Despite his break from Marxism, Baudrillard's work retains elements of Marxist critique, particularly in its focus on the ways in which power operates through representation and consumption. However, Baudrillard takes this critique in a radically different direction, moving away from Marxism's focus on material conditions and economic exploitation to explore the symbolic and cultural dimensions of power in a world where the real has been replaced by the simulated. His rejection of Marxism reflects his belief that traditional categories like class, value, and labor no longer provide a sufficient framework for understanding the complexities of late capitalist society, where media, technology, and consumption have become the primary forces shaping human experience.

In conclusion, Baudrillard's criticism of Marxism marks a significant departure from the traditional materialist and economic analysis of society. While he initially engaged with Marxist ideas, particularly in his early work on consumer society, Baudrillard ultimately rejected Marxism as inadequate for understanding the complexities of the postmodern world. He critiqued Marxism's emphasis on production, class struggle, and revolution, arguing that these concepts no longer applied in a society dominated by media, simulation, and consumption. Baudrillard's critique highlights the ways in which power operates through signs, symbols, and desires in a hyperreal world, where the real has been replaced by the simulated and the possibility of revolutionary change has been absorbed into the spectacle. By moving beyond Marxism, Baudrillard offers a radical rethinking of power, class, and ideology in the postmodern era, challenging us to reconsider how control is exercised in a world where reality itself has been transformed.

Symbolic Exchange and Death

Jean Baudrillard's concept of *symbolic exchange and death* is a key component of his critique of modernity, capitalism, and the nature of social relations. This idea, which he elaborates in his 1976 book *Symbolic Exchange and Death*, presents a radical alternative to the dominant logic of capitalist society, where value, meaning, and human relationships are defined by systems of production, consumption, and exchange. Baudrillard's theory of symbolic exchange seeks to recover a more primal, pre-capitalist mode of interaction, rooted in reciprocity, gift-giving, and the cyclical nature of life and death. For Baudrillard, symbolic exchange represents a form of social relation that stands in opposition to the capitalist system's obsession with accumulation, control, and the denial of death. In this context, *death* is not merely an end but a crucial aspect of symbolic exchange, embodying the ultimate form of reciprocity and transformation.

To fully understand Baudrillard's notion of symbolic exchange, it is important to contrast it with the capitalist mode of exchange. In capitalist economies, social relations are mediated by the exchange of commodities, which are assigned a value based on their use or exchange value, according to the logic of supply and demand. This system of exchange is linear and accumulative, with individuals seeking to maximize wealth, productivity, and consumption. In this context, exchange is reduced to a calculable transaction, stripped of any deeper social or spiritual meaning. Baudrillard saw this system of exchange as fundamentally alienating because it reduces all human interactions to abstract relations of value and ownership, severing the connection between individuals and the deeper, symbolic meanings of their actions.

In contrast, symbolic exchange refers to a form of interaction based on reciprocity and the circulation of gifts, values, and signs that are not reducible to economic calculation. Baudrillard draws on anthropological studies of gift-giving in so-called "primitive" societies, particularly the work of Marcel Mauss, who argued that in traditional cultures, the giving of a gift creates a bond of reciprocity between the giver and the receiver. This gift must be returned, not in a direct, calculable way, but through the creation of an ongoing cycle of giving and receiving, which strengthens social ties and maintains a balance within the community. The value of the gift is not determined by its material worth but by its symbolic meaning and the social relationship it fosters.

Baudrillard extends this concept of symbolic exchange to challenge the entire structure of capitalist society, where economic and social relations are governed by the logic of accumulation and rationalization. In a world dominated by production and consumption, Baudrillard argues that true exchange—an exchange that creates meaningful social bonds—has been lost. The capitalist system denies the possibility of symbolic exchange because it operates on the principle of accumulation without end, refusing to acknowledge the inevitability of loss, waste, and death. This refusal to engage with loss or to embrace the cyclical nature of existence, Baudrillard suggests, leads to a society that is obsessed with the preservation of life, the prolongation of consumption, and the avoidance of death.

Here, Baudrillard introduces death as a key component of symbolic exchange. In traditional societies, death is not simply the end of life; it is a fundamental aspect of the cycle of exchange. Death represents the ultimate form of reciprocity—an inevitable return or giving back to the world, to the community, or to the cosmos. In these societies, rituals surrounding death—such as funerals, sacrifices, or mourning rites—are symbolic acts that reinforce the continuity of life and the social order. Death, in this sense, is not an individual tragedy to be avoided but a shared event that affirms the bonds between the living and the dead, between individuals and their community.

Baudrillard contrasts this symbolic understanding of death with the way death is treated in modern capitalist societies, where it is seen as a taboo, something to be feared, hidden, and avoided. In these societies, the goal is to prolong life at all costs, to delay death through technology, medicine, and consumption. Death is no longer integrated into the cycle of life and exchange; instead, it is externalized, medicalized, and commodified. The denial of death is, for Baudrillard, symptomatic of a society that is obsessed with accumulation and growth, refusing to acknowledge the limits of life, the inevitability of loss, and the necessity of symbolic giving and receiving.

For Baudrillard, the capitalist refusal to engage with death is also reflected in the way the system handles waste, destruction, and loss. In a world where everything is commodified and valued for its utility, waste is seen as something to be eliminated, managed, or recycled, rather than accepted as part of the natural cycle of exchange. In traditional societies, rituals of sacrifice or destruction were ways of returning something to the gods, the ancestors, or the earth, acknowledging the limits of human accumulation and affirming the importance of balance and reciprocity. In contrast, modern capitalist societies are structured around the constant production of value, with no room for waste, destruction, or loss. This refusal to accept the inevitability of loss, Baudrillard argues, is part of the system's broader denial of death, leading to a society that is out of balance, obsessed with accumulation and growth but disconnected from the deeper, symbolic meanings of life and death.

Baudrillard's concept of symbolic exchange and death also has profound implications for how we understand power and control in modern society. In the capitalist system, power is exercised through the control of production, consumption, and accumulation. However, Baudrillard suggests that true power lies not in accumulation but in the ability to give, to sacrifice, and to engage in symbolic exchange. This is because symbolic exchange operates outside the logic of capital, where everything is calculated and accounted for. In symbolic exchange, there is always an element of unpredictability, risk, and loss, which creates a form of power that cannot be controlled or commodified. The power of the gift lies in its ability to create bonds of reciprocity and to circulate beyond the confines of economic calculation.

In this sense, symbolic exchange represents a form of resistance to the logic of capitalism, a way of undermining the system's obsession with accumulation, control, and the denial of death. Baudrillard argues that symbolic exchange, with its emphasis on reciprocity, loss, and the acceptance of death, offers a way of rethinking social relations and power outside the framework of capitalism.

By embracing the symbolic aspects of exchange, rather than reducing everything to value, individuals and communities can resist the alienating effects of the capitalist system and reconnect with the deeper, more primal meanings of life and death.

One of the most radical aspects of Baudrillard's concept of symbolic exchange and death is his argument that death is the ultimate form of symbolic exchange because it represents the final, irreversible giving back. In death, the individual returns to the community, to nature, or to the cosmos, completing the cycle of life and exchange. For Baudrillard, this return is not a tragic or negative event; it is a necessary part of the symbolic order, which affirms the continuity of life through the acceptance of death. In a capitalist society that seeks to deny death, prolong life, and accumulate endlessly, the acceptance of death represents a radical challenge to the system's refusal to engage with loss and mortality.

Baudrillard's idea of symbolic exchange and death also connects to his broader critique of modernity, where he argues that the capitalist system's obsession with production, consumption, and accumulation has led to the disappearance of meaning in social life. In a world dominated by signs, images, and commodities, the symbolic meanings of life and death have been eroded, replaced by a superficial culture of endless consumption. Symbolic exchange, with its focus on reciprocity, giving, and the cyclical nature of life and death, offers a way of recovering meaning in a world that has lost touch with these deeper, symbolic structures.

In conclusion, Jean Baudrillard's concept of *symbolic exchange and death* offers a powerful critique of capitalist society and its obsession with accumulation, consumption, and the denial of death. By drawing on pre-capitalist forms of exchange, Baudrillard challenges the linear, calculable logic of the capitalist system and offers an alternative vision of social relations rooted in reciprocity, gift-giving, and the cyclical nature of life and death. For Baudrillard, symbolic exchange represents a form of resistance to the alienating effects of capitalism, offering a way of rethinking power, value, and meaning in a world where death is not denied but embraced as a fundamental part of the human experience.

Technology and the Deconstruction of Reality

Jean Baudrillard's critique of technology plays a crucial role in his broader philosophical exploration of how reality has been transformed in the postmodern world. Central to Baudrillard's thought is the idea that technology, particularly through media, digital communication, and virtual environments, has led to the *deconstruction of reality*. This deconstruction does not simply mean that reality has been replaced by false representations or illusions; rather, it refers to the way that technology has dismantled the traditional concept of reality itself, replacing it with simulations, signs, and hyperreal environments that blur the boundaries between the real and the artificial. In Baudrillard's view, technology doesn't just distort reality—it creates a new kind of reality that renders the distinction between truth and fiction increasingly irrelevant.

Baudrillard's analysis begins with his theory of *simulation* and *hyper reality*. For Baudrillard, modern society is dominated by simulations—representations of reality that have no connection to any original, real-world counterpart. These simulations don't simply imitate the real; they replace it. This process of replacement is most evident in the media, where images, narratives, and information are constructed and circulated without any direct reference to an underlying reality. News, entertainment, advertisements, and digital content all participate in this creation of a simulated world, where what is seen, heard, and consumed is often a fabrication designed to evoke certain emotions, desires, or reactions. Over time, these simulations become more real than reality itself, creating what Baudrillard calls *hyper reality*, a state where the boundary between the real and the artificial dissolves, and where people accept simulations as their primary reality.

In this context, technology plays a fundamental role in the deconstruction of reality. The rise of digital media, virtual reality, and the internet has accelerated the process of simulation, allowing for the creation of entire worlds that exist only as digital constructs. Virtual reality (VR) technology, for example, enables users to immerse themselves in environments that feel real, even though they are entirely artificial. In these virtual spaces, users can interact with objects, people, and scenarios that mimic reality, but are fundamentally disconnected from any real-world referent. For Baudrillard, this marks a profound shift in the way humans experience the world: technology no longer simply mediates or enhances reality—it replaces it with something else entirely, something that exists only as a simulation.

Baudrillard's critique of technology and its deconstructive effects can also be seen in his analysis of *digital communication* and *social media*. In the digital age, communication is increasingly mediated through screens, platforms, and devices that filter, curate, and shape how people interact with each other and the world. Social media platforms like Facebook, Instagram, and Twitter encourage users to create highly curated versions of their lives, where images, statuses, and posts are carefully constructed to present an idealized persona. This digital self often bears little resemblance to the actual, lived experience of the individual, but it becomes the version of the self that is most real to others. For Baudrillard, this represents another layer of simulation, where the self is no longer an authentic expression of identity but a performance designed for public consumption.

The deconstruction of reality through digital technology also extends to *news and information*. In Baudrillard's view, the media no longer reports on events or reality in any meaningful sense. Instead, it produces narratives and images that are designed to evoke emotional responses, shape public opinion, and reinforce certain ideologies. News stories are often constructed as spectacles, where the line between entertainment and information becomes blurred. This creates a situation where events are not understood in terms of their real-world significance but are consumed as media products, designed to attract attention and engagement. The result is a hyperreal world where information is detached from truth, and where the reality of events is less important than the way they are presented, packaged, and consumed by audiences.

Baudrillard's concept of *the implosion of meaning* is closely tied to his analysis of technology's role in deconstructing reality. In the digital age, where information is constantly produced and circulated, the sheer volume of data, images, and messages overwhelms the capacity for meaningful understanding. In Baudrillard's view, more information does not lead to greater knowledge or clarity; instead, it leads to confusion, disorientation, and the collapse of meaning. Technology enables the proliferation of images and information to such an extent that reality becomes fragmented, incoherent, and ultimately irrelevant. The more data people are exposed to, the less they are able to discern what is true, real, or significant. This implosion of meaning, facilitated by technology, contributes to the deconstruction of reality, as the distinction between truth and falsehood, real and fake, becomes impossible to maintain.

One of the most striking aspects of Baudrillard's critique of technology is his analysis of *virtual reality* and *artificial intelligence* (AI), which he saw as the ultimate expressions of the hyperreal world. Virtual reality, by creating immersive environments that simulate the real, challenges the very notion of what it means to experience reality. In a VR world, the user can interact with a simulated environment that feels real, even though it has no physical existence. For Baudrillard, this raises profound questions about the nature of reality itself. If technology can create experiences that feel just as real as those in the physical world, what does that mean for our understanding of reality? Are these virtual experiences less real, or do they represent a new kind of reality that is equally valid?

Artificial intelligence takes this deconstruction of reality even further, as AI systems are designed to simulate human thought, decision-making, and creativity. In fields like art, literature, and music, AI can now produce works that are indistinguishable from those created by humans. This blurs the line between human and machine, raising questions about the authenticity and originality of creative expression. For Baudrillard, AI represents the ultimate extension of simulation, where machines not only replicate human functions but replace them, creating a world where human creativity, decision-making, and even existence are no longer necessary. In this world, the real is no longer defined by human experience but by the simulations produced by machines, further deconstructing the traditional boundaries of reality.

Baudrillard's critique of technology is not simply a rejection of technological progress or an argument for a return to some pre-digital past. Instead, he is interested in exploring the ways in which technology transforms the very nature of reality and our experience of it. For Baudrillard, technology's deconstruction of reality is both inevitable and irreversible. The more advanced technology becomes, the more it dismantles the structures of reality that have traditionally anchored human existence. This process cannot be stopped or reversed; it is the logical outcome of a society that has become fully immersed in the world of simulations, signs, and images.

In Baudrillard's view, the deconstruction of reality through technology also has profound implications for *power* and *control*. In traditional societies, power was exercised through physical force, coercion, and domination. However, in the hyperreal world created by technology, power operates not through direct control but through the manipulation of signs, images, and simulations. Those who control the media, digital platforms, and technological systems have the power to shape reality itself, determining what people see, believe, and understand about the world. This form of power is subtle and invisible, as it does not rely on overt repression or violence but on the ability to construct and control the simulations that define reality. For Baudrillard, this represents a new kind of power, one that is more insidious and totalizing because it operates at the level of perception and experience, rather than through physical coercion.

In conclusion, Jean Baudrillard's analysis of technology and the deconstruction of reality provides a powerful critique of how digital media, virtual environments, and AI have transformed the way we experience and understand the world. For Baudrillard, technology does not merely distort reality; it replaces it with simulations that become more real than the real itself. This process of deconstruction, facilitated by the rise of digital communication, social media, and virtual reality, leads to the collapse of traditional notions of truth, meaning, and authenticity. Baudrillard's critique challenges us to consider the implications of living in a world where technology shapes not just how we interact with reality but what we understand reality to be. In this hyperreal world, the boundaries between the real and the simulated blur, leaving us in a state where reality itself is constantly being deconstructed and reconstructed by the forces of technology.

The Impact of Simulation on Identity

Jean Baudrillard's concept of *simulation* and its relationship to *hyper reality* profoundly impacts how we understand *identity* in the modern, technology-driven world. In Baudrillard's view, the rise of media, digital technologies, and consumer culture has led to the erosion of traditional, stable identities. Instead of individuals forming their identities through personal experiences, relationships, and authentic self-reflection, identity in the age of simulation is constructed through images, signs, and representations that are often disconnected from any deeper reality. In this hyperreal environment, identity becomes fluid, fragmented, and performative, shaped more by external symbols and media representations than by an internal sense of self.

Baudrillard's analysis of simulation begins with the idea that in the postmodern world, *simulacra*—copies without an original—have replaced the real. In the realm of identity, this means that the self is no longer something stable or authentic but is instead created through a series of simulations that reflect cultural and societal expectations. These simulations of identity are produced and reinforced by the media, advertising, social networks, and other systems of representation. As individuals navigate this world of simulations, their sense of self is increasingly defined by external images and symbols rather than by an inner core of authenticity or unique personal identity.

One of the most significant ways simulation impacts identity is through *consumer culture*, where products, brands, and lifestyles become markers of identity. In a society dominated by consumption, individuals are encouraged to define themselves through the goods they buy, the clothes they wear, the technology they use, and the lifestyles they adopt. A smartphone, for instance, is not just a tool for communication—it is a symbol of status, identity, and belonging in a digital world. Fashion, similarly, is not merely about clothing but about the performance of identity through carefully curated appearances. These consumer choices become simulations of identity, where the individual adopts signs and symbols to project a desired image of themselves to the outside world. The identity formed through these simulations is inherently unstable, as it is dependent on external validation and constantly subject to change based on shifting trends and cultural expectations.

Social media has amplified the impact of simulation on identity, creating platforms where users can construct and curate idealized versions of themselves. Platforms like Instagram, Facebook, and TikTok encourage individuals to perform their identity in front of an audience, using images, posts, and videos to craft a digital persona. These personas are often carefully edited, filtered, and designed to present an idealized version of the self—one that may bear little resemblance to the individual's actual, lived experience. In this way, identity on social media becomes a simulation, a hyperreal version of the self that is more real to the audience than the actual person behind the screen.

Baudrillard would argue that in the hyperreal world of social media, the distinction between the real self and the simulated self collapses. The digital persona, though a construction, becomes the dominant reality for both the individual and their audience. The individual's sense of self-worth, identity, and social status is increasingly tied to the performance of this digital persona, rather than to any authentic, internal sense of identity. As a result, identity becomes fragmented, with individuals performing different versions of themselves across various platforms and contexts. The self becomes a fluid, shifting construct, defined by the simulations that are most effective in gaining validation, likes, and followers in the digital space.

Baudrillard's analysis of identity in the age of simulation also highlights the *performative* nature of identity in modern culture. In a hyperreal world, individuals are constantly engaged in the act of *performing* their identity for others, adopting roles and personas that are shaped by the expectations of society, media, and consumer culture. This performative aspect of identity is not just limited to social media but extends to everyday life, where individuals navigate a world of signs and symbols that dictate how they should behave, dress, and present themselves in various social situations.

For Baudrillard, this performative identity is not necessarily a reflection of an inner, authentic self; instead, it is a response to the demands of the hyperreal world, where appearances and representations matter more than reality. In this context, identity is no longer something stable or essential; it is something that is constantly being created and recreated through performance. The individual becomes a kind of actor, constantly adjusting their identity to fit the demands of the simulated environment in which they live.

Another important aspect of Baudrillard's critique is the *commodification* of identity. In consumer culture, identity itself becomes a commodity, something that can be bought, sold, and consumed. Brands and products are marketed as tools for identity formation, offering individuals the promise of a better, more desirable self through consumption. A perfume ad, for example, does not just sell a fragrance; it sells an identity—a vision of beauty, sophistication, and allure. In this sense, identity is no longer something inherent or personal but something that is constructed through the act of consumption. The individual becomes a consumer not only of goods but of identities, adopting different personas based on the products they purchase and the lifestyles they aspire to.

Baudrillard's concept of *the hyperreal* also suggests that identity is no longer anchored in the real world but is shaped by media and cultural representations that create a distorted version of reality. In the hyperreal world, individuals are constantly bombarded with images and narratives that tell them what it means to be successful, attractive, or fulfilled. These representations often present idealized, unattainable versions of reality, creating a sense of disconnection between the individual's lived experience and the simulated world they see in the media. As a result, individuals may feel pressure to conform to these hyperreal representations, adopting identities that are shaped by media images rather than by their own authentic experiences.

Baudrillard's critique of identity in the age of simulation also extends to his analysis of *power* and *control*. In traditional societies, power was exercised through direct forms of control, such as laws, institutions, and authority figures. However, in the hyperreal world, power operates more subtly, through the manipulation of signs, images, and identities. The media, advertising, and digital platforms shape not only what people see and believe but also how they perceive themselves and others. In this sense, power is exercised through the creation and reinforcement of simulated identities that conform to societal norms and expectations. Individuals internalize these simulations, adopting identities that fit within the framework of the hyperreal world, even as they lose touch with their own authentic sense of self.

Baudrillard's analysis of the *depersonalization* of identity is another key aspect of his critique. In the hyperreal world, individuals may feel increasingly disconnected from their own sense of self, as their identity becomes fragmented and shaped by external forces. This depersonalization can lead to a sense of alienation, where individuals feel that their identity is not something they control but something that is imposed on them by the systems of media, technology, and consumer culture. In this context, the individual becomes a passive participant in the construction of their own identity, adopting roles and personas that are dictated by the hyperreal world rather than by their own desires or experiences.

Baudrillard's critique of identity in the age of simulation forces us to question the nature of identity itself. Is identity something inherent and stable, or is it a construction shaped by the systems of representation that dominate modern life? For Baudrillard, the answer is clear: in a world of simulations, identity is no longer something that exists independently of the signs and symbols that define it. Instead, identity is constructed through the act of performance, consumption, and representation, shaped by the hyperreal world in which we live.

In conclusion, Jean Baudrillard's exploration of the impact of simulation on identity provides a profound critique of how modern society, shaped by media, technology, and consumer culture, has transformed the way individuals understand and construct their sense of self. In the hyperreal world, identity becomes fluid, fragmented, and performative, shaped more by external symbols and simulations than by internal authenticity. Baudrillard's critique challenges us to consider how much of our identity is shaped by the world of signs, images, and representations that dominate our lives, and whether it is possible to find an authentic sense of self in a world where simulation and hyper reality have replaced the real.

Disneyland as a Model of the Hyperreal

Jean Baudrillard's concept of *hyper reality* finds one of its most vivid and illustrative examples in Disneyland. For Baudrillard, Disneyland is not merely a theme park filled with fantastical rides and characters—it is a model of how hyper reality operates in modern society. In his view, Disneyland exemplifies the process by which reality is replaced by simulations, creating a world where the distinction between the real and the artificial collapses. Disneyland does not pretend to represent reality; rather, it creates a completely self-contained universe of fantasy that feels more real, more perfect, and more controlled than reality itself. This phenomenon is at the heart of Baudrillard's critique of hyper reality, where the simulated world becomes more real than the reality it is meant to imitate.

Baudrillard's analysis of Disneyland begins with the observation that the park is a meticulously constructed simulation, designed to offer visitors an escape into a world of idealized fantasy. In this sense, Disneyland is an example of what Baudrillard calls a *simulacrum*—a copy or representation of something that has no original. The castles, streets, and characters within Disneyland are not meant to refer to any real-world place or event; they are pure simulations, existing solely within the boundaries of the theme park. However, what makes Disneyland a model of the hyperreal is not just its simulated nature, but the way in which it creates a reality that is more compelling and desirable than the world outside its gates. Visitors to Disneyland are not simply observing a representation of reality; they are participating in a world that feels more enchanting, more orderly, and more satisfying than everyday life.

Baudrillard's concept of *hyper reality* suggests that in the postmodern world, simulations do not merely imitate reality—they replace it. In Disneyland, the simulation is so complete and immersive that it becomes the dominant reality for those who experience it. The theme park offers a carefully curated, controlled environment where everything—from the architecture to the behavior of the employees—is designed to create a seamless fantasy experience. There is no disorder, no unpredictability, and no flaws in this simulated world. For many visitors, this artificial world can feel more real and desirable than the chaotic and often disappointing reality outside. In this sense, Disneyland exemplifies how simulations can create a hyperreal environment that becomes more attractive and compelling than the real world it is meant to reflect.

One of the key aspects of Disneyland's hyper reality is its ability to create an idealized version of reality, one that is free from the complexities, contradictions, and problems of the real world. Disneyland offers a sanitized, idealized version of history, culture, and fantasy, where the darker aspects of life are excluded. The various lands within Disneyland—such as Frontierland, Adventureland, and Fantasyland—offer a simplified, romanticized version of the past or of imagined worlds, where conflict and tragedy are absent, and everything operates according to a clear, predictable narrative. This process of simplification is central to hyper reality, where the messy, complicated aspects of life are stripped away, leaving only a polished, idealized simulation of reality.

Baudrillard's analysis of Disneyland also extends to its role as a *mask* for the hyper reality of American culture. In his view, Disneyland exists to reinforce the illusion that the outside world—the "real" world—is still grounded in reality, even as it too is increasingly dominated by simulations. Disneyland presents itself as a place of escape, a fantasy world distinct from the everyday reality of modern life. However, Baudrillard argues that the very existence of Disneyland, with its hyperreal simulations, is a way of concealing the fact that the outside world is also a simulation. In other words, Disneyland is not a separate fantasy world but a model for the hyperreal nature of American culture as a whole. By visiting Disneyland, people reinforce the belief that the rest of their lives are real, even though, according to Baudrillard, the entire social and cultural landscape has become a simulation.

Baudrillard illustrates this point by comparing Disneyland to the broader American landscape, where cities, shopping malls, and media are all part of a hyperreal environment. For Baudrillard, American culture is dominated by the production of signs and images that no longer refer to any underlying reality. In this sense, Disneyland is not an exception but a model for how the entire culture operates—through simulations that replace the real. The clean, orderly, and controlled environment of Disneyland is mirrored in the way suburban neighborhoods, shopping centers, and media outlets present a carefully constructed version of reality, one that is designed to be consumed and enjoyed without questioning its authenticity.

Baudrillard's critique of Disneyland also touches on the idea of *participation* in the hyperreal. Disneyland is not just a place to observe; it is a place to engage, to participate in the fantasy. Visitors are not passive spectators; they become part of the simulated world, interacting with characters, riding attractions, and immersing themselves in the fantasy narrative. This active participation is key to understanding the seductive power of hyper reality. In Disneyland, visitors willingly suspend their disbelief, accepting the simulation as reality for the duration of their visit. This suspension of disbelief is central to Baudrillard's idea of hyper reality, where people accept simulations not as imitations of reality but as reality itself.

The commodification of experience in Disneyland is another key aspect of its hyper reality. Every aspect of the Disneyland experience is commodified, from the tickets to the rides to the souvenirs. Visitors consume not just goods but experiences, paying for the privilege of participating in the fantasy world that Disneyland creates. In this sense, Disneyland is a perfect example of how hyper reality operates within consumer culture, where experiences themselves are commodified and sold as products. The park offers an experience of happiness, wonder, and nostalgia, all of which are carefully crafted, packaged, and sold to visitors. This commodification of experience reinforces the hyperreal nature of Disneyland, where even emotions and memories are constructed and consumed as part of the simulation.

Baudrillard's analysis of Disneyland also touches on the *social control* inherent in hyper reality. In Disneyland, every aspect of the environment is controlled and regulated, from the cleanliness of the streets to the behavior of the employees. This control is invisible but total, creating an illusion of freedom and spontaneity within a highly regulated system. Visitors are free to explore and enjoy the park, but their experience is carefully orchestrated to ensure that they remain within the boundaries of the simulation.

This form of social control is emblematic of the hyperreal world more broadly, where people are given the illusion of freedom and choice, even as their experiences are shaped by the systems of media, technology, and consumerism that define the hyperreal environment.

In conclusion, Jean Baudrillard's analysis of Disneyland as a model of the hyperreal offers a powerful critique of how modern society, particularly in the context of American culture, is dominated by simulations that replace reality. Disneyland, with its idealized, controlled, and commodified world of fantasy, exemplifies the process by which hyper reality is constructed and maintained. For Baudrillard, Disneyland is not just a theme park but a microcosm of the larger cultural landscape, where reality is replaced by simulations that are more attractive, more controlled, and more compelling than the real world. Through his critique of Disneyland, Baudrillard challenges us to question how much of our experience of reality is shaped by simulations and to consider the implications of living in a world where the boundaries between the real and the artificial have collapsed into hyper reality.

The Mirror of Production: Critique of Political Economy

In *The Mirror of Production* (1973), Jean Baudrillard launches a critique of traditional Marxist political economy and its focus on production as the central force shaping society. Baudrillard argues that Marxism, while intending to critique capitalism, actually mirrors and perpetuates many of its underlying assumptions, particularly its emphasis on labor, productivity, and material progress. For Baudrillard, this focus on production—whether in capitalist or Marxist terms—overlooks the symbolic and cultural dimensions of human existence, reducing social life to economic relations and material exchanges. In this work, Baudrillard calls for a radical rethinking of how we understand value, labor, and social relations, offering an alternative vision that emphasizes symbolic exchange over the traditional political economy's obsession with production.

At the core of Baudrillard's critique is his argument that Marxism, despite its revolutionary aspirations, is ultimately grounded in the same framework of production that defines capitalist societies. Marxist theory, like capitalism, views history and society through the lens of labor and productivity, focusing on the exploitation of workers and the struggle over the means of production. In this view, economic forces drive social change, and the liberation of the working class comes through seizing control of production from capitalists. For Marx, the ultimate goal is a classless society in which workers collectively own the means of production and control the fruits of their labor.

Baudrillard, however, sees this as a limited and problematic perspective. He argues that by focusing so heavily on production, both Marxism and capitalism reduce human existence to material labor and economic exchange, overlooking the symbolic, cultural, and non-material aspects of life that give it meaning. In this sense, Baudrillard sees Marxism as a kind of "mirror" of capitalism—it critiques the system but remains trapped within the same logic of production and materialism. By framing liberation solely in terms of economic control and productive labor, Marxism, according to Baudrillard, fails to escape the capitalist worldview that values people only in relation to their productive capacity.

Baudrillard's alternative to this emphasis on production is his theory of *symbolic exchange*, a concept he develops as a way to understand human relations outside the framework of economic value and labor. Symbolic exchange refers to the non-economic, non-productive forms of social interaction that are based on reciprocity, gift-giving, and the circulation of symbolic meanings. Drawing on anthropological studies of pre-capitalist societies, Baudrillard highlights how these societies were not organized around production or accumulation but around forms of symbolic exchange that maintained social bonds and reinforced communal values. In such societies, objects were not valued for their material function or productive capacity but for their symbolic meanings, which were tied to rituals, relationships, and the cyclical nature of life and death.

Baudrillard contrasts this with the logic of capitalist (and Marxist) production, which seeks to accumulate, control, and maximize output. In capitalist societies, value is determined by labor, production, and exchange value, reducing social relations to economic transactions. This process of commodification, Baudrillard argues, strips objects and relationships of their symbolic significance, replacing them with a purely materialist logic. In this context, even human labor is commodified, with workers valued only for their ability to produce and generate surplus value for capitalists.

In *The Mirror of Production*, Baudrillard takes issue with Marxism's focus on *labor* as the central defining feature of human life. For Marx, labor is what makes humans unique, and it is through their productive activity that they realize their potential and reshape the world. Marx's vision of socialism is one where workers regain control over the means of production, thus liberating themselves from exploitation and alienation. Baudrillard, however, argues that this focus on labor as the essence of humanity is problematic because it reduces human existence to economic production. By defining people primarily as producers, both Marxism and capitalism perpetuate a worldview that sees individuals as tools of production rather than as complex beings engaged in a wide range of symbolic, social, and cultural activities.

Baudrillard's critique of Marxism also extends to its view of *history* as a linear process driven by material forces, specifically the development of productive capacities and class struggle. For Marx, history unfolds through stages—feudalism, capitalism, socialism—each driven by changes in the mode of production and the conflicts between different classes. This view of history as a rational, progressive movement toward a higher stage of social organization mirrors the capitalist narrative of progress and growth, where increased productivity and technological advancement are seen as the markers of human development.

Baudrillard, however, rejects this linear, materialist view of history. He argues that history cannot be reduced to the logic of production or class struggle. In fact, he questions whether history, as traditionally understood, still exists in the postmodern world, where technological advancements and media simulations create a state of *hyper reality* that erases the boundaries between past, present, and future. In Baudrillard's view, Marxism's historical materialism is outdated because it fails to account for the ways in which media, technology, and simulation have transformed our experience of time, space, and social relations.

One of Baudrillard's most radical departures from Marxist thought is his critique of the idea of *revolution* as a means of liberating society from capitalism. For Marx, revolution is the culmination of class struggle, when the working class overthrows the capitalist system and seizes control of the means of production. Baudrillard, however, argues that the very notion of revolution is itself a product of the same logic of production that sustains capitalism. In his view, the idea of revolution assumes that human freedom can be achieved through control over production and material resources, but this only reinforces the capitalist emphasis on labor, productivity, and economic relations.

Baudrillard is particularly skeptical of the possibility of revolutionary change in the modern, post-industrial world, where media and technology have created a state of hyper reality in which even resistance and rebellion are co-opted by the system. In the hyperreal world, revolutionary movements are often absorbed into the spectacle of media and consumer culture, becoming just another form of entertainment or simulation. Baudrillard argues that traditional forms of revolution, rooted in the seizure of the means of production, no longer offer a path to liberation because they remain trapped within the capitalist framework of economic production and materialism.

Instead of revolution, Baudrillard calls for a radical rethinking of *value* itself, moving away from the materialist focus on production and consumption toward an understanding of human life based on symbolic exchange. In his view, the key to breaking free from the capitalist system is not to seize control of production but to reject the logic of production altogether, embracing forms of social interaction and value that are not tied to economic accumulation or productivity. This means revaluing the non-productive, symbolic aspects of life—rituals, festivals, gift-giving, art, and play—that exist outside the capitalist economy and resist its logic of accumulation and control.

Baudrillard's critique of political economy in *The Mirror of Production* is also closely tied to his rejection of the concept of *alienation* as understood by Marx. For Marx, alienation occurs when workers are estranged from the products of their labor, from the process of production, and from their own creative potential. The solution, according to Marx, is for workers to regain control over the means of production, thus overcoming alienation and realizing their true potential as producers. Baudrillard, however, argues that this focus on overcoming alienation through production is flawed because it assumes that labor and production are the essence of human life. Instead, he suggests that true freedom lies in escaping the logic of production and reconnecting with the symbolic, non-productive dimensions of existence.

In conclusion, Jean Baudrillard's *The Mirror of Production* presents a radical critique of Marxist political economy, challenging its focus on labor, production, and materialism. Baudrillard argues that both Marxism and capitalism share a common obsession with production, reducing human life to economic relations and overlooking the symbolic and cultural dimensions of existence. In contrast, Baudrillard calls for a shift away from the logic of production toward an understanding of value and social relations based on symbolic exchange, reciprocity, and the rejection of accumulation. By critiquing the central role of production in Marxist and capitalist thought, Baudrillard offers a new way of thinking about freedom, value, and human existence outside the framework of political economy.

Baudrillard and Science Fiction

Jean Baudrillard's philosophy, particularly his ideas about simulation, hyper reality, and the collapse of the real, has had a significant impact on the genre of science fiction. His concepts are reflected not only in academic circles but also in the narrative structures and thematic concerns of many science fiction works. Science fiction, as a genre, often explores the boundaries between reality, technology, and the human condition, making it a natural fit for Baudrillard's theories on how reality is increasingly mediated and replaced by simulations. Through the lens of science fiction, Baudrillard's ideas about the dissolution of the real and the rise of hyper reality come to life, providing a framework for understanding the genre's engagement with futuristic technologies, virtual realities, artificial intelligence, and post-humanism.

One of the most notable intersections between Baudrillard's work and science fiction is his influence on *The Matrix* (1999), a film that directly engages with his ideas about simulation and hyper reality. Baudrillard's book *Simulacra and Simulation* appears in the film, symbolizing the collapse of the distinction between reality and the virtual world. The Matrix itself—a computer-generated simulation that the human characters experience as reality—embodies Baudrillard's notion of *hyper reality*, where simulations no longer reflect or distort reality but replace it entirely. In *The Matrix*, individuals live inside a simulated world, unaware that their perceptions, experiences, and identities are constructed by a vast artificial system. This perfectly mirrors Baudrillard's claim that in postmodern societies, people live in a state of hyper reality, where simulations are more real than the real world itself.

Baudrillard's reaction to *The Matrix* was complex. Despite the filmmakers openly acknowledging his influence, Baudrillard himself distanced his ideas from the film, arguing that *The Matrix* did not fully capture the essence of his critique of hyper reality. According to Baudrillard, *The Matrix* assumes that there is a real world outside the simulation that can be accessed and reclaimed, whereas his theory suggests that in the age of hyper reality, the distinction between the real and the simulated has collapsed entirely. There is no longer a "real" world to return to—only layers of simulations that obscure the absence of an underlying reality. In Baudrillard's view, the film's narrative of breaking free from the Matrix reinforces a binary opposition between the real and the simulated that no longer holds in the postmodern condition.

Beyond *The Matrix*, Baudrillard's ideas resonate with broader themes in science fiction, particularly in works that explore the consequences of advanced technologies, artificial intelligence, and virtual realities. His theory of *simulacra*—copies without an original—plays out in stories where reality is manufactured, and characters struggle to distinguish between what is real and what is artificial. In many science fiction narratives, the boundaries between human and machine, real and virtual, or organic and artificial are blurred, reflecting Baudrillard's contention that technology has led to the erosion of traditional categories that once defined human existence.

Philip K. Dick, one of the most influential science fiction writers, frequently explores themes that align with Baudrillard's philosophy. In works like *Do Androids Dream of Electric Sheep?* (1968)—which was adapted into the film *Blade Runner* (1982)—Dick examines the nature of reality, identity, and humanity in a world where humans and artificial beings (androids) are almost indistinguishable. The question of what it means to be real, or human, in a world where simulations and artificial life forms exist, echoes Baudrillard's concerns about the dissolution of reality in the age of advanced technology. In Dick's world, reality is fragile, constantly undermined by illusions, technological constructs, and artificial identities, making it difficult to determine what is "authentic" or "real."

Baudrillard's influence is also felt in the *cyberpunk* subgenre of science fiction, which emerged in the 1980s and 1990s and focuses on the interaction between technology, society, and human identity. Cyberpunk authors like William Gibson and Bruce Sterling explore dystopian futures where virtual realities, artificial intelligence, and corporate control define human existence. In Gibson's seminal work *Neuromancer* (1984), the concept of cyberspace—a virtual environment where people interact with digital representations of reality—mirrors Baudrillard's hyperreal world, where the boundaries between the virtual and the real collapse. In *Neuromancer*, the protagonist navigates a world where digital simulations dominate, and the distinction between flesh and code, body and machine, becomes increasingly tenuous. Baudrillard's ideas about simulation and the replacement of the real with the virtual are central to the cyberpunk vision of a future where technology has irrevocably altered the human experience.

In addition to cyberspace and virtual reality, Baudrillard's critique of the *implosion of meaning* in a media-saturated world is reflected in science fiction's portrayal of information overload and the collapse of truth. In a hyperreal world, Baudrillard argues, the constant flow of images, signs, and information overwhelms people's ability to make sense of reality, leading to a state where meaning itself collapses. Science fiction often explores this theme through stories set in futures where information is so abundant and easily manipulated that it becomes impossible to distinguish truth from falsehood. Films like *Total Recall* (1990) and *Inception* (2010) play with the idea of constructed memories and manufactured realities, where characters must question whether their experiences are real or artificial. These narratives reflect Baudrillard's contention that in the postmodern age, reality is no longer a stable or knowable category, as it is constantly mediated and constructed by technological systems of representation.

Baudrillard's influence on science fiction also extends to his exploration of *artificial intelligence* and the post-human. In his view, the rise of AI and technological replication marks a shift toward a world where machines not only mimic human abilities but begin to replace them, creating a situation where the distinction between human and machine dissolves. This idea is reflected in science fiction narratives that question the nature of consciousness, identity, and what it means to be human. Films like *Ex Machina* (2014) and *Her* (2013) explore relationships between humans and AI, blurring the boundaries between human emotions and artificial simulations of love, desire, and communication. Baudrillard's notion of the *death of the real* is evident in these stories, where the human experience is increasingly mediated by machines and artificial constructs, raising questions about the authenticity of relationships, emotions, and identity in a technologically dominated world.

Baudrillard's work also engages with the broader *ethical implications* of living in a hyperreal world, a theme that is frequently explored in science fiction. In a world where simulations replace reality and technology mediates every aspect of life, traditional ethical categories—such as responsibility, freedom, and agency—are called into question. Science fiction often grapples with the consequences of living in a world where individuals no longer control their identities or environments but are instead subject to systems of surveillance, control, and manipulation. In *The Matrix*, the idea that humans are unknowingly trapped in a simulated reality controlled by machines raises profound ethical questions about free will, autonomy, and the nature of reality itself. Similarly, in stories like *The Terminator* series and *Westworld*, the rise of AI and the potential for machines to develop consciousness challenge the ethical boundaries between creator and creation, human and machine.

In conclusion, Jean Baudrillard's ideas about simulation, hyper reality, and the collapse of the real have had a profound impact on the genre of science fiction, shaping its engagement with technology, identity, and reality. His philosophy offers a framework for understanding the ways in which science fiction explores the blurred boundaries between the real and the artificial, the human and the machine, and the authentic and the simulated. From films like *The Matrix* and *Blade Runner* to the cyberpunk visions of *Neuromancer* and the AI-driven futures of *Ex Machina* and *Her*,

Baudrillard's critique of modern society resonates with science fiction's exploration of the technological forces that shape human existence. Through the lens of science fiction, Baudrillard's theories come to life, offering a powerful critique of the postmodern condition and its implications for the future of reality, identity, and human experience.

The Dangers of Simulation in a Technological World

Jean Baudrillard's exploration of *simulation* and *hyper reality* reveals deep concerns about the dangers these phenomena pose in a technologically driven world. According to Baudrillard, the rise of digital technologies, media, and virtual environments has led to the *collapse of reality*, creating a world where simulations have replaced the real, and the distinction between truth and falsehood, reality and fiction, has become blurred. Baudrillard's critique highlights the ways in which simulations, while often perceived as harmless or entertaining, have profound consequences for human identity, social relations, and the ability to perceive and engage with reality. In this context, the dangers of simulation are not just philosophical or abstract concerns but have real-world implications for how people understand themselves, interact with others, and make sense of the world.

One of the primary dangers of simulation, as Baudrillard sees it, is the *erosion of reality*. In a world where simulations dominate, people lose their connection to the real world, as their experiences and perceptions are increasingly mediated through artificial environments, images, and signs. Baudrillard argues that in the postmodern era, simulations no longer merely reflect or distort reality—they *replace* it entirely, creating what he calls *hyper reality*. Hyper reality is a state in which the simulated becomes more real than reality itself, and people come to accept the artificial as their primary reality. This process leads to the *death of the real*, as the distinctions between reality and simulation collapse, leaving individuals unable to discern what is real and what is artificial.

The technological world amplifies this problem, as digital media, virtual reality (VR), and social media platforms create immersive, hyperreal environments that feel more compelling and desirable than the physical world. Social media platforms like Instagram, Facebook, and TikTok, for example, encourage users to construct idealized versions of their lives through carefully curated images and posts. These digital personas often bear little resemblance to the individual's real-life experiences, but they become the dominant reality in the virtual space. Baudrillard would argue that this process of *self-simulation* leads to a fragmented and performative sense of identity, where individuals are constantly engaged in the act of performing and presenting a version of themselves for public consumption.

The *dissolution of identity* in a simulated world is one of the most profound dangers that Baudrillard identifies. In the hyperreal environment created by digital media and virtual technologies, individuals increasingly define themselves through external symbols, signs, and representations rather than through internal reflection or authentic self-expression. The result is a sense of self that is fluid, unstable, and disconnected from any grounded reality. Identity becomes a *performance*, constantly shaped and reshaped by external forces, including the media, advertising, and social expectations. In this hyperreal world, people lose their sense of agency and autonomy, as their identities are constructed not by their own choices or experiences but by the simulations they inhabit.

Baudrillard's critique also extends to the *implosion of meaning* in the technological world. As media and information systems proliferate, the sheer volume of data, images, and narratives overwhelms individuals' ability to make sense of reality. In a world where everything is mediated through screens and digital interfaces, the distinction between truth and fiction collapses, and meaning becomes fragmented and incoherent. Baudrillard argues that the constant flow of information creates a situation where *meaning implodes*—instead of greater clarity or understanding, individuals are left disoriented and confused by the endless stream of images and messages. This implosion of meaning is dangerous because it undermines the ability to engage with reality critically or to distinguish between what is real and what is artificial.

One of the clearest examples of this danger is in the realm of *news and information*. In the age of digital media, news is often presented as entertainment, with sensationalized stories, dramatic images, and emotional appeals taking precedence over facts and analysis. The rise of *fake news*, conspiracy theories, and disinformation campaigns further blurs the line between truth and falsehood, leaving individuals uncertain about what to believe. Baudrillard's concept of hyper reality helps explain how news media creates simulations that are consumed as reality, even when they distort or obscure the truth. In this context, the danger is not just the spread of misinformation but the erosion of trust in any kind of objective reality, leading to a state where people are disconnected from any shared understanding of truth or facts.

In the technological world, *virtual reality* (VR) and *augmented reality* (AR) present another set of dangers related to simulation. These technologies create immersive, artificial environments that simulate real-world experiences but are entirely fabricated. While VR and AR offer exciting possibilities for entertainment, education, and communication, Baudrillard would argue that they also pose a risk of further detaching individuals from reality. In virtual environments, users can interact with simulated worlds that feel real, even though they are completely artificial. As these technologies become more advanced and immersive, the danger is that individuals may begin to prefer the virtual world to the real one, leading to a form of *escapism* where reality is abandoned in favor of the more controlled, idealized simulations offered by technology.

This form of escapism is particularly dangerous because it reinforces the *commodification* of experience. In the hyperreal world, experiences themselves become commodities to be bought, sold, and consumed. Theme parks like Disneyland, which Baudrillard famously analyzed, offer carefully curated simulations of reality that are designed to provide visitors with idealized, commodified experiences. Similarly, VR environments offer users the opportunity to experience new realities, from exploring virtual worlds to engaging in simulations of real-world activities. However, these experiences are often packaged and sold as products, reinforcing the capitalist logic of consumption. The danger here is that individuals come to see their experiences, emotions, and relationships as things to be consumed, further disconnecting them from authentic, unmediated experiences of the real world.

Baudrillard also critiques the role of *artificial intelligence (AI)* and *automation* in the technological world, arguing that the rise of intelligent machines further destabilizes human identity and autonomy. As AI systems become more sophisticated, they increasingly take over tasks that were once the domain of human intelligence and creativity, from writing and art to decision-making and problem-solving. Baudrillard's concept of simulation suggests that AI and automation represent a new form of hyper reality, where human activities are simulated by machines, replacing the need for real human engagement. The danger here is twofold: first, the potential loss of human creativity and autonomy as machines take over more aspects of life, and second, the blurring of boundaries between human and machine, as AI systems become increasingly integrated into daily life.

Baudrillard's critique of simulation in a technological world also raises questions about the *ethics of representation* and *surveillance*. In the hyperreal environment of digital media and social networks, individuals are constantly subjected to surveillance, with their behaviors, preferences, and identities tracked, recorded, and analyzed by algorithms. This creates a situation where identity is no longer private or autonomous but is instead shaped by the systems of control that monitor and manipulate individuals' interactions with the digital world. The rise of surveillance capitalism, where personal data is commodified and sold, is another danger of the technological world that Baudrillard's work anticipates. In a hyperreal world, individuals become products themselves, with their behaviors and desires shaped by the algorithms and simulations that track and predict their actions.

In conclusion, Jean Baudrillard's critique of simulation and hyper reality offers a powerful warning about the dangers of living in a technologically driven world where the boundaries between the real and the artificial collapse. The erosion of reality, the fragmentation of identity, the implosion of meaning, and the commodification of experience are all consequences of the rise of simulation in the postmodern world. As digital media, virtual reality, and artificial intelligence continue to shape human experiences, Baudrillard's ideas challenge us to consider the implications of living in a world where reality itself is increasingly mediated and replaced by simulations. The dangers of simulation are not just philosophical concerns but have real-world consequences for how individuals understand themselves, interact with others, and engage with the world around them.

Baudrillard on Globalization and Power Structures

Jean Baudrillard's critique of globalization and power structures reflects his broader concerns with *hyper reality*, *simulation*, and the changing nature of power in the postmodern world. For Baudrillard, globalization is not simply an economic or political phenomenon; it represents the spread of a *hyperreal* world where the traditional structures of power, control, and domination are no longer exercised through direct force or coercion but through the manipulation of images, signs, and symbols. As globalization expands, it brings with it the collapse of local cultures and realities, replacing them with a homogenized, global system of simulations that obscures the real and creates new forms of control and domination.

Baudrillard's analysis of globalization begins with his concept of *simulation*—the idea that in the postmodern world, reality is increasingly replaced by simulations that do not reflect or represent reality but instead *produce* their own reality. In the context of globalization, this means that global media, corporations, and cultural forces create a homogenized world of simulations that erase local differences and impose a standardized, hyperreal version of reality across the globe. Globalization, for Baudrillard, is not just the spread of capitalist markets or Western culture; it is the expansion of a *simulated reality* that dominates and subsumes all other realities. This process of homogenization leads to the erosion of cultural diversity and the disappearance of local traditions, identities, and values, as everything is absorbed into the global system of hyper reality.

One of the key ways globalization operates, according to Baudrillard, is through the *global media*. The rise of global media networks, particularly in the age of satellite television, the internet, and social media, has created a situation where information, images, and narratives circulate instantaneously around the world. This constant flow of media content creates a global *hyperreal environment*, where people from different parts of the world are exposed to the same images, ideas, and narratives, regardless of their local context. The media does not simply report on events or reality; it constructs a simulated version of reality that becomes the dominant way people perceive the world. In this sense, global media plays a central role in creating and sustaining the *hyper reality* of globalization, where the distinction between reality and representation collapses.

Baudrillard argues that this global media-driven hyper reality creates new forms of *power and control*. In traditional societies, power was exercised through direct control over land, resources, and people. In the modern world, power was tied to the control of economic production and the state. However, in the postmodern world, power is increasingly exercised through the control of *images, signs, and representations*. The global media plays a crucial role in this process, as it shapes how people perceive reality, what they believe to be true, and how they understand their place in the world. For Baudrillard, this form of power is more insidious than traditional forms of domination because it operates invisibly, through the creation of a simulated reality that people accept as real.

Baudrillard's concept of *soft power* reflects this shift in the nature of control in the globalized world. Soft power refers to the ability to shape the preferences and beliefs of others through cultural and ideological influence, rather than through direct force or coercion. In the context of globalization, soft power is exercised through the global spread of media, entertainment, technology, and consumer culture. Hollywood movies, global brands like Coca-Cola and Apple, and social media platforms like Facebook and Instagram all exert soft power by shaping how people around the world think, act, and define themselves. This form of power is not imposed by governments or military forces; it is spread through cultural and media systems that create a global hyperreal environment where people's desires, identities, and values are shaped by simulations of reality.

Baudrillard also critiques the idea that globalization represents a kind of *universal progress* or *global unity*. While globalization is often framed as a process of bringing the world closer together through increased economic, cultural, and technological integration, Baudrillard sees it as a form of domination that erases differences and creates a world of *sameness*. Globalization, in his view, is a process of homogenization, where local cultures, languages, and traditions are absorbed into the global system of hyper reality. The result is a loss of diversity, as everything is standardized and commodified for global consumption. For Baudrillard, this is a form of violence, not in the traditional sense of physical force, but in the sense of cultural erasure and the imposition of a single, global reality that leaves no room for alternatives.

Baudrillard's critique of globalization is closely tied to his analysis of *consumer culture*. He argues that globalization spreads not just markets and products but a global system of consumption that defines people's identities and social relations. In the globalized world, individuals are no longer defined by their local cultures or traditions but by their participation in the global economy of signs and commodities. Consumer goods, brands, and media content circulate globally, creating a shared set of symbols and identities that transcend national or cultural boundaries. This global system of consumption is driven by the logic of *simulation*, where people's desires and identities are shaped by images and signs that have no connection to reality. The result is a global hyperreal environment where individuals define themselves through the products they consume and the media they watch, rather than through their connection to a particular culture or community.

For Baudrillard, this global system of consumption is a form of *domination*, as it reduces people to consumers of images and commodities, stripping them of their autonomy and agency. In a globalized, hyperreal world, individuals are constantly bombarded with messages, advertisements, and images that tell them what to desire, how to behave, and what to value. This creates a situation where people's identities are shaped not by their own experiences or choices but by the global system of simulation that defines what is real, desirable, and valuable. This form of domination is particularly dangerous because it operates through the creation of illusions and simulations that people willingly participate in, without recognizing that they are being controlled.

Baudrillard also critiques the *political dimension* of globalization, particularly the idea that global governance and international organizations can create a more just or equitable world. In his view, globalization leads not to greater equality or democracy but to new forms of *global domination* that operate through the control of information, media, and technology. International institutions, multinational corporations, and global media conglomerates exert power not by enforcing laws or military might but by shaping the way people understand the world and their place in it. Baudrillard argues that this form of power is more subtle and more pervasive than traditional forms of political control because it operates through the manipulation of signs and symbols, creating a global hyperreal environment where political reality is constructed and managed by those in control of the media and information systems.

In the globalized world, Baudrillard suggests that traditional forms of *resistance*—such as political protests, revolutionary movements, or local activism—are increasingly absorbed into the global system of hyper reality. In his view, even acts of resistance are often commodified and turned into media spectacles, losing their effectiveness as tools of political change. Protests, revolutions, and political movements are often reduced to *simulacra*—representations that are consumed as entertainment or symbols of rebellion but have little impact on the actual power structures that define globalization. For Baudrillard, this is another way in which globalization maintains its dominance, by absorbing and neutralizing resistance through the creation of simulations that give the illusion of political engagement without challenging the underlying structures of power.

Baudrillard's analysis of globalization also touches on the concept of *the implosion of power*. In the globalized, hyperreal world, power no longer operates in a clear, hierarchical manner. Instead, it becomes diffuse, decentralized, and difficult to locate. This is because power is no longer exercised through direct control over land, resources, or institutions but through the manipulation of images, symbols, and signs. In the hyperreal world, power is everywhere and nowhere at the same time, as it operates invisibly through the global media and cultural systems that shape how people see and understand reality. This makes it difficult to resist or challenge global power structures because they are no longer concentrated in a single place or controlled by a single entity. Instead, power operates through the global system of simulation that defines the hyperreal environment in which people live.

In conclusion, Jean Baudrillard's critique of globalization and power structures reveals a deep concern with the ways in which globalization creates a *hyperreal world* where reality is replaced by simulations, and power is exercised through the manipulation of signs and images. For Baudrillard, globalization is not just an economic or political process but a cultural and symbolic one, where local identities and realities are erased and replaced by a homogenized, global system of hyper reality. This system of simulation creates new forms of power and domination that operate through the media, consumer culture, and global networks of information and technology. Baudrillard's analysis challenges us to consider the dangers of living in a world where reality is increasingly mediated by simulations, and where power operates invisibly through the global systems that shape our perceptions, desires, and identities.

Why Baudrillard Matters Today

Jean Baudrillard's philosophy remains deeply relevant today, as his ideas about *hyper reality*, *simulation*, and the transformation of power in a mediated world offer profound insights into the complexities of contemporary society. Baudrillard's critiques of media, technology, globalization, and consumer culture speak directly to the challenges we face in an age dominated by digital communication, virtual environments, and global networks. As we navigate a world where reality is increasingly constructed and mediated through screens, algorithms, and simulations, Baudrillard's work provides a powerful framework for understanding how these forces shape not only our perceptions of the world but also our sense of identity, meaning, and power.

One of the primary reasons Baudrillard matters today is his analysis of *hyper reality*, the state in which simulations and representations become more real and impactful than reality itself. In the digital age, where social media, virtual reality, and online platforms dominate much of our lives, Baudrillard's concept of hyper reality helps explain how digital spaces often replace face-to-face interactions and authentic experiences. On platforms like Instagram, TikTok, and Facebook, people curate idealized versions of themselves, constructing and sharing carefully edited representations that are often far removed from the messy, complex realities of daily life. Baudrillard's ideas reveal the dangers of living in a world where these hyperreal simulations replace genuine human engagement, leading to a fractured sense of self and a disconnection from the real world.

This shift toward hyper reality is particularly evident in the rise of *virtual reality* (VR) and *augmented reality* (AR) technologies, which offer immersive experiences that blur the line between the real and the virtual. Baudrillard's concern with the replacement of reality by simulations is directly applicable to these technologies, as they create environments where users can interact with digital worlds that feel just as real—if not more real—than physical reality. As VR and AR become more advanced and integrated into everyday life, Baudrillard's warnings about the *death of the real* take on new urgency. His work encourages us to question how much of our lives and identities are shaped by artificial environments and to consider the potential consequences of living in a world where reality is increasingly mediated by technology.

Baudrillard's analysis of *consumer culture* and the commodification of experience also remains relevant in today's world, where global capitalism continues to shape how we live, think, and consume. Baudrillard argued that in late capitalist societies, consumption becomes a form of identity, with individuals defining themselves through the products they buy, the brands they wear, and the lifestyles they adopt. This process of commodification extends to every aspect of life, as even emotions, experiences, and relationships are packaged and sold as commodities. Today, this phenomenon is amplified by *influencer culture* and the rise of the *experience economy*, where individuals are encouraged to monetize their personal lives and turn every moment into a marketable product. Baudrillard's critique of consumerism exposes the emptiness of this hyperreal world, where identity and meaning are reduced to mere signs and symbols, disconnected from any deeper or authentic experience.

In addition to his critique of consumer culture, Baudrillard's concept of *soft power* and the manipulation of signs and images offers a powerful lens for understanding the dynamics of *media and political power* today. In the age of global media networks, 24-hour news cycles, and social media platforms, Baudrillard's ideas about the power of media to shape perceptions and control reality have only become more relevant. The manipulation of news, the rise of *fake news*, and the spread of *disinformation* reflect Baudrillard's contention that the media no longer simply reports on reality but creates and constructs it. Political events are often framed as media spectacles, where the presentation of images and narratives becomes more important than the actual substance of events. This media-driven hyper reality makes it increasingly difficult to distinguish between truth and fiction, fact and fabrication, as people's understanding of the world is shaped by the simulations they consume rather than by direct engagement with reality.

This is particularly evident in the context of *social media algorithms*, which curate and filter the information individuals receive based on their preferences and behaviors. These algorithms create *filter bubbles*, where users are exposed only to information that reinforces their existing beliefs, further blurring the line between reality and simulation. Baudrillard's warnings about the implosion of meaning in a media-saturated world are more relevant than ever, as the constant flow of information and images makes it difficult to discern what is real or true. His work encourages us to question how media and technology shape our perceptions of reality and to remain vigilant in a world where power is increasingly exercised through the control of signs, images, and information.

Baudrillard's *critique of globalization* also remains a critical tool for understanding contemporary power structures. In an era of global interconnectedness, Baudrillard's insights into how globalization homogenizes culture, erases local identities, and creates a hyperreal world of simulations resonate deeply. The spread of global media, consumer goods, and corporate brands creates a world where cultural diversity is replaced by a standardized global culture dominated by signs and symbols that circulate endlessly without reference to any specific local context. Baudrillard's critique reveals how globalization, far from creating greater equality or unity, often imposes a single reality—a global hyper reality—that obscures the complexities of local cultures and identities. His work pushes us to consider the consequences of living in a world where globalization creates not just economic or political uniformity but a uniformity of experience, identity, and meaning.

One of the most pressing aspects of Baudrillard's relevance today is his critique of *artificial intelligence (AI)* and the *posthuman*. Baudrillard's work anticipates the rise of AI systems that simulate human thought, creativity, and decision-making, raising profound questions about the nature of humanity, autonomy, and agency. In a world where AI is increasingly integrated into everyday life, from smart assistants to autonomous vehicles, Baudrillard's concerns about the blurring of boundaries between human and machine take on new significance. His theory of simulation suggests that AI systems, by replicating human behavior and intelligence, create new forms of hyper reality, where the distinction between human creativity and machine-generated output becomes increasingly difficult to maintain.

The ethical implications of living in a world dominated by AI, automation, and simulation are profound. Baudrillard's work forces us to confront the ways in which technology not only transforms our environment but also redefines what it means to be human. As AI systems take over more aspects of life—decision-making, creativity, and even emotional interaction—Baudrillard's critique challenges us to consider the potential consequences of living in a world where human agency and autonomy are increasingly replaced by machine-driven simulations.

Baudrillard also offers an important critique of *resistance and activism* in the hyperreal world. In his view, traditional forms of resistance—political protests, revolutionary movements, or direct action—are often absorbed into the system of hyper reality, becoming part of the spectacle rather than genuine challenges to power. In today's world, where social movements and political causes are often reduced to social media hashtags or media events, Baudrillard's insights into the commodification of resistance are especially relevant. His work suggests that in a hyperreal world, even acts of rebellion can become simulacra—representations that give the illusion of resistance without challenging the underlying structures of power. This critique pushes us to rethink how resistance can be effective in a world where even dissent is commodified and turned into a spectacle.

In conclusion, Jean Baudrillard's work remains deeply relevant in today's world, offering crucial insights into the ways in which media, technology, globalization, and consumer culture shape our reality. His concepts of hyper reality, simulation, and the implosion of meaning help us navigate a world where the boundaries between the real and the artificial are increasingly blurred. Baudrillard's critiques of power, identity, and resistance challenge us to think critically about how technology and media shape our lives and to remain vigilant in a world where reality itself is increasingly constructed and controlled by the forces of simulation. As we move further into the digital age, Baudrillard's philosophy provides a powerful framework for understanding the complexities of modern life and the dangers of living in a hyperreal world.

Baudrillard's Analysis of Modern Warfare

Jean Baudrillard's analysis of modern warfare is one of the most striking aspects of his critique of postmodern society, particularly through his concept of *simulation* and *hyper reality*. Baudrillard contends that in the postmodern world, war has become a spectacle, an event that is no longer grounded in the brutal reality of combat and suffering but is instead mediated and constructed by the global media. In modern warfare, the boundary between reality and representation has collapsed, transforming war into a hyperreal experience where simulations, media portrayals, and virtual narratives replace the actual horrors of conflict. Baudrillard's examination of modern warfare, particularly in relation to events like the Gulf War, reflects his broader concerns about the ways in which media, technology, and simulation shape our understanding of violence, conflict, and power.

One of Baudrillard's most famous works on this topic is his provocative assertion that *The Gulf War Did Not Take Place*. Baudrillard's argument is not that the Gulf War, fought between Iraq and a U.S.-led coalition in 1990-1991, literally did not occur. Rather, he is making a more profound philosophical claim: the war, as it was presented to the global public through media coverage, was not a real war but a simulation. In Baudrillard's view, the Gulf War was not experienced as a series of real battles with real consequences but as a carefully constructed media spectacle, designed to appear clean, efficient, and technologically superior. The war was mediated through images of precision bombing, satellite footage, and military briefings that gave the impression of a sanitized, almost bloodless conflict. The reality of civilian casualties, destruction, and chaos was hidden behind the hyperreal version of the war presented on television screens around the world.

For Baudrillard, the Gulf War was a prime example of how modern warfare has been transformed into a *hyperreal event*, where the media's representation of the conflict becomes more real than the actual events on the ground. The war was constructed as a spectacle for global audiences, with the focus on technological superiority, military precision, and the righteousness of the coalition forces. In this sense, the Gulf War, as presented by the media, was a simulation—a representation of war that was disconnected from the actual human suffering and destruction taking place. Baudrillard's critique highlights how modern warfare, mediated through global media networks, becomes a hyperreal event where the reality of violence and death is obscured by the spectacle of military power.

Baudrillard's analysis of modern warfare also touches on the role of *technology* in transforming the nature of conflict. In traditional wars, combat was a direct, physical experience, with soldiers and civilians confronting the brutal realities of violence and death. In modern warfare, however, technology increasingly mediates the experience of war, distancing both soldiers and the public from the realities of combat. The use of precision-guided missiles, drones, and other advanced military technologies creates an illusion of control, where war appears to be a clean, surgical operation that minimizes human suffering. Baudrillard argues that this technological mediation is itself a form of simulation, where the actual violence of war is hidden behind the façade of precision and efficiency.

This technological mediation extends to the way war is experienced by the general public. In modern warfare, the global media plays a central role in shaping how people perceive conflict, often reducing complex geopolitical events to simplified narratives and dramatic visuals. Baudrillard argues that the media's portrayal of war as a spectacle of power and control creates a *detached, passive experience* for the public, where they consume images of war without confronting its real consequences. The violence, destruction, and human suffering of war are reduced to images and signs that are consumed like entertainment, further reinforcing the hyperreal nature of modern warfare.

Baudrillard's critique of modern warfare also highlights the *political implications* of war as a simulation. In his view, the transformation of war into a media spectacle serves the interests of political and military elites by obscuring the true costs and consequences of conflict. By presenting war as a clean, efficient operation, the media and governments can maintain public support for military interventions without exposing the public to the horrors of war. This process of simulation allows political leaders to wage war with minimal political risk, as the public remains disconnected from the reality of the violence being inflicted in their name. In this sense, modern warfare, as a hyperreal event, becomes a tool of political control, where the true nature of conflict is hidden behind the spectacle of military power.

Baudrillard's concept of *virtual war* also extends to his critique of how modern warfare blurs the lines between the real and the virtual. In the postmodern era, the development of advanced military technologies, such as drones and cyber warfare, has created a situation where war is increasingly fought in virtual spaces rather than on traditional battlefields. Drones allow military forces to carry out attacks from a distance, often operated by soldiers thousands of miles away from the conflict zone. Cyber warfare, meanwhile, takes place in the digital realm, where attacks on infrastructure, communication networks, and financial systems can have devastating consequences without any physical confrontation. Baudrillard argues that this shift toward virtual war represents a new stage in the evolution of conflict, where the physical realities of violence and combat are replaced by digital simulations and remote-controlled operations.

In this context, Baudrillard's analysis of modern warfare resonates with broader concerns about the *ethical implications* of technological warfare. The use of drones, for example, raises questions about the dehumanization of combat, as soldiers engage in violence from a distance, often without confronting the human consequences of their actions. Similarly, the rise of cyber warfare challenges traditional notions of sovereignty and conflict, as attacks can be carried out by anonymous actors across borders, blurring the lines between war and peace. Baudrillard's critique of simulation and hyper reality helps us understand how these new forms of warfare, while technologically advanced, further disconnect both combatants and the public from the realities of violence and destruction.

Another key aspect of Baudrillard's analysis of modern warfare is his critique of the *spectacle of terrorism*. Baudrillard argues that terrorism, like conventional warfare, has become a form of hyper reality in the postmodern world. In the age of global media, terrorist acts are not just acts of violence; they are carefully staged events designed to capture the attention of global audiences.

Baudrillard's analysis of the 9/11 attacks, for example, highlights how terrorism operates as a spectacle, where the destruction of the Twin Towers was not just a military or political act but a symbolic event designed to resonate in the hyperreal world of media and images. In Baudrillard's view, terrorism, like modern warfare, operates in the realm of hyper reality, where the symbolic power of an act often outweighs its physical consequences.

Baudrillard's analysis of terrorism also extends to his critique of how governments and media respond to terrorist acts. In his view, the media's coverage of terrorism often amplifies the spectacle, turning it into a global event that reinforces the power of the terrorist act. By focusing on the dramatic visuals and symbolic meanings of terrorist attacks, the media helps transform these acts into hyperreal events that resonate far beyond their immediate impact. This process of mediation and amplification, according to Baudrillard, contributes to the spread of fear and paranoia, creating a climate where the distinction between real threats and imagined dangers becomes increasingly difficult to discern.

In conclusion, Jean Baudrillard's analysis of modern warfare offers a powerful critique of how conflict has been transformed in the postmodern world. His concepts of simulation, hyper reality, and virtual war help explain how the realities of violence, destruction, and suffering are increasingly obscured by the media's portrayal of war as a controlled, sanitized spectacle. Baudrillard's critique reveals how modern warfare, whether in the form of drone strikes, cyber attacks, or terrorism, operates in the realm of hyper reality, where the boundaries between the real and the virtual collapse. His work challenges us to confront the ethical, political, and social implications of living in a world where war is no longer a direct, physical experience but a mediated event, consumed and interpreted through the lens of simulation.

The Political Economy of the Sign

Jean Baudrillard's *The Political Economy of the Sign* (1972) represents a pivotal moment in his intellectual development, marking his departure from traditional Marxist theory and the exploration of how signs, symbols, and representation have come to dominate contemporary social and economic life. Baudrillard's central argument in this work is that the traditional Marxist focus on production, labor, and material goods is no longer sufficient for understanding the complexities of late capitalism. Instead, Baudrillard argues that in modern consumer society, value is not determined by labor or the use of objects but by *sign-value*—the symbolic meanings and associations attached to commodities. In this context, Baudrillard introduces a new way of thinking about *political economy*, one that shifts from the economic analysis of goods to the analysis of signs and their role in shaping social relations, identity, and power.

At the core of Baudrillard's critique is the distinction between *use-value, exchange-value*, and *sign-value*. In Marxist theory, use-value refers to the practical, material utility of a commodity, while exchange-value represents its worth in the marketplace as determined by labor and supply-demand dynamics. However, Baudrillard argues that in modern consumer society, neither use-value nor exchange-value fully explain how commodities are valued. Instead, he introduces the concept of *sign-value*, which refers to the symbolic meaning that commodities carry within a cultural or social context. In Baudrillard's view, modern capitalism is less about the production of goods for their utility or market price and more about the creation of signs and symbols that shape identity, social status, and desires.

For example, a luxury car such as a Ferrari is not valued simply for its use as a mode of transportation (its use-value) or for the labor and materials that went into producing it (its exchange-value). Rather, the car's value is largely symbolic—it serves as a sign of wealth, power, and status. In this sense, the Ferrari's *sign-value* far outweighs its practical or material aspects. Baudrillard argues that this shift toward sign-value transforms the way people relate to commodities and to one another. In a society dominated by sign-value, individuals no longer consume goods for their practical uses or even for their monetary value; they consume them for the symbolic meanings they represent. The act of consumption becomes an act of communication, where individuals signal their identity, status, and belonging through the signs attached to the goods they purchase.

Baudrillard's analysis of the *political economy of the sign* also addresses the ways in which commodities are increasingly detached from their material origins and take on a life of their own as *signifiers* in a system of cultural meaning. In the traditional Marxist view, commodities are tied to the labor that produces them, with value being extracted from the worker's labor-power. However, Baudrillard argues that in a post-industrial society dominated by media, advertising, and consumer culture, commodities are no longer valued for the labor that went into them but for the images, narratives, and symbols they evoke. In this sense, commodities become part of a vast system of *simulacra*, where signs circulate independently of any material reality, creating a hyperreal environment where meaning is generated through the play of signs rather than through direct reference to the real world.

The concept of *simulacra* plays a key role in Baudrillard's critique of the political economy of the sign. In a world dominated by sign-value, objects are no longer tied to a specific material function or reality; they become *simulations*—copies without an original. A brand logo, for instance, may no longer refer to the quality or function of a product but instead evoke a set of symbolic associations that consumers find desirable. These simulations create a world where signs and images proliferate, and reality is replaced by a network of representations that bear little relation to the material world. Baudrillard's theory of simulacra highlights how the economy of signs transforms both commodities and social relations, creating a hyperreal world where individuals engage in the constant exchange of symbolic meanings, detached from any direct reference to the real.

In *The Political Economy of the Sign*, Baudrillard also critiques the role of *advertising* and *media* in shaping the system of sign-value. In traditional economies, advertising was simply a tool for promoting products and increasing sales. However, Baudrillard argues that in the modern economy, advertising plays a far more central role in creating and sustaining the system of sign-value. Through advertisements, commodities are imbued with symbolic meanings that go beyond their material utility or exchange value. Advertising, in Baudrillard's view, is not just about selling products; it is about selling *signs*, constructing narratives that attach desirable identities and lifestyles to commodities. As a result, consumers are not just buying goods—they are buying the symbolic meanings that these goods represent.

This process of commodification extends beyond material goods to encompass *experiences*, *emotions*, and even *relationships*. In Baudrillard's view, everything in the modern world becomes subject to the logic of sign-value, where the symbolic meanings attached to goods and experiences take precedence over their actual content or material function. For instance, travel, once an experience of exploration and discovery, becomes commodified as a symbol of status and identity. A luxury vacation is no longer valued simply for the experience itself but for the symbolic capital it confers on the traveler, who can display their travels on social media, signaling their wealth, taste, and sophistication.

Baudrillard's critique of the political economy of the sign also touches on the ways in which sign-value creates new forms of *social control* and *domination*. In traditional Marxist theory, the capitalist system exploits workers by extracting surplus value from their labor. Baudrillard, however, argues that in the postmodern economy, power operates not primarily through the control of production but through the control of signs and images. In a society dominated by sign-value, individuals are controlled not through direct force or economic coercion but through their participation in the system of consumption, where their desires, identities, and social status are shaped by the signs they consume. This form of control is more subtle and pervasive than traditional forms of domination because it operates through the construction of desires and the manipulation of symbolic meanings, making individuals complicit in their own subjugation.

The political economy of the sign also has profound implications for *identity formation* and *social relations*. In Baudrillard's view, individuals in modern consumer society no longer construct their identities through work, community, or family ties. Instead, they define themselves through the commodities they consume and the signs they display. This process of identity formation is inherently unstable, as individuals are constantly engaged in the act of consuming new signs in order to construct and maintain their social identities. In this sense, identity becomes a *performance*—a constant process of adopting and displaying signs in order to communicate one's place within the social order. This performative aspect of identity is tied to the larger system of sign-value, where individuals are not defined by their inherent qualities or abilities but by the symbolic meanings attached to the goods and experiences they consume.

Baudrillard's analysis also highlights the ways in which sign-value creates *social hierarchies* and reinforces *inequalities*. In a society dominated by sign-value, individuals are differentiated not by their productive capacities or labor but by their ability to consume and display the right signs. The accumulation of sign-value becomes a marker of social status, where those who can afford to consume luxury goods, experiences, and lifestyles are elevated within the social hierarchy, while those who lack access to these signs are marginalized. This system of differentiation creates a new form of inequality, where social status is determined not by one's relationship to the means of production but by one's ability to participate in the economy of signs.

In conclusion, Jean Baudrillard's *The Political Economy of the Sign* offers a radical rethinking of traditional Marxist political economy by shifting the focus from the production of goods to the production of *signs*. In a world dominated by consumer culture, advertising, and media, Baudrillard argues that commodities are no longer valued for their material utility or exchange value but for the symbolic meanings they carry. This shift toward *sign-value* transforms social relations, identity, and power, creating a world where individuals are controlled not through direct force or economic coercion but through their participation in the system of consumption and the display of signs. Baudrillard's analysis challenges us to reconsider the ways in which modern capitalism operates, not only as an economic system but as a cultural and symbolic one, where the politics of the sign are central to understanding the dynamics of power, identity, and social control in the postmodern world.

The Real and the Imaginary in Popular Culture

Jean Baudrillard's exploration of the *real* and the *imaginary* offers a profound lens through which to understand the dynamics of *popular culture* in the postmodern world. According to Baudrillard, the boundaries between the real and the imaginary have become increasingly blurred in a world dominated by media, consumerism, and technology. Popular culture—comprising movies, television, music, fashion, and social media—plays a central role in creating and sustaining this blurring, as it constructs a reality that is shaped more by simulations, representations, and images than by direct experiences. Baudrillard's concepts of *simulation* and *hyper reality* provide a powerful framework for analyzing how popular culture both reflects and creates a world where the imaginary becomes more real than reality itself.

At the heart of Baudrillard's critique is the idea that popular culture, through media and entertainment, produces *simulacra*—copies or representations of reality that have no original. These simulacra replace the real with a hyperreal version of reality that is more attractive, compelling, and believable than the actual world. In this context, the *imaginary* becomes not just an escape from reality but a dominant force that shapes how people understand and engage with the world. Popular culture constructs and disseminates these simulacra through films, TV shows, music videos, and digital platforms, creating a version of reality that is increasingly disconnected from material reality but accepted as more real by the public.

One of the clearest examples of this phenomenon is the *Hollywood film industry*, which plays a central role in creating hyperreal narratives and representations of the world. Films, by their very nature, are fictional creations, yet they are designed to appear as realistic and believable as possible. Special effects, CGI, and advanced production techniques create immersive worlds that feel more real than reality itself. For instance, science fiction films like *Star Wars* or *The Avengers* construct elaborate, imaginary universes that captivate audiences, offering a more exciting and engaging experience than the ordinary, everyday world. Baudrillard would argue that these films are not simply entertainment; they are simulations that shape how people perceive reality. The line between the real and the imaginary blurs as audiences become immersed in these fictional worlds, accepting them as part of their lived experience.

Baudrillard's concept of *hyper reality* is particularly relevant when analyzing the *superhero genre*, which has come to dominate popular culture in the 21st century. Superhero films present exaggerated, idealized versions of reality, where moral absolutes are clear, heroes are physically and morally perfect, and conflicts are resolved through grandiose acts of violence or sacrifice. These films present a hyperreal version of reality where the stakes are higher, the visuals are more spectacular, and the characters are larger than life. Baudrillard would argue that this creates a form of escapism, where the imaginary becomes more compelling than the real. Audiences are drawn into these hyperreal worlds, where the problems and complexities of real life are simplified or ignored in favor of dramatic, black-and-white narratives.

The *reality TV* genre offers another striking example of how the imaginary can replace the real in popular culture. Reality TV purports to show "real" people in unscripted situations, yet these shows are often carefully edited, scripted, and manipulated to create compelling narratives and characters. Shows like *Keeping Up with the Kardashians*, *Big Brother*, or *Survivor* blur the line between reality and fiction, presenting highly stylized, dramatized versions of everyday life that are consumed as reality by audiences. Baudrillard would argue that reality TV represents a form of *simulation*, where real-life situations are transformed into entertainment products that bear little resemblance to actual reality. The participants become *simulacra* of themselves, performing exaggerated versions of their personalities for the camera, further contributing to the hyperreal environment in which the imaginary overtakes the real.

Baudrillard's critique extends to the world of *social media*, where the distinction between the real and the imaginary becomes even more blurred. Platforms like Instagram, TikTok, and YouTube encourage users to create and curate idealized versions of their lives, presenting highly edited, filtered, and staged representations of reality. These digital personas often bear little resemblance to the actual experiences of the users, yet they are consumed by audiences as authentic representations of real life. Baudrillard's concept of *the implosion of meaning* helps explain this phenomenon: in the digital age, the constant flow of images, videos, and posts creates a situation where meaning becomes fragmented and unstable. The line between what is real and what is performed, edited, or constructed collapses, leaving users trapped in a hyperreal world where the imaginary is indistinguishable from reality.

In the world of *fashion* and *advertising*, Baudrillard's insights are particularly poignant. Fashion, for Baudrillard, operates as a system of *signs* where clothing and accessories are not valued for their material utility but for the symbolic meanings they convey. In modern consumer society, clothing becomes a way of signaling identity, status, and taste, turning the act of dressing into a form of communication. The fashion industry thrives on the creation of imaginary ideals—beauty standards, body images, and lifestyles—that are presented as achievable through the consumption of specific products. Advertising reinforces this system of sign-value by creating narratives and images that attach symbolic meanings to commodities, transforming ordinary goods into symbols of success, happiness, or desirability. In this sense, the fashion industry creates a hyperreal world where the imaginary ideals presented in advertisements and fashion shows become more real and influential than the actual lives and bodies of consumers.

Baudrillard's analysis of the *music industry* also sheds light on the relationship between the real and the imaginary in popular culture. In contemporary music, especially pop and hip-hop, the personas of artists are often highly constructed, with performers adopting exaggerated, stylized versions of themselves that align with the themes of their music. Musicians like Beyoncé, Lady Gaga, and Kanye West, for example, cultivate highly curated public images that blur the line between their real identities and the personas they present to the world. Their music videos, performances, and social media presence contribute to a hyperreal version of their identity that is consumed by fans as both real and imaginary. Baudrillard would argue that these artists, like characters in a film, become *simulacra*—copies without originals—where the distinction between their real selves and their performative personas collapses.

Baudrillard's critique also addresses the *political implications* of the collapse between the real and the imaginary in popular culture. In a hyperreal world, where the imaginary becomes indistinguishable from reality, politics itself is transformed into a form of entertainment or spectacle. Political leaders, like celebrities, craft public personas that are mediated through images, sound bites, and performances. Baudrillard's concept of the *implosion of meaning* applies to the way political discourse is reduced to slogans, catchphrases, and emotional appeals, often detached from substantive issues or policies. The rise of *celebrity politicians* and the increasing *mediatization of politics* reflect Baudrillard's concern that in a hyperreal world, the imaginary dominates the political sphere, making it difficult to distinguish between genuine political engagement and mere performance.

Baudrillard's analysis of popular culture also extends to the *ethical implications* of living in a world where the real and the imaginary are so deeply intertwined. In the hyperreal world of popular culture, individuals are constantly exposed to representations of idealized beauty, success, and happiness that are often unattainable. This creates a sense of alienation, as people compare their own lives to the imaginary ideals presented in the media and find themselves lacking. Baudrillard's critique suggests that the constant consumption of hyperreal images and narratives leads to a disconnection from the real world, as individuals become trapped in a cycle of desire, consumption, and performance, always chasing after imaginary ideals that can never be fully realized.

In conclusion, Jean Baudrillard's analysis of the *real* and the *imaginary* in popular culture provides a powerful critique of how media, entertainment, and consumerism shape our understanding of reality. In the hyperreal world of films, TV shows, social media, fashion, and music, the line between the real and the imaginary collapses, creating a world where simulations and representations dominate. Baudrillard's concepts of *simulation, sign-value,* and *hyper reality* offer a framework for understanding how popular culture constructs a version of reality that is more compelling and influential than the actual, material world. His work challenges us to question how much of our experience of reality is shaped by the imaginary worlds of popular culture and to consider the ethical and political implications of living in a world where the real and the imaginary are increasingly indistinguishable.

Baudrillard on the Collapse of History

Jean Baudrillard's notion of the *collapse of history* is one of his most provocative and challenging ideas, offering a deep critique of how modern society understands and engages with time, memory, and the past. According to Baudrillard, in the postmodern era, history has lost its linear, coherent structure, and has been replaced by a fragmented, *simulated* version of itself. Rather than viewing history as a continuous narrative that shapes the present and future, Baudrillard argues that we now experience history as a series of *simulacra*—representations and images disconnected from any real events or causes. This collapse of history is tied to the rise of media, technology, and consumer culture, which have transformed the way we engage with the past and understand historical events. For Baudrillard, history has not only lost its meaning but has become a *spectacle*—a hyperreal construct that is consumed as entertainment or nostalgia rather than as a serious engagement with the real past.

Baudrillard's critique begins with the idea that in the postmodern world, *history* no longer functions as a linear, progressive narrative. In traditional societies, history was seen as a process of development and evolution, where events unfolded in a logical sequence and contributed to the progress of human civilization. This historical narrative provided a sense of continuity and purpose, linking the past, present, and future in a meaningful way. However, Baudrillard argues that in the postmodern era, this linear sense of history has collapsed. Historical events are no longer understood as part of a larger story or trajectory; instead, they are fragmented, decontextualized, and reduced to isolated images and signs that circulate in the media and popular culture.

One of the key factors contributing to the collapse of history is the role of *media and technology* in shaping how we engage with the past. In Baudrillard's view, the media does not simply report on historical events; it constructs and mediates them, transforming them into spectacles that can be consumed by global audiences. The constant flow of images, news, and narratives creates a situation where historical events are no longer experienced as real, lived moments but as mediated representations. For example, major historical events like the fall of the Berlin Wall, the 9/11 attacks, or the Gulf War are experienced by most people not through direct involvement but through the images and reports broadcast on television and the internet. These media representations create a *hyperreal* version of history, where the reality of the events is obscured by the spectacle of their representation.

Baudrillard's concept of *simulation* plays a central role in his critique of the collapse of history. In his view, modern media and technology create *simulacra* of historical events—copies or representations that have no connection to any original, real event. These simulations replace the real, creating a hyperreal version of history that is consumed as if it were reality. For instance, historical films, documentaries, and television series often present highly stylized, dramatized versions of past events that are designed to entertain and engage audiences rather than provide an accurate portrayal of the past. These simulations create a version of history that is more compelling and believable than the actual events, leading people to accept the simulated version as the real one.

One striking example of this phenomenon is the way historical events are presented in *Hollywood films*. Movies like *Braveheart*, *Gladiator*, and *Saving Private Ryan* offer dramatized, fictionalized versions of historical events that, while based on real moments in history, are primarily designed to evoke emotional responses and create compelling narratives. Baudrillard would argue that these films create *simulacra* of history, where the representation of the past is more real to the audience than the actual events. This process contributes to the collapse of history, as the line between historical reality and fictional representation becomes blurred. In the hyperreal world of postmodern society, the past is no longer something that can be directly accessed or understood; it is mediated, represented, and consumed through simulations.

Baudrillard's concept of the *implosion of meaning* also applies to his analysis of the collapse of history. As historical events are transformed into simulations and representations, their meaning becomes fragmented and unstable. In a world saturated with media images and narratives, the sheer volume of information and representations makes it difficult to discern what is real or significant. Historical events lose their depth and context, becoming just another set of images or symbols circulating in the media. This *implosion of meaning* leads to a situation where history no longer functions as a coherent narrative that shapes our understanding of the present and future. Instead, it becomes a series of disjointed moments, consumed for their entertainment or nostalgic value rather than for their historical significance.

Baudrillard's critique of *nostalgia* is central to his understanding of the collapse of history. In the postmodern era, Baudrillard argues, history is often consumed as *nostalgia*—a longing for an idealized, simplified version of the past that never really existed. This nostalgic version of history is not based on a serious engagement with the complexities and contradictions of the past but on a desire to return to a more stable, comforting world. In this sense, nostalgia functions as a form of escapism, where people retreat into an imagined past to avoid confronting the uncertainties and anxieties of the present. Baudrillard would argue that popular culture, particularly through films, television shows, and advertising, plays a key role in producing and disseminating these nostalgic images of the past. Whether it's the romanticized portrayal of the 1950s in films like *Back to the Future* or the revival of vintage fashion and music, nostalgia creates a hyperreal version of history that offers comfort and familiarity but obscures the real complexities of the past.

Baudrillard also critiques the way *historical memory* is shaped by the process of simulation. In his view, the postmodern world is characterized by a loss of authentic historical memory, as the past is increasingly mediated through images, representations, and simulations. This process leads to the creation of what Baudrillard calls *historical amnesia*, where the real, lived experiences of history are forgotten or replaced by hyperreal representations. For example, many people's understanding of historical events like World War II, the Civil Rights Movement, or the Vietnam War is shaped not by direct experience or study but by the films, documentaries, and television shows that depict these events. As a result, the real history is forgotten or overshadowed by the simulated versions that circulate in the media. Baudrillard argues that this loss of historical memory contributes to the collapse of history, as the past is no longer something that can be accessed or understood in any meaningful way.

The collapse of history, for Baudrillard, also has *political implications*. In a world where history is reduced to simulations and representations, it becomes difficult to engage in meaningful political action or change. Baudrillard argues that the collapse of history creates a sense of *detachment* and *disillusionment*, as people are no longer able to connect their present struggles with the larger historical narratives that once gave meaning and purpose to political movements. In this sense, the collapse of history contributes to the rise of a *post-political* world, where politics is reduced to spectacle and performance, and genuine political engagement is replaced by simulations of activism and resistance. Baudrillard's critique challenges us to consider how the collapse of history undermines our ability to engage with the present and imagine alternative futures.

Baudrillard's analysis of *hyper reality* and the collapse of history also extends to his critique of the *future*. In the traditional view of history, the past, present, and future were understood as distinct temporal categories, with history providing a narrative of progress and development that shaped the future. However, Baudrillard argues that in the postmodern world, the distinction between past, present, and future has collapsed. The future is no longer seen as an open, unknown space of possibility; instead, it is increasingly experienced as a continuation of the present, shaped by the simulations and hyperreal narratives that dominate our understanding of time. This collapse of the future leads to a sense of *stasis* or *repetition*, where the same images, narratives, and simulations are endlessly recycled without any possibility of real change or progress.

In conclusion, Jean Baudrillard's analysis of the *collapse of history* offers a profound critique of how modern society understands and engages with the past. In the postmodern world, history is no longer experienced as a coherent, linear narrative but as a series of *simulacra*—representations and images that replace the real events of the past. This process of simulation, driven by media, technology, and popular culture, creates a hyperreal version of history that is consumed as entertainment or nostalgia rather than as a serious engagement with the complexities of the past. Baudrillard's critique challenges us to consider the political and ethical implications of living in a world where history has collapsed, and the past is no longer something we can access or understand in any meaningful way. In a hyperreal world, where the boundaries between the real and the imaginary have blurred, history becomes just another spectacle, consumed and forgotten in the endless flow of images and signs that define postmodern life.

Images, Power, and the Loss of Truth

Jean Baudrillard's critique of modern society revolves around the profound impact that *images* and *representations* have on *power* and the concept of *truth*. In his analysis, Baudrillard argues that in the postmodern world, images have gained unprecedented power, not simply as representations of reality but as producers of a new kind of *hyper reality*. In this state of hyper reality, images no longer reflect or distort the truth but replace it, creating a reality that is constructed through simulations. As a result, the relationship between truth, reality, and representation collapses, leading to what Baudrillard describes as the *loss of truth*. This loss of truth is not just a philosophical or abstract problem; it has serious implications for how power operates in modern society, as those who control images and representations hold immense influence over how reality is perceived and understood.

At the core of Baudrillard's analysis is his concept of *simulation*—the idea that in the postmodern world, reality is increasingly replaced by simulations that bear no relation to any original truth or real-world referent. These simulations create a *hyperreal* environment in which images, signs, and representations take precedence over material reality. In this context, truth becomes unstable and elusive, as the line between the real and the simulated is blurred or erased. Baudrillard argues that in a world dominated by images and simulations, people no longer engage with reality directly but through *mediated representations*, which construct a version of reality that is often more compelling and convincing than the real world itself.

One of the key ways in which images gain power in the postmodern world is through the media. Baudrillard's critique of the *media* highlights how news, television, films, and social media platforms create a constant flow of images and narratives that shape how people understand the world. The media does not simply report on reality; it constructs and mediates it, often creating a version of reality that is shaped by the demands of entertainment, ideology, or commercial interests. News stories are often selected, framed, and presented in ways that generate emotional reactions or reinforce specific narratives, creating a hyperreal version of events that may bear little resemblance to the underlying reality.

Baudrillard's analysis of *power* in the age of hyper reality suggests that those who control images and representations hold immense power over how reality is perceived. In traditional societies, power was exercised through direct control over land, resources, and people. In the modern world, power operates more subtly through the control of *signs*, *symbols*, and *representations*. Those who control the media, advertising, and popular culture hold the ability to shape public perceptions, define what is true or real, and influence the way people think and behave. This form of power is more insidious than traditional forms of domination because it operates invisibly, shaping people's understanding of reality without the need for direct force or coercion.

One of Baudrillard's most striking examples of how images replace truth is his analysis of the *Gulf War* in the essay *The Gulf War Did Not Take Place*. In this work, Baudrillard argues that the Gulf War, as it was presented to the global public, was not a real war but a *media spectacle*.

The images of precision bombing, clean surgical strikes, and military technology that dominated the media's coverage of the conflict created a hyperreal version of the war that obscured the real violence, destruction, and human suffering. According to Baudrillard, the media's portrayal of the war was more real to the global audience than the actual events on the ground, leading to the collapse of truth and reality. The war, in this sense, became a simulation—a representation that replaced the actual experience of war with a hyperreal version designed for consumption by television viewers.

Baudrillard's critique of the *loss of truth* extends beyond the media to the world of *advertising* and *consumer culture*. In a consumer-driven society, products are not sold based on their material utility or value but through the images and narratives attached to them. Advertising creates symbolic meanings and associations that turn ordinary commodities into signs of success, happiness, beauty, or status. In this context, the truth of a product's material qualities becomes irrelevant; what matters is the symbolic value it conveys. A luxury car, a designer handbag, or a smartphone are not simply objects—they are symbols that communicate social status, identity, and desire. Baudrillard argues that this system of *sign-value* leads to the loss of any objective truth about products or consumption, as people's desires and identities are shaped by the images they consume rather than by any material reality.

The rise of *social media* further amplifies Baudrillard's concerns about the loss of truth in a world dominated by images. Platforms like Instagram, Facebook, and TikTok encourage users to create and curate idealized versions of their lives, presenting highly edited, filtered, and stylized images of themselves and their experiences. These digital personas often bear little resemblance to the actual lives of the users, yet they are consumed by audiences as authentic representations of reality. Baudrillard would argue that social media creates a hyperreal environment where the line between truth and performance collapses, as users craft images of themselves that are more compelling and desirable than their real lives. This process of self-simulation leads to the loss of truth in identity, as individuals become trapped in a cycle of performing and consuming simulated versions of themselves.

Baudrillard's concept of the *implosion of meaning* is central to his critique of how images and simulations undermine truth. In a world where images and representations proliferate endlessly, the sheer volume of signs and symbols creates a situation where meaning becomes fragmented, unstable, and incoherent. The constant flow of images, news, and narratives overwhelms people's ability to make sense of reality, leading to a state where truth itself becomes elusive. In this hyperreal environment, the distinction between true and false, real and fake, becomes impossible to maintain, as all representations are consumed in the same way, regardless of their connection to reality. This implosion of meaning leads to a form of *historical amnesia*, where people lose their connection to the real past and live in a perpetual present of simulations and representations.

The *political implications* of Baudrillard's critique of images and the loss of truth are profound. In a hyperreal world, where images and representations dominate, political power is increasingly exercised through the control of *narratives* and *perceptions* rather than through direct force or coercion. Political leaders, like media corporations, use images, sound bites, and media spectacles to construct a version of reality that serves their interests.

Baudrillard's analysis of the mediatisation of politics highlights how political discourse is reduced to *spectacle*, where images and performances take precedence over substantive debate or policy. In this environment, the truth of political events or issues becomes secondary to the power of the images used to represent them. Elections, campaigns, and political movements are often framed as media events, where the success or failure of a candidate or cause depends not on their ideas or policies but on their ability to create compelling images and narratives.

Baudrillard's critique of the loss of truth also extends to the concept of *fake news* and *disinformation*, phenomena that have become increasingly prevalent in the digital age. In Baudrillard's view, the rise of fake news reflects the collapse of truth in a world dominated by simulations. In the hyperreal environment of the internet and social media, fake news stories are consumed and shared in the same way as real news, creating a situation where the distinction between truth and falsehood is blurred. This process of simulation creates a *crisis of truth*, where people are unable to trust the information they receive or discern what is real from what is fabricated. Baudrillard's critique challenges us to consider the ethical and political consequences of living in a world where truth is no longer a stable or reliable concept, and where reality is constantly mediated and constructed by images and simulations.

In conclusion, Jean Baudrillard's analysis of *images*, *power*, and the *loss of truth* offers a powerful critique of how modern society is shaped by the dominance of images, simulations, and representations. In the postmodern world, images no longer reflect reality; they create it, constructing a *hyperreal* environment where truth is elusive and unstable. This loss of truth has profound implications for how power is exercised, as those who control images and representations hold immense influence over how reality is perceived and understood. Baudrillard's work challenges us to consider the consequences of living in a world where the line between reality and simulation has collapsed, and where truth itself is lost in the endless flow of images and signs that define modern life.

The Reversal of Meaning: From Reality to Simulation

Jean Baudrillard's theory of *the reversal of meaning* is a fundamental aspect of his critique of the postmodern world, focusing on how reality has been replaced by *simulation* in modern society. Baudrillard argues that the process of meaning has undergone a profound shift, where once meaning was tied to tangible reality and direct experience, it is now constructed and mediated through images, symbols, and simulations. This shift from reality to simulation represents a reversal in the way meaning is generated and understood. Rather than deriving meaning from lived experiences and the material world, individuals in the postmodern age derive meaning from representations and simulations that no longer reference any original reality. This process has led to the creation of *hyper reality*, where simulations become more real than reality itself, and meaning is detached from any grounding in the real world.

Baudrillard's concept of *simulation* is central to understanding the reversal of meaning. In traditional societies, meaning was derived from a direct relationship between *signifiers* (words, images, symbols) and *signified* objects or experiences in the real world. A sign referred to something concrete or tangible, and meaning was rooted in the relationship between the sign and its referent. However, Baudrillard argues that in the postmodern era, this relationship has collapsed. Signs no longer refer to anything real; instead, they refer to other signs or images in an endless chain of representations that never lead back to any original, material reality. This creates a world of *simulacra*—copies without originals—where meaning is constantly generated and exchanged but no longer tied to any objective truth or reality.

One of the most profound consequences of this reversal of meaning is the rise of *hyper reality*. Hyper reality refers to a state in which simulations and representations are perceived as more real, more desirable, and more meaningful than the actual reality they were meant to represent. In the hyperreal world, simulations not only distort reality but replace it entirely, creating a version of reality that feels more authentic than the real world itself. For example, theme parks like *Disneyland* offer highly controlled, idealized versions of reality that are more attractive and compelling than the ordinary, messy, and unpredictable world outside. In this context, meaning is generated not from actual experiences but from the simulated worlds that people inhabit and consume. Baudrillard would argue that in the case of Disneyland, the simulated reality becomes so pervasive and convincing that it replaces any notion of a real, external world.

The *media* and *advertising* industries play a crucial role in the reversal of meaning by constantly producing and circulating images, signs, and narratives that construct hyperreal versions of reality. Baudrillard's critique of the media highlights how news, entertainment, and advertising are not merely passive reflections of the world but active producers of meaning. Through carefully crafted images, stories, and symbols, the media constructs a version of reality that is often disconnected from actual events or material truths. The result is a world where meaning is no longer derived from lived experiences but from the mediated representations that circulate through television, social media, and digital platforms.

Advertising is particularly emblematic of the reversal of meaning in postmodern society. In Baudrillard's view, advertising does not simply inform consumers about products; it creates a symbolic universe where products are imbued with meanings that go far beyond their material use or function. A luxury car, for example, is not just a vehicle; it becomes a sign of wealth, status, and identity. Through the power of advertising, products are transformed into *signs* that carry symbolic meanings, creating a hyperreal world where commodities are valued not for their practical utility but for the meanings they convey. In this sense, the material reality of the product becomes secondary to the symbolic meaning attached to it, illustrating how meaning is reversed and detached from reality.

Baudrillard's analysis of the reversal of meaning also applies to the realm of *politics*, where political discourse is increasingly shaped by images, symbols, and media performances rather than substantive debate or policy. In the postmodern political landscape, meaning is constructed through the careful management of appearances, sound bites, and spectacles designed to appeal to emotions and perceptions rather than reason or truth. Baudrillard would argue that political campaigns and media events have become hyperreal simulations, where the performance of politics becomes more important than the actual policies or decisions being made. The result is a *spectacle of politics*, where politicians are valued for their image, charisma, and ability to generate media attention rather than for their leadership or vision. This process leads to the reversal of meaning, where the *appearance* of political action is more significant than the reality of governance.

Baudrillard's critique of the reversal of meaning extends to the concept of *identity* in the postmodern world. In traditional societies, identity was tied to concrete roles, relationships, and experiences. A person's identity was shaped by their work, family, community, and social position. However, in the hyperreal world, identity is increasingly constructed through *performance*, *consumption*, and *representation*. Social media platforms like Instagram, Facebook, and TikTok encourage users to create idealized versions of themselves, presenting highly edited, filtered, and stylized images of their lives for public consumption. These digital personas often bear little resemblance to the actual experiences or identities of the users, yet they are consumed by audiences as authentic representations of the self. Baudrillard would argue that this process represents a reversal of meaning, where identity is no longer rooted in reality but in the simulations and performances created for others.

Baudrillard's theory also addresses the implications of the reversal of meaning for *truth* and *knowledge*. In a hyperreal world, where meaning is detached from reality and constructed through simulations, the concept of objective truth becomes increasingly unstable. Baudrillard argues that in the postmodern era, the distinction between truth and falsehood, reality and fiction, has collapsed. The constant flow of information, images, and narratives creates a situation where meaning is fragmented, unstable, and endlessly shifting. The rise of *fake news* and *disinformation* in the digital age reflects this collapse of truth, as people are increasingly exposed to competing versions of reality that are constructed and disseminated through social media, news outlets, and digital platforms. Baudrillard's critique challenges us to consider how the reversal of meaning undermines our ability to engage with truth in a meaningful way, as reality itself becomes indistinguishable from the simulations that surround us.

In *popular culture*, the reversal of meaning is particularly evident in the world of *entertainment*, where films, television shows, and video games construct hyperreal versions of reality that often feel more compelling and engaging than actual life. Baudrillard would argue that popular culture creates simulations of reality that are consumed as more real and meaningful than the world outside. For instance, reality television shows, which claim to depict real-life situations and individuals, are often heavily scripted, edited, and produced to create dramatic narratives that bear little resemblance to actual reality. Yet these shows are consumed as authentic representations of real life, illustrating the collapse of meaning and the replacement of reality with simulation.

Baudrillard's analysis also extends to the realm of *virtual reality (VR)* and *augmented reality (AR)* technologies, which create immersive, simulated environments that feel more real and engaging than the physical world. In the hyperreal worlds created by VR and AR, individuals can experience fully constructed realities that are designed to be more exciting, more beautiful, or more perfect than the actual world. Baudrillard's critique suggests that as these technologies become more advanced and widespread, the reversal of meaning will intensify, as people increasingly derive meaning and fulfillment from simulations rather than from real-world experiences.

Baudrillard's concept of *symbolic exchange* offers a possible counterpoint to the process of meaning reversal. In contrast to the world of signs and simulations, symbolic exchange refers to forms of social interaction that are not mediated by economic value, consumerism, or representation. Symbolic exchange involves direct, reciprocal interactions between individuals that are rooted in shared experiences, rituals, and relationships. Baudrillard sees symbolic exchange as a way to reclaim meaning from the hyperreal world of simulations and return to a more authentic form of social engagement. However, he remains skeptical about the possibility of recovering this kind of meaning in a world so thoroughly dominated by signs, symbols, and simulations.

In conclusion, Jean Baudrillard's theory of *the reversal of meaning* from reality to simulation offers a powerful critique of how modern society constructs meaning in the postmodern age. Through the process of simulation, meaning is no longer derived from lived experiences or material reality but from images, signs, and representations that circulate in a hyperreal world. This reversal of meaning has profound implications for how we understand identity, politics, truth, and culture, as the line between reality and simulation collapses and meaning becomes increasingly unstable. Baudrillard's critique challenges us to reconsider how we engage with reality in a world dominated by simulations and to question whether it is possible to recover any sense of authentic meaning in the age of hyper reality.

Baudrillard's Philosophy on the Media and Spectacle

Jean Baudrillard's philosophy on the *media* and *spectacle* plays a central role in his broader critique of postmodern society. Baudrillard viewed the media as a primary force in creating what he famously termed *hyper reality*—a state in which the distinction between reality and simulation has collapsed, and representations become more real and influential than reality itself. His concept of *spectacle*, influenced by Guy Debord's theory in *The Society of the Spectacle*, expands upon this idea by analyzing how media transforms not only entertainment but also politics, culture, and everyday life into a continuous, immersive spectacle. For Baudrillard, the media doesn't simply transmit information or reflect reality; rather, it constructs a version of reality that becomes more dominant and impactful than the reality it is supposed to represent. This manufactured reality obscures truth, creates passive spectators, and transforms social and political events into consumable, commodified spectacles.

The Media as a Producer of Hyper reality

At the heart of Baudrillard's critique of the media is his concept of *hyper reality*. In the postmodern world, Baudrillard argues, the media does not reflect reality but *produces* it through a process of *simulation* and *representation*. Media creates images, signs, and narratives that are detached from any original reality, transforming events into hyperreal versions of themselves. These simulations then become accepted as reality by the public, to the point that people's understanding of the world is shaped more by media representations than by their direct experiences.

Baudrillard's analysis of television, news, and film exemplifies this. Television, in particular, plays a critical role in constructing hyper reality. News programs, reality shows, and political broadcasts present a *mediated reality* that is filtered, edited, and framed to create specific emotional responses, narratives, or ideologies. For example, news coverage often emphasizes dramatic or sensational aspects of an event, amplifying its impact while obscuring the complexity or nuance of the situation. This manufactured reality is then consumed by viewers as if it were the whole truth, even though it is a simulation crafted to fit within the media's commercial or ideological interests.

Baudrillard's critique goes beyond the traditional notion of media bias; he suggests that the very act of media representation transforms events into *spectacles*—performances designed to entertain, shock, or engage viewers rather than provide accurate depictions of reality. In this process, the media becomes a powerful force in shaping public consciousness, as people internalize the hyperreal images and narratives that are constantly produced and consumed.

The Spectacle: Politics and Society as Performance

Baudrillard's concept of the *spectacle* draws heavily on the ideas of Guy Debord, who argued that modern capitalist societies increasingly turn all aspects of life into a spectacle. For Baudrillard, the media plays a central role in this process by turning *everything*—from entertainment and consumerism to politics and war—into a continuous, self-sustaining spectacle. Social and political events, in Baudrillard's analysis, are not only reported on by the media but are *constructed* by the media in such a way that they become part of a larger performance, designed to generate viewership, ratings, and consumption.

One of Baudrillard's most famous analyses of media spectacle is his commentary on the *Gulf War* in his essay *The Gulf War Did Not Take Place*. Here, Baudrillard does not claim that the war was fictional; rather, he argues that the media transformed the war into a *spectacle*, where the images of precision bombing, military technology, and strategic strikes overshadowed the brutal reality of the conflict. The war was represented as a clean, controlled, and almost bloodless event—far removed from the chaos and human suffering that occurred on the ground. Baudrillard's provocative assertion that the war "did not take place" refers to the fact that the public only experienced the hyperreal version of the war, the media spectacle, not the actual war itself. The spectacle, for Baudrillard, becomes more real and influential than the real event.

In a similar vein, Baudrillard critiques the way *politics* has been transformed into a spectacle in the media-dominated world. Political campaigns, debates, and even governance itself are often reduced to performances, where appearances, image management, and sound bites become more important than substantive policies or actions. Politicians are often judged not on their ideas or leadership but on how effectively they perform on television, in debates, or on social media. The political spectacle, according to Baudrillard, is about *managing perceptions* rather than engaging with reality, reducing political engagement to a form of passive consumption.

Baudrillard also applies his theory of the spectacle to *celebrity culture*, where individuals become objects of fascination not for their achievements or personal qualities but for their ability to generate media attention and symbolic meaning. Celebrities function as *simulacra*—images that represent nothing beyond themselves, yet carry immense symbolic value in a hyperreal world. Their lives, mediated and performed through the lens of the media, become part of the larger spectacle of entertainment and consumption, reinforcing the idea that image, representation, and performance have become more important than reality.

The Media's Role in the Loss of Meaning

For Baudrillard, the media not only constructs hyper reality and spectacle but also contributes to the *implosion of meaning* in contemporary society. In a world where images, signs, and symbols proliferate endlessly through television, social media, and advertising, the sheer volume of representations overwhelms people's ability to make sense of reality. This *over-saturation* of meaning creates a situation where meaning itself becomes fragmented and unstable. Events, images, and narratives are consumed at such a rapid pace that they lose their depth, context, and significance, becoming interchangeable parts of the larger media spectacle.

Baudrillard argues that the media creates a kind of *simulation overload*, where the constant flow of information and representations leads to the collapse of any stable understanding of truth or reality. In this hyperreal world, distinctions between truth and falsehood, reality and fiction, become increasingly blurred. The media spectacle reduces complex social and political issues to *simplified narratives* or *emotional sound bites*, stripping them of their real-world significance and turning them into easily consumable images. This process leads to the *loss of meaning* in modern society, as people become passive spectators in a world of endless simulations.

The Spectacle and Consumerism

Baudrillard also links the media spectacle to the logic of *consumerism*, arguing that the media serves as a vehicle for promoting and sustaining consumer culture. In Baudrillard's view, the media creates *desire* by constructing idealized images of lifestyles, products, and experiences that people are encouraged to aspire to and consume. Advertisements, television shows, and films all work to reinforce the spectacle of consumerism, where identity and meaning are constructed through the act of consumption. In this way, the media spectacle becomes a powerful tool for reinforcing the *ideology of consumption*, as people are encouraged to define themselves through the products they buy and the images they consume.

Baudrillard's analysis of *advertising* is particularly revealing. He argues that advertising does not simply promote products; it creates symbolic meanings that transform products into signs of status, success, and identity. In this sense, advertising is part of the larger media spectacle that shapes how people understand themselves and their place in the world. Products are no longer valued for their material utility but for the symbolic meanings they carry within the hyperreal world of consumer culture.

The Passive Spectator

One of Baudrillard's key concerns about the media spectacle is its impact on *agency* and *engagement*. In a world dominated by media spectacle, Baudrillard argues, people become passive spectators rather than active participants in their own lives. The constant consumption of images and representations creates a sense of *detachment* from reality, as people are more likely to engage with the spectacle on their screens than with the real world around them. This passivity reinforces the power of the spectacle, as individuals are conditioned to accept the hyperreal version of reality presented by the media rather than questioning or challenging it.

Baudrillard's critique of *reality TV* illustrates this dynamic. In reality shows, ordinary people are transformed into characters in a media spectacle, their lives edited, scripted, and performed for the entertainment of viewers. The audience, in turn, consumes these hyperreal representations as authentic depictions of reality, further reinforcing the idea that spectacle is more real than reality itself. This process encourages passivity, as viewers become absorbed in the spectacle of other people's lives rather than engaging with their own.

Jean Baudrillard's philosophy on the media and spectacle offers a powerful critique of how modern society is shaped by the dominance of images, simulations, and representations. The media, in Baudrillard's view, does not simply report on reality; it constructs it, creating a hyperreal world where the spectacle of events, politics, and consumption becomes more real and significant than the actual events themselves. This process leads to the loss of meaning, the blurring of reality and fiction, and the rise of passive spectatorship, as individuals are conditioned to engage with the media spectacle rather than with the real world. Baudrillard's work challenges us to critically examine the role of the media in shaping our perceptions of reality and to consider the consequences of living in a world where spectacle dominates every aspect of life.

The Influence of Baudrillard on New Age Thinkers

Jean Baudrillard's philosophy has had a significant impact on *New Age thinkers*, particularly those concerned with the evolving relationship between reality, technology, media, and consciousness in the postmodern world. His concepts of *simulation*, *hyper reality*, and the *collapse of meaning* have resonated with New Age thinkers, who often explore the boundaries between material reality and spiritual or metaphysical dimensions of existence. Baudrillard's ideas have provided a critical framework for understanding how contemporary society, through media, technology, and consumerism, constructs reality in ways that can obscure deeper spiritual or existential truths. For many New Age thinkers, Baudrillard's work helps illuminate the tensions between the material world and the quest for higher consciousness, authenticity, and self-awareness in an age of media saturation and technological mediation.

Hyper reality and the Illusion of the Material World

One of the key aspects of Baudrillard's philosophy that resonates with New Age thinkers is his concept of *hyper reality*, the state in which simulations and representations become more real and impactful than reality itself. In the hyperreal world, the line between reality and illusion is blurred, and people engage more with mediated representations of reality—through media, advertising, and technology—than with direct experiences of the real world.

For New Age thinkers who explore the nature of reality and consciousness, Baudrillard's notion of hyper reality offers a powerful critique of how modern society creates a *false sense of reality*. In many New Age philosophies, the material world is often viewed as an illusion or a lower form of consciousness that distracts individuals from deeper spiritual truths. Baudrillard's idea that hyperreal simulations replace reality echoes this sentiment, as it suggests that people are trapped in a world of images and signs that obscure their true connection to the deeper, more authentic aspects of existence.

Baudrillard's critique of consumer culture, where people define themselves through the consumption of images, commodities, and signs rather than through authentic, lived experiences, aligns with New Age thinkers who advocate for *spiritual awakening* and *self-realization*. For these thinkers, the hyperreal world created by media and consumerism represents a distraction from the pursuit of higher consciousness. Baudrillard's philosophy provides a framework for understanding how people are drawn into a false reality, constructed by technology and consumerism, which keeps them from engaging with more profound aspects of human existence, such as spiritual growth and enlightenment.

Simulation and the Nature of Consciousness

Baudrillard's concept of *simulation*—the idea that representations no longer refer to an original reality but instead create a world of signs and symbols that generate their own reality—has been influential in New Age thinking, particularly in discussions about the nature of consciousness and reality. For many New Age thinkers, the world we perceive through our senses is not the ultimate reality but a construction of the mind.

Baudrillard's notion of simulation aligns with this perspective, as it suggests that what we take to be real is often a product of constructed, mediated images and ideas rather than direct, unmediated experience.

This concept is particularly relevant to New Age ideas about the *illusory nature of reality* and the belief that consciousness itself shapes the world we perceive. For many New Age thinkers, the material world is seen as a kind of *simulation* created by collective consciousness or the limitations of human perception. The goal of spiritual practice, in this view, is to transcend these simulations and reach a higher state of awareness that allows individuals to see beyond the illusions of the material world. Baudrillard's philosophy provides a critical lens for understanding how modern society's simulations, mediated through technology and media, further entrench individuals in a false sense of reality that prevents them from accessing higher levels of consciousness.

The Collapse of Meaning and the Search for Authenticity

Baudrillard's critique of the *implosion of meaning* in contemporary society—the idea that the endless circulation of images, signs, and information creates a state where meaning becomes fragmented, unstable, and incoherent—also resonates with New Age thinkers. Many New Age philosophies emphasize the importance of finding *authentic meaning* in life, whether through personal spiritual journeys, mindfulness practices, or alternative ways of understanding reality. Baudrillard's notion of the collapse of meaning speaks to the sense of *alienation* and *disconnection* that many people feel in a world dominated by media and technology.

In New Age thought, this collapse of meaning is often seen as a symptom of the larger spiritual crisis facing modern society. The media-saturated world, with its focus on superficial images and material consumption, is viewed as a barrier to true self-awareness and spiritual fulfillment. Baudrillard's analysis of how meaning becomes destabilized in a hyperreal world aligns with New Age critiques of modern society's fixation on the material and the superficial. For New Age thinkers, the challenge is to *transcend* the meaningless simulations of the material world and reconnect with deeper, more authentic sources of meaning, often found through spiritual exploration, meditation, or practices that emphasize inner awareness and self-discovery.

Media, Consciousness, and Spirituality

Baudrillard's exploration of how media shapes reality also intersects with New Age concerns about the *impact of technology* on consciousness and spirituality. Many New Age thinkers argue that media and technology, particularly social media and digital communication, have a profound effect on how people perceive themselves and the world around them. Baudrillard's idea that media creates a hyperreal world where simulations replace reality mirrors New Age concerns about the *fragmentation of consciousness* in the digital age.

For some New Age thinkers, media and technology are seen as tools that can either *hinder* or *aid* in the quest for higher consciousness. On the one hand, media is often viewed as a distraction that pulls people away from direct, lived experience and immerses them in a world of artificial representations. On the other hand, some New Age thinkers see the potential for media and technology to facilitate spiritual growth by spreading alternative ideas, connecting like-minded individuals, and providing access to new forms of knowledge. Baudrillard's critique of media as a creator of hyper reality provides a framework for understanding the *double-edged nature* of technology in the New Age movement—both as a source of distraction and as a tool for spiritual awakening.

Postmodern Spirituality and the Blurring of Boundaries

Baudrillard's influence on New Age thinkers is also evident in the way his ideas about *postmodernism* intersect with *New Age spirituality*. In the postmodern world, traditional boundaries—between reality and fiction, truth and illusion, the material and the spiritual—are increasingly blurred. Baudrillard's analysis of how these boundaries collapse in a hyperreal world resonates with New Age thinkers who embrace the idea that reality is fluid, interconnected, and multi-dimensional. New Age spirituality often rejects rigid, dualistic thinking in favor of a more holistic understanding of reality, where material and spiritual realms are interconnected and mutually influencing.

Baudrillard's critique of postmodernism, with its focus on the dissolution of fixed meanings and stable identities, complements New Age explorations of *non-linear* thinking, *alternative realities*, and *multiple dimensions of consciousness*. For New Age thinkers, the collapse of boundaries between reality and illusion is not necessarily a negative development; it opens up new possibilities for exploring alternative ways of being and understanding the world. Baudrillard's philosophy provides a critical framework for thinking about how the dissolution of traditional structures in the postmodern era creates both challenges and opportunities for spiritual growth and self-awareness.

The Role of Simulation in New Age Thought

Baudrillard's concept of *simulation* has also found resonance in New Age theories about the *nature of reality* and *spiritual dimensions*. In some New Age philosophies, the idea of simulation is explored through metaphysical concepts such as the *holographic universe*, which posits that reality itself is a kind of simulation or projection of consciousness. Baudrillard's critique of simulation as a force that creates hyper reality is echoed in New Age discussions about the illusory nature of the material world and the possibility that reality is a construct of the mind or a reflection of higher dimensions.

Some New Age thinkers use Baudrillard's ideas to explore the possibility that human existence is part of a larger *simulation* or cosmic design, where the material world is just one layer of reality that can be transcended through spiritual practices. This view aligns with Baudrillard's notion that the reality we experience may be a *copy without an original*, a simulation that obscures the deeper, more profound realities that lie beyond material perception.

Conclusion: Baudrillard's Legacy in New Age Thought

Jean Baudrillard's philosophy has had a profound influence on New Age thinkers, particularly in their exploration of reality, consciousness, and the search for meaning in the postmodern world. Baudrillard's ideas about hyper reality, simulation, and the collapse of meaning provide a critical framework for understanding how modern society creates artificial realities that obscure deeper spiritual truths. For New Age thinkers, Baudrillard's critique of media, consumerism, and technology resonates with their concerns about the ways in which contemporary society distracts individuals from the pursuit of higher consciousness and spiritual fulfillment.

By highlighting the ways in which simulations replace reality, Baudrillard's philosophy encourages New Age thinkers to question the authenticity of the material world and to seek out alternative, more profound sources of meaning and self-awareness. His work challenges individuals to move beyond the hyperreal constructions of modern society and to engage with the deeper, more authentic dimensions of existence that lie beyond the illusions of the material world.

Baudrillard on Terrorism: The Illusion of Destruction

Jean Baudrillard's analysis of *terrorism*, particularly after the 9/11 attacks, offers one of the most striking and controversial aspects of his philosophical work. Baudrillard argues that terrorism, in the postmodern context, functions not merely as an act of violence or political rebellion but as a form of *spectacle* and *symbolic challenge* to the hyperreal world created by modern media, technology, and globalization. His interpretation of terrorism reflects his broader critique of *hyper reality* and *simulation*—the idea that the modern world operates more on the level of images, signs, and representations than on direct experiences of reality. For Baudrillard, terrorism is both a response to and a product of the hyperreal world. It is not just about causing destruction but about creating an *illusion of destruction*, a challenge to the symbolic order of Western power, media, and global capitalism.

Terrorism as a Symbolic Act

Baudrillard's view of terrorism begins with the idea that it is not simply a political or military strategy but a *symbolic* act, designed to disrupt and challenge the established order. In his analysis, terrorist acts—particularly large-scale events like the 9/11 attacks—are aimed at creating a powerful symbolic rupture, exposing the vulnerabilities of the global system and shaking the confidence of the Western world. Baudrillard argues that terrorism represents a form of *counter-spectacle* to the hyperreal, media-saturated world of the West, where images and signs dominate reality. In this context, the act of terrorism functions as a kind of *theatrical performance*, designed to be consumed by global audiences through the media.

Baudrillard famously described the 9/11 attacks as a *symbolic event* rather than a purely material or political one. For him, the destruction of the Twin Towers was not just about the physical damage or loss of life but about the symbolic meaning of the act. The Twin Towers, as symbols of global capitalism, modernity, and Western power, represented the pinnacle of the hyperreal world that Baudrillard critiques throughout his work. The attack on these symbols, then, was a direct challenge to the *hyperreal system* that the towers embodied—a system of economic, political, and technological power that had become increasingly detached from any material reality.

In this sense, Baudrillard argues that terrorism operates on the same level as the media spectacle, using the logic of *images and representation* to create its impact. The goal of terrorism, in Baudrillard's view, is not just to inflict physical destruction but to generate powerful *symbolic images* that disrupt the hyperreal world. The 9/11 attacks, for instance, were immediately consumed and reproduced as images on television and the internet, becoming part of the global media spectacle. These images of destruction, endlessly replayed and disseminated, created a sense of *hyperreal terror*, where the event itself was experienced more as a media representation than as a material reality.

The Illusion of Destruction

One of Baudrillard's most provocative claims is his suggestion that terrorism, particularly in the context of 9/11, creates an *illusion of destruction*. In his analysis, the true impact of terrorism lies not in the material damage caused but in the way it exposes the fragility and artificiality of the hyperreal world. For Baudrillard, the destruction of the Twin Towers symbolized the destruction of the *illusion* of Western invulnerability, of the seemingly unassailable power of global capitalism and technological supremacy. The spectacle of destruction, in this case, was more significant than the actual destruction itself.

Baudrillard argues that the media's role in amplifying the spectacle of terrorism further reinforces the illusion of destruction. The relentless coverage of the 9/11 attacks, for example, transformed the event into a *global media phenomenon*, where the images of the collapsing towers took on a life of their own, detached from the actual event. This process of mediation, Baudrillard argues, creates a hyperreal version of the event, where the destruction is experienced more as an image or symbol than as a physical reality. The real destruction—both the material collapse of the towers and the human suffering involved—is overshadowed by the media spectacle that the event generates.

In this sense, Baudrillard suggests that terrorism operates within the same logic of *simulation* and *hyper reality* that defines the modern world. Just as the media creates hyperreal simulations of reality through its representations, so too does terrorism create a *hyperreal illusion* of destruction through its symbolic acts. The power of terrorism, in Baudrillard's view, lies not in its ability to cause physical harm but in its ability to manipulate the symbolic order and create powerful images of destruction that resonate in the hyperreal world of media and representation.

The Reversal of Power: Terrorism as a Challenge to Globalization

Baudrillard's analysis of terrorism also addresses the *reversal of power* that occurs in the act of terrorism. In his view, terrorism represents a form of *symbolic revenge* against the global system of Western power, technology, and capitalism. The hyperreal world of globalization, driven by media, technology, and consumerism, creates a system of domination that seems omnipresent and invulnerable. However, Baudrillard argues that this very system contains the seeds of its own destruction. The hyperreal world is fragile precisely because it is built on simulations and representations rather than on material realities.

Terrorism, in Baudrillard's analysis, exploits this fragility by attacking the *symbols* of power rather than the structures themselves. The 9/11 attacks, for example, targeted the Twin Towers not just as physical buildings but as *symbols* of American capitalism and global dominance. By attacking these symbols, terrorism reveals the vulnerability of the hyperreal system, showing that even the most powerful structures can be brought down by a single symbolic act.

Baudrillard's theory of the *reversal of power* suggests that terrorism operates as a kind of *mirror image* of the global system it opposes. Just as the global media system generates power through images, signs, and representations, so too does terrorism create its impact through the manipulation of symbols and images. In this sense, Baudrillard argues that terrorism is not external to the hyperreal world but is a product of it—an inevitable consequence of the way power operates in a world dominated by images and simulations.

The Absurdity of Rational Explanations for Terrorism

Another key aspect of Baudrillard's analysis of terrorism is his critique of *rational explanations* for acts of terror. Baudrillard argues that the Western world's attempts to rationalize and explain terrorism through political, economic, or psychological frameworks miss the symbolic and irrational nature of terrorist acts. In his view, terrorism operates outside the logic of conventional power structures and cannot be fully understood through the lens of rationality.

For Baudrillard, terrorism represents a form of *symbolic violence* that challenges the very foundations of rational, modern society. It is not motivated solely by political or economic grievances but by a deeper desire to disrupt and challenge the symbolic order of the hyperreal world. In this sense, Baudrillard suggests that terrorism is not just an act of destruction but a form of *symbolic communication*, aimed at exposing the contradictions and weaknesses of the global system.

Baudrillard's critique of rational explanations for terrorism is linked to his broader analysis of how the Western world constructs meaning through media and representation. He argues that in the hyperreal world, meaning is generated through simulations and representations rather than through direct engagement with reality. Terrorism, in this context, represents a challenge to this system of meaning-making, as it operates outside the logic of rationality and defies the conventional narratives that the media and political systems rely on to make sense of the world.

Terrorism and the Spectacle of Fear

Baudrillard also addresses the role of *fear* in the spectacle of terrorism. In his view, the real impact of terrorism is not in the immediate destruction it causes but in the way it generates a *spectacle of fear* that resonates far beyond the event itself. The media's amplification of terrorist acts creates an atmosphere of fear and uncertainty that extends into everyday life, transforming the hyperreal world into a space of *perpetual anxiety*.

This spectacle of fear, Baudrillard argues, serves to reinforce the power of both terrorism and the media system that amplifies it. By generating images of destruction and chaos, terrorism creates a climate of fear that destabilizes the social order and undermines the sense of security that the hyperreal world is built upon. The media, in turn, perpetuates this fear by endlessly reproducing the images of terrorist acts, creating a cycle in which the spectacle of fear becomes self-sustaining.

Baudrillard's analysis of the spectacle of fear highlights the way in which terrorism, like the media, operates through the manipulation of symbols and images rather than through direct material impact. The fear generated by terrorism is not just a response to the physical danger posed by terrorist acts but to the *symbolic disruption* that these acts represent. In this sense, Baudrillard suggests that terrorism creates a *hyperreal fear*, where the threat of terrorism is amplified through the media spectacle to the point that it becomes more real and immediate than the actual danger posed by terrorist groups.

Conclusion: The Illusion of Destruction and the Power of Symbols

Jean Baudrillard's analysis of terrorism offers a radical and challenging perspective on how terrorist acts function in the postmodern, hyperreal world. For Baudrillard, terrorism is not simply about causing destruction or advancing political goals; it is about creating powerful *symbolic ruptures* in the hyperreal system of media, technology, and globalization. Terrorism operates within the same logic of images, signs, and representations that defines the hyperreal world, using the *spectacle of destruction* to expose the fragility and contradictions of global power. In this sense, Baudrillard argues that terrorism creates an *illusion of destruction*, where the real impact lies not in the physical damage caused but in the symbolic disruption of the established order.

Baudrillard's theory of *hyper reality* helps explain how terrorism functions within the mediated world. Acts of terror are designed to generate media attention, becoming spectacles consumed by global audiences. These spectacles operate within the realm of *simulation*, where the symbolic meaning of the terrorist act becomes more significant than the act itself. The 9/11 attacks, for instance, were not just destructive; they were a symbolic assault on the imagery of Western capitalism and power. The images of the Twin Towers collapsing became more enduring and impactful than the physical destruction, as they were endlessly replayed and consumed within the media ecosystem.

The *reversal of power* that Baudrillard identifies in terrorism shows that while Western powers dominate the world economically, militarily, and technologically, terrorism destabilizes this dominance through symbolic acts. Terrorists use the very tools of the hyperreal world—images and symbols—to expose the vulnerabilities of the system, demonstrating that even the most powerful nations are not immune to disruption. This symbolic warfare turns the logic of power on its head, showing that the hyperreal system, with all its media-driven representations of invulnerability, is built on an illusion.

Baudrillard's *critique of rational explanations* for terrorism further deepens his analysis. He challenges the notion that terrorism can be understood purely through political or economic motivations. Instead, he emphasizes the symbolic dimension of terrorism, which operates outside the rational frameworks used by governments and media to interpret and respond to it. This symbolic dimension, Baudrillard argues, is what makes terrorism so difficult to combat. It defies the conventional logic of warfare and political struggle, functioning instead as a *symbolic challenge* to the entire global system of power and meaning.

Finally, Baudrillard's exploration of the *spectacle of fear* highlights how terrorism's real power lies in its ability to generate ongoing fear and uncertainty. The media's role in amplifying this fear turns terrorism into a *hyperreal threat*, where the fear of potential attacks becomes more pervasive than the attacks themselves. This fear infiltrates daily life, creating a constant sense of anxiety and vulnerability that the media continues to reproduce through its coverage. For Baudrillard, this cycle of fear perpetuates the power of terrorism, reinforcing its symbolic challenge to the stability of the hyperreal world.

In conclusion, Jean Baudrillard's analysis of terrorism as the *illusion of destruction* provides a profound critique of how terrorism functions in the postmodern, media-saturated world. By focusing on the symbolic, mediated aspects of terrorism, Baudrillard reveals how terror operates not only through violence but through the manipulation of images, signs, and symbols. In a world defined by hyper reality, where representations often carry more weight than the material reality they depict, terrorism becomes a form of *symbolic warfare*, aimed at exposing the fragility of the global system. Baudrillard's work challenges us to reconsider how we understand terrorism, suggesting that its real power lies in its ability to disrupt the symbolic order of the hyperreal world, creating an illusion of destruction that resonates far beyond the physical damage caused.

The Future of Reality in Baudrillard's Thought

Jean Baudrillard's exploration of *the future of reality* reflects his deep concerns about the increasing dominance of *simulation* and *hyper reality* in modern life. For Baudrillard, the future of reality is marked by the continued blurring of the boundaries between the real and the simulated, as technological advancements, media saturation, and the expansion of virtual environments redefine how we perceive and experience the world. In his philosophy, reality itself is at risk of disappearing altogether, replaced by a world of signs, images, and simulations that bear no connection to material reality. As we move deeper into the postmodern condition, Baudrillard foresees a future in which reality as we once knew it is replaced by a fully constructed, artificial world—a world where *hyper reality* dominates, and the distinction between truth and illusion becomes impossible to discern.

The Decline of the Real

Baudrillard's analysis of the future of reality begins with his concept of the *decline of the real*. In the traditional view, reality was understood as a stable, material world that could be directly experienced and known. Meaning was derived from the relationship between objects, people, and events, and the real was something that could be distinguished from illusions or representations. However, Baudrillard argues that in the postmodern world, this stable sense of reality has been undermined by the rise of *simulation*.

Simulation, in Baudrillard's view, is the process by which representations and images come to replace and even create reality. As simulations proliferate through media, advertising, and digital technologies, they begin to overshadow the material world. The result is *hyper reality*—a state in which simulations become more real and significant than the reality they are supposed to represent. In this hyperreal world, the real is no longer something that exists independently of representations. Instead, reality is continuously constructed, mediated, and redefined by the signs, symbols, and images that circulate in the media and technological systems.

For Baudrillard, the future of reality is one in which this process of simulation continues to accelerate, leading to the *total disappearance of the real*. As simulations become more advanced and immersive, particularly with the rise of *virtual reality* (VR) and *augmented reality* (AR) technologies, Baudrillard foresees a world where the boundary between reality and illusion is entirely erased. People will no longer be able to distinguish between what is real and what is simulated, as the hyperreal world becomes the only reality they know. This loss of the real represents a profound shift in how we understand existence, identity, and truth.

The Role of Technology in the Future of Reality

Technology plays a central role in Baudrillard's vision of the future of reality. He argues that the rise of digital technologies, the internet, and virtual environments has accelerated the collapse of the real. These technologies create *simulated experiences* that often feel more real and engaging than the physical world. For instance, virtual reality environments offer users the ability to immerse themselves in fully constructed, artificial worlds that simulate sensory experiences in ways that can feel just as convincing as real-life interactions. In Baudrillard's view, these technologies represent the future of reality—a future in which people increasingly live within simulated environments, detached from material reality.

The expansion of *augmented reality* (AR) technologies also contributes to the future of hyper reality. AR overlays digital information and images onto the physical world, creating a hybrid reality where the real and the simulated coexist. In Baudrillard's framework, this blending of the real and the virtual further erodes the boundary between reality and illusion. As AR becomes more integrated into daily life—through devices like smartphones, smart glasses, and wearable technology—the physical world itself becomes *augmented* by simulations, creating a situation where the real and the simulated are indistinguishable.

Baudrillard's vision of the future also includes the *convergence of human consciousness with technology*, particularly through artificial intelligence (AI) and neural interfaces. In a world where AI systems simulate human intelligence, creativity, and interaction, the line between human reality and machine-generated simulations becomes increasingly blurred. Baudrillard suggests that the future of reality may involve a *post-human condition*, where human consciousness is mediated and shaped by technologies that simulate human experiences, thoughts, and emotions. In this future, the real becomes a matter of technological mediation, and human identity itself is redefined through simulations.

Virtual Reality and the Disappearance of the Real

One of the key technologies that Baudrillard sees as central to the future of reality is *virtual reality* (VR). VR technologies allow users to enter fully immersive, digital worlds that simulate real-life experiences in a way that feels authentic and convincing. For Baudrillard, VR represents the next stage in the evolution of *hyper reality*, where simulations become so advanced that they replace the need for actual experiences. In the future, Baudrillard predicts that people will increasingly live within virtual environments, where their interactions, relationships, and identities are constructed through simulations rather than through direct engagement with the physical world.

Baudrillard's analysis of VR reflects his broader concerns about the disappearance of the real. As virtual environments become more sophisticated and accessible, they create a world where the boundaries between reality and simulation collapse entirely. In these virtual worlds, people can experience sensations, emotions, and relationships that are indistinguishable from those in the real world.

However, because these experiences are simulations, they lack the grounding in material reality that once defined human existence. Baudrillard suggests that the future of reality may involve a complete immersion in virtual environments, where people lose touch with the physical world and live entirely within simulated realities.

This future of *total immersion* in virtual reality raises profound questions about the nature of existence, identity, and truth. In a world where simulations replace reality, what does it mean to be human? What happens to concepts like truth, authenticity, and meaning when the real is replaced by the virtual? Baudrillard's critique suggests that the future of reality may involve a profound loss of these concepts, as people become increasingly detached from the material world and live within a hyperreal environment where everything is constructed, mediated, and simulated.

The Implosion of Meaning

Baudrillard's vision of the future of reality also includes the *implosion of meaning*—a process in which the proliferation of images, signs, and simulations leads to the collapse of any stable or coherent sense of meaning. In the hyperreal world, meaning becomes fragmented and unstable, as people are bombarded with endless representations that no longer refer to any underlying reality. This implosion of meaning is a key feature of Baudrillard's critique of postmodern society, and he argues that it will only intensify in the future.

In the future of hyper reality, Baudrillard predicts that meaning itself will become increasingly *fluid* and *arbitrary*, as people are overwhelmed by the sheer volume of information, images, and simulations they encounter daily. The distinction between truth and falsehood, reality and illusion, becomes impossible to maintain, as all representations are consumed in the same way, regardless of their connection to reality. This implosion of meaning creates a world where people are constantly engaged with simulations but are unable to make sense of them in any meaningful way.

Baudrillard's analysis suggests that the future of reality will involve a profound *alienation* from meaning and truth. As simulations replace the real, people become disconnected from any stable sense of reality or purpose. In this future, reality becomes a *surface phenomenon*, where everything is mediated through images and signs, and nothing has any deeper significance or meaning. Baudrillard's critique challenges us to consider the implications of living in a world where reality is constantly constructed and reconstructed through simulations, and where meaning is constantly shifting, elusive, and fragmented.

The Future of Identity in a Hyperreal World

Baudrillard's vision of the future of reality also has profound implications for *identity*. In the hyperreal world, identity is no longer something that is rooted in material reality or personal experience. Instead, identity is constructed through the consumption of images, signs, and simulations. In the future, Baudrillard predicts that people will increasingly define themselves through the virtual environments they inhabit, the digital personas they create, and the simulations they engage with.

This process of *identity construction* through simulations is already evident in the rise of social media platforms like Instagram, TikTok, and Facebook, where people create idealized versions of themselves and curate their online personas for public consumption. In the future, Baudrillard suggests that this process will intensify, as people live more of their lives within virtual environments and define themselves through their interactions with simulations. Identity becomes a performance, a *simulation of the self*, rather than a reflection of material reality or lived experience.

The future of identity in a hyperreal world raises profound questions about the nature of the self. If identity is constructed entirely through simulations, what does it mean to be *authentic*? Can there be any sense of an *authentic self* in a world where reality itself has disappeared? Baudrillard's critique suggests that the future of identity may involve a profound *loss of authenticity*, as people become increasingly detached from the material realities that once defined their sense of self.

Conclusion: Baudrillard's Vision of a Hyperreal Future

Jean Baudrillard's vision of the future of reality is a provocative and unsettling critique of the postmodern world. He argues that the future will be defined by the continued dominance of *hyper reality*, where simulations replace reality, and the distinction between truth and illusion becomes impossible to maintain. As media, technology, and virtual environments continue to evolve, Baudrillard predicts that people will increasingly live within simulated worlds, detached from the material realities that once defined existence.

In this hyperreal future, reality becomes a *construct*, constantly mediated and redefined by images, signs, and simulations. Meaning becomes fragmented and *unstable*, as the endless proliferation of images and simulations overwhelms people's ability to engage with the world in a meaningful way. The distinction between what is real and what is simulated collapses entirely, creating a world where *truth*, *authenticity*, and *materiality* no longer hold the same significance they once did.

Baudrillard's vision of the future is one in which the *implosion of meaning* leads to a profound sense of *alienation*. Individuals find themselves adrift in a world dominated by simulations, where the real has been replaced by a hyperreal version of itself—one that is more compelling, more immersive, and ultimately more detached from anything material or concrete. This world of hyper reality offers endless possibilities for *entertainment*, *self-creation*, and *consumption*, but it also presents deep challenges for those seeking connection, purpose, or truth.

The Future of Identity and Human Interaction

In Baudrillard's view, as simulations dominate the future of reality, *identity* and *human interaction* will also undergo significant transformations. With the rise of *virtual realities*, *digital avatars*, and *AI-driven environments*, people will increasingly engage with each other and the world through *simulated identities* and *constructed personas*. The self will no longer be defined by physical presence or personal history but by one's ability to navigate and manipulate virtual spaces, perform within hyperreal environments, and project carefully curated images of the self.

Social media platforms already provide a glimpse of this future, where users create and sustain multiple, often idealized versions of themselves online. In Baudrillard's hyperreal future, this process will deepen, as people spend more time inhabiting digital and virtual spaces, constructing identities that are fluid, flexible, and adaptable to different simulations. The traditional markers of identity—such as nationality, gender, and class—may become increasingly irrelevant, as virtual realities allow individuals to reinvent themselves according to the logic of the simulation they inhabit.

Moreover, the way people relate to each other will be increasingly shaped by *mediated interactions* through virtual platforms. Direct, physical interactions may become secondary to the engagement that takes place in digital worlds, where relationships are formed, maintained, and performed through images, text, and avatars. Baudrillard would argue that these relationships, while potentially rich in symbolic and emotional content, remain disconnected from the *real* in a material sense, as they exist within a world of simulation rather than lived experience.

The Challenge of Finding Meaning in a Hyperreal World

One of the central challenges Baudrillard identifies for the future is the difficulty of finding *meaning* in a world dominated by hyper reality. As simulations become more immersive and compelling, they begin to replace traditional sources of meaning, such as *religion, community, work*, or *personal experience*. The hyperreal world, with its endless production of images, narratives, and spectacles, offers a constant stream of entertainment, but it also creates a sense of *emptiness* and *detachment*.

In Baudrillard's view, the future of reality may be one in which people are caught in a cycle of consuming simulations, constantly seeking new experiences, but never finding lasting meaning or fulfillment. This endless pursuit of stimulation without deeper engagement leads to what Baudrillard describes as a state of *hyper-passivity*—a condition where individuals are no longer active agents in their own lives but passive consumers of the realities constructed for them by media, technology, and corporate systems.

Baudrillard's critique suggests that the *search for meaning* in the hyperreal future will be increasingly difficult, as the traditional markers of reality and truth become obscured by simulations. In a world where everything is a representation or a performance, where can one find something *authentic*, something that transcends the hyperreal world of images and signs? Baudrillard offers no simple solutions to this problem, but his work challenges us to critically examine the ways in which the hyperreal world shapes our understanding of reality and to consider the consequences of living in a world where meaning has become fragmented and elusive.

The End of History and the Future of Reality

Baudrillard's analysis of the future of reality is also deeply connected to his concept of the *end of history*. For Baudrillard, the traditional narrative of history as a linear progression of events, leading toward a clear future, has collapsed in the postmodern world. In the hyperreal future, history itself becomes *simulated*, as events are constantly reinterpreted, replayed, and mediated through images and representations. The future, therefore, does not represent a break from the present or a continuation of historical progress but becomes a *repetition* of the same simulations, endlessly reproduced and reconfigured within the hyperreal world.

This *cyclical nature of time* in the hyperreal world creates a future where *novelty* and *innovation* are simulated rather than real. Baudrillard suggests that the future will be marked by an endless recycling of cultural forms, ideas, and experiences, with no clear sense of direction or progress. In this sense, the future of reality may feel increasingly stagnant, as the hyperreal world reproduces itself in infinite variations without moving toward any genuine transformation or change.

Baudrillard's critique of the end of history also raises questions about the future of *human agency*. In a world where reality is constructed and mediated by simulations, what role do individuals have in shaping their own future? If the future is simply a continuation of the hyperreal present, where simulations dominate and meaning is fragmented, then the possibility of genuine *agency* or *resistance* becomes increasingly difficult. Baudrillard suggests that in the hyperreal future, individuals may find themselves trapped in a system of representation that limits their ability to engage with reality in any meaningful way.

Conclusion: Baudrillard's Dystopian Vision of the Future

Jean Baudrillard's vision of the future of reality is deeply *dystopian*, offering a critique of how modern media, technology, and consumer culture shape our understanding of the world. For Baudrillard, the future is one where *hyper reality* dominates, where simulations replace the real, and where meaning becomes increasingly unstable and fragmented. In this hyperreal world, individuals are alienated from both material reality and from themselves, as identity, experience, and truth are all constructed through simulations.

Baudrillard's work challenges us to consider the consequences of living in a world where reality is constantly mediated by images, signs, and technology. His critique raises important questions about the future of *truth, authenticity*, and *human experience* in a world where simulations increasingly define our existence. While Baudrillard offers no simple solutions to the challenges posed by the hyperreal future, his philosophy encourages us to critically examine the ways in which modern society constructs reality and to seek out ways of engaging with the world that go beyond the superficial, simulated experiences of hyper reality.

The Illusion of Freedom in a Simulated World

Jean Baudrillard's exploration of *freedom* in the postmodern world reveals a deeply unsettling reality: what many consider freedom is, in fact, an *illusion* shaped by a world dominated by *simulation* and *hyper reality*. In Baudrillard's view, modern society, with its pervasive media, technological advances, and consumer culture, has constructed a version of freedom that is detached from any real autonomy or agency. Instead of true freedom—the capacity to act meaningfully and autonomously—individuals are given *simulated choices*, which serve only to reinforce the systems of control that govern their lives. In this simulated world, freedom becomes a carefully constructed *performance*, where individuals feel empowered but are, in fact, bound by the invisible structures of a hyperreal system.

The Illusion of Choice in Consumer Culture

One of the key ways in which Baudrillard critiques the illusion of freedom is through his analysis of *consumer culture*. In modern capitalist societies, individuals are constantly presented with a vast array of choices—what to buy, where to live, how to dress, and so on. This abundance of choices creates the illusion of freedom, as people believe that they are making autonomous decisions about how to shape their lives. However, Baudrillard argues that these choices are superficial and predetermined by the logic of *consumerism* and *market forces*. The system offers a vast range of options, but these options are confined within the limits of *consumer choice*, where decisions are shaped by advertising, trends, and social pressures rather than by true autonomy.

For Baudrillard, the choices presented by consumer culture are part of a larger system of *sign-value*, where commodities are not valued for their practical utility but for the symbolic meanings they carry. In this context, individuals are not free to make meaningful choices; rather, they are trapped in a cycle of consumption, where their choices are dictated by the need to display *status*, *identity*, and *belonging*. The illusion of freedom is maintained through the appearance of choice, but in reality, individuals are constrained by the system of signs and symbols that define their options.

Baudrillard's critique suggests that consumer culture creates a form of *pseudo-freedom*, where individuals are free to choose between different products and lifestyles, but these choices serve only to reinforce the system of consumption. This system, in turn, shapes people's desires, aspirations, and identities, leaving little room for genuine autonomy. The freedom to choose within the confines of consumer culture is not a form of liberation; it is a form of *control*, where individuals are guided by the logic of consumption rather than by their own independent will.

The Media and the Performance of Freedom

Baudrillard's analysis of the media further deepens his critique of the illusion of freedom in a simulated world. In his view, the media plays a central role in constructing the *hyperreal world*, where simulations replace reality and where freedom is performed rather than exercised. The media, through its endless production of images, narratives, and representations, creates a world in which individuals believe they are free to choose their own identities, lifestyles, and beliefs. However, these choices are shaped by the media itself, which presents a carefully curated set of options that conform to the dominant *ideologies* and *social norms* of the time.

The media creates the illusion of freedom by offering individuals the opportunity to participate in the *spectacle* of modern life. Whether through television, social media, or advertising, people are encouraged to construct and display their identities in ways that align with the images and narratives promoted by the media. This process creates a sense of empowerment, as individuals feel that they are in control of their own self-presentation and life choices. However, Baudrillard argues that this empowerment is illusory, as the media dictates the parameters of choice and shapes the very desires that individuals believe are their own.

In the hyperreal world of the media, freedom becomes a *performance*, where individuals act out the roles and identities presented to them by the media. These roles are not chosen freely but are shaped by the images and narratives that dominate the hyperreal world. Baudrillard's critique suggests that the media creates a form of *symbolic freedom*, where people are free to choose between different representations of reality, but these representations are all part of the same simulated system. The freedom to choose between different media spectacles, whether in politics, entertainment, or lifestyle, is a form of control that limits genuine autonomy.

Political Freedom in the Hyperreal World

Baudrillard's critique of political freedom in the postmodern world is particularly striking. He argues that political systems, especially in Western democracies, offer an *illusion of political freedom*, where citizens are encouraged to believe that they have a meaningful say in the governance of their societies. Elections, political campaigns, and public debates create the appearance of democratic engagement, but Baudrillard contends that these processes are largely *performative*, designed to maintain the status quo rather than to enable real political change.

In Baudrillard's view, modern political systems function within the logic of *hyper reality*, where politics is mediated through the media and transformed into a spectacle. Political leaders become *media figures*, whose success is determined not by their policies or leadership but by their ability to perform effectively in the media spotlight. Elections and political debates are reduced to *spectacles*, where the emphasis is on image, rhetoric, and emotional appeal rather than substantive issues. This creates a situation where citizens are given the illusion of political choice, but the choices they are offered are limited to the candidates and platforms that conform to the logic of the media spectacle.

Baudrillard's critique of political freedom suggests that the hyperreal world of media and simulation has *eroded the possibility of genuine democratic engagement*. The choices offered in elections are *pre-packaged* and shaped by the media, leaving little room for alternative voices or meaningful dissent. In this sense, political freedom becomes another form of *symbolic freedom*, where the act of voting or participating in political debate is a performance that reinforces the illusion of democracy but does not lead to real change.

The Illusion of Autonomy in the Digital Age

The rise of *digital technologies* and *social media* has further complicated the notion of freedom in the simulated world. Baudrillard's critique of technology suggests that the digital age has created new forms of *control* and *surveillance*, even as it presents itself as a space of *individual empowerment* and *freedom*. In the digital world, individuals are given the tools to create their own identities, share their thoughts and experiences, and connect with others across the globe. This creates the appearance of autonomy, as people feel that they have control over their digital lives.

However, Baudrillard would argue that this digital freedom is another form of *simulated freedom*. Social media platforms, for example, operate within a system of *algorithms*, *data collection*, and *monetization*, where individuals' choices and behaviors are constantly monitored, analyzed, and shaped by unseen forces. The freedom to express oneself online is constrained by the algorithms that determine what content is seen, shared, or promoted. In this sense, digital freedom is *illusory*, as individuals are guided by invisible structures of control that shape their interactions and limit their autonomy.

The digital age also amplifies Baudrillard's critique of *identity as performance*. On social media platforms, individuals are encouraged to construct idealized versions of themselves, curating their images, thoughts, and experiences for public consumption. This process of *self-curation* creates a sense of freedom, as people believe they are in control of how they present themselves to the world. However, Baudrillard would argue that this is another form of *symbolic freedom*, where individuals are performing within the confines of the platform's logic, conforming to the expectations of their audience, and shaped by the desire for *likes*, *followers*, and *validation*.

The Role of Surveillance in the Simulated World

Baudrillard's concept of the *panopticon*—a system of control where individuals are constantly monitored—also plays a role in his critique of the illusion of freedom. In the simulated world, *surveillance* technologies, from CCTV cameras to data tracking, create a situation where individuals are constantly observed, shaping their behavior in subtle but pervasive ways. This surveillance is often justified in the name of *security* or *convenience*, but it also serves to reinforce systems of control.

In this context, the freedom that individuals believe they have is compromised by the fact that they are constantly being monitored, both by the state and by corporate entities. The choices they make, the content they consume, and the interactions they engage in are all tracked and used to shape future behaviors. Baudrillard's analysis suggests that this creates a form of *self-regulation*, where individuals internalize the logic of surveillance and conform to the expectations of the system without realizing they are doing so.

This form of surveillance is particularly relevant in the digital age, where data collection and algorithmic analysis shape almost every aspect of online life. From targeted advertising to content recommendations, individuals are constantly guided by invisible forces that limit their autonomy, even as they believe they are freely choosing what to engage with. In this sense, the *panopticon of the digital age* creates a situation where the illusion of freedom is maintained, but the reality is one of profound control and manipulation.

Conclusion: The Illusion of Freedom in a Simulated World

Jean Baudrillard's critique of *freedom* in the postmodern world challenges the very foundation of what many people understand as *autonomy* and *choice*. In a world dominated by *simulation*, *media*, *consumer culture*, and *digital technologies*, Baudrillard argues that freedom has become an *illusion*—a performance that disguises the systems of control that govern modern life. Whether in consumer culture, politics, or the digital realm, Baudrillard suggests that individuals are trapped in a system where their choices are predetermined and shaped by forces beyond their control. This system maintains the appearance of freedom, offering countless options and opportunities for self-expression, but these options are confined within the boundaries set by *consumerism*, *media representation*, and *technological surveillance*. In reality, Baudrillard argues, this *simulated freedom* only serves to reinforce the existing power structures, ensuring that individuals remain passive participants in a hyperreal world where autonomy and true agency are increasingly eroded.

Freedom as a Simulation

One of Baudrillard's key insights is that freedom in the postmodern world has been reduced to a *simulation*—a hollow concept that no longer carries the meaning it once did. In traditional terms, freedom was understood as the ability to act according to one's own will, free from external constraints. However, in a world dominated by simulations, the *conditions of freedom* have been transformed. What people perceive as freedom today is not rooted in real autonomy or independent thought but in a carefully controlled system of *representation* and *performance*.

In Baudrillard's analysis, this simulation of freedom manifests most clearly in the realm of *consumer choice*. The vast array of products, services, and experiences offered in modern society creates the illusion that individuals have unprecedented freedom to shape their lives according to their desires. But Baudrillard argues that this freedom is a mirage—choices are largely dictated by advertising, cultural norms, and the capitalist system that encourages consumption as a way of defining identity and meaning.

The more choices people are given, the more they are absorbed into the *sign-value* system, where commodities represent not utility but status and identity. Freedom, in this context, is reduced to the ability to choose between *pre-fabricated identities* and *lifestyles* that conform to the logic of consumerism.

Political Freedom as Spectacle

Baudrillard extends his critique of freedom to the realm of *politics*, where democratic processes are increasingly shaped by *media spectacle* rather than substantive engagement. Elections, campaigns, and political debates are mediated through the lens of television, social media, and advertising, transforming political participation into a *performance* rather than a true exercise of power. Political figures are marketed like celebrities, and the success of a candidate depends more on their media presence and ability to generate *emotional responses* than on their ideas or policies.

In this mediated environment, Baudrillard argues, political freedom becomes another *illusion*. Citizens are encouraged to participate in the democratic process, but the choices they are offered are limited to the candidates and platforms that align with the interests of the media and political elites. The act of voting, which is held up as the ultimate expression of democratic freedom, is reduced to a symbolic gesture, where the outcome has already been shaped by the forces of media, money, and corporate power.

Baudrillard's analysis suggests that modern politics operates within the same framework as consumer culture. Just as individuals are offered the illusion of freedom through consumer choice, they are given the illusion of political freedom through participation in a spectacle that offers little real change or challenge to the existing order. The system of representation, both in politics and in media, ensures that the choices available are always aligned with the interests of those in power, while maintaining the appearance of freedom and democracy.

Digital Freedom and Algorithmic Control

In the digital age, Baudrillard's critique of simulated freedom becomes even more relevant, as *algorithms* and *data-driven systems* increasingly shape the choices individuals make. Social media platforms, search engines, and online marketplaces use complex algorithms to curate the content people see, the advertisements they are shown, and the products they are recommended. These algorithms are designed to optimize engagement, maximize profits, and reinforce certain behaviors, all while creating the illusion that individuals are in control of their digital experiences.

For Baudrillard, this form of *algorithmic control* represents a new dimension of the illusion of freedom. On social media platforms, users believe they have the freedom to express themselves, connect with others, and access information, but their behavior is constantly monitored, analyzed, and influenced by unseen forces.

The *personalization* of content, which is presented as a way to enhance the user experience, is actually a form of control that limits the scope of what individuals can see and engage with. In this digital panopticon, individuals are free to choose within the parameters set by the algorithms, but these parameters are designed to guide their choices in ways that benefit the platform or its advertisers.

This *digital enclosure* of freedom is perhaps most evident in the rise of *filter bubbles* and *echo chambers*, where users are shown content that reinforces their existing beliefs and preferences, further limiting their exposure to alternative viewpoints or ideas. Baudrillard's critique suggests that this form of digital freedom is illusory, as individuals are trapped in a feedback loop of their own preferences, curated by algorithms that shape their behavior and reinforce the system of *hyperreal* engagement.

Surveillance and Self-Regulation

Baudrillard's analysis of *surveillance* in the postmodern world also reveals how the illusion of freedom is maintained through *self-regulation*. In a society where individuals are constantly monitored—whether by governments, corporations, or digital platforms—surveillance creates a system of control that is both visible and invisible. The presence of cameras, data collection tools, and tracking technologies leads individuals to regulate their own behavior, conforming to the norms and expectations set by the system.

Baudrillard argues that this form of surveillance reinforces the illusion of freedom by making individuals feel that they are choosing to conform, when in reality their behavior is being shaped by the knowledge that they are always being watched. The rise of *self-surveillance* through social media, where individuals voluntarily share intimate details of their lives, further deepens this illusion. People believe they are exercising their freedom to express themselves, but they are actually participating in a system that collects, analyzes, and profits from their personal data.

The more individuals engage with this system of surveillance, the more they internalize its logic, adjusting their behavior to fit the expectations of the platforms, algorithms, or social norms that govern their digital interactions. This process creates a form of *voluntary conformity*, where individuals believe they are exercising freedom but are actually reinforcing the very structures of control that limit their autonomy.

The Erosion of True Autonomy

At the heart of Baudrillard's critique is the idea that true *autonomy*—the ability to act freely and independently—has been eroded in the hyperreal world. As individuals navigate a world shaped by media, consumer culture, politics, and technology, they are given the illusion of freedom, but their choices are largely predetermined by the structures of *simulation* that define modern life. The vast array of options available, whether in consumer goods, political candidates, or digital content, creates the appearance of freedom, but these options are confined within a system that limits real autonomy.

Baudrillard's work challenges the modern understanding of freedom, revealing it to be a *performance* that masks deeper systems of control. In the hyperreal world, individuals are free to make choices, but these choices are shaped by *representations*, *algorithms*, and *spectacles* that dictate the terms of engagement. True autonomy, in Baudrillard's view, would require breaking free from these simulations and engaging with reality in a more direct, meaningful way—a task that becomes increasingly difficult as the boundaries between reality and simulation collapse.

Conclusion: The Illusion of Freedom in a Simulated World

Jean Baudrillard's exploration of *freedom* in the postmodern world reveals the profound ways in which freedom has been transformed into an *illusion*. In a world dominated by *simulation, consumerism, media spectacles*, and *digital technologies*, the choices individuals make are shaped by invisible systems of control, creating the appearance of freedom but limiting real autonomy. Baudrillard's critique challenges us to reconsider what it means to be free in a world where identity, politics, and even self-expression are mediated through simulations and performances. True freedom, according to Baudrillard, may be impossible to achieve in a hyperreal world, where every action is already shaped by the logic of the system. Instead, individuals are left with a *simulated freedom*—a carefully constructed performance that disguises the deeper structures of control that govern their lives.

Violence, Media, and the Spectacle of the Real

Jean Baudrillard's analysis of *violence*, especially in the context of modern media and the spectacle it creates, offers a provocative examination of how violence is transformed in the postmodern world. Baudrillard argues that violence, once a direct, tangible act with real consequences, has increasingly been transformed into a *spectacle*—a performance mediated and amplified by the media. In this context, violence becomes less about the immediate harm it causes and more about the *symbolic power* it exerts through representation. The media does not simply report on violence; it turns it into a *hyperreal* event, where the boundaries between reality and its representation collapse, creating a world where the spectacle of violence is consumed as entertainment, detached from its real-world consequences.

Violence as Spectacle

Baudrillard's concept of the *spectacle* draws from Guy Debord's theory in *The Society of the Spectacle*, but he extends it to explore the role of violence in the media-saturated world. For Baudrillard, the *real* violence of war, terrorism, crime, and conflict is increasingly subsumed by its *representation* in the media. News outlets, films, television shows, and social media platforms all participate in transforming violence into a *spectacle*—a mediated event that is consumed by a global audience. In this process, violence is stripped of its material consequences and transformed into a series of *images*, *sound bites*, and *narratives* that serve to entertain, shock, or manipulate viewers.

One of the key ideas in Baudrillard's analysis is that the media's portrayal of violence creates a form of *hyper reality*, where the line between the real and the represented violence is blurred. For example, the constant bombardment of violent imagery on the news—images of wars, terrorist attacks, mass shootings, and natural disasters—numbs viewers to the actual suffering and destruction caused by these events. Violence, in this sense, becomes something that people *watch* and *consume*, rather than something they directly experience or understand in its full gravity. The *real* violence is obscured by its transformation into a media event, where the spectacle of destruction becomes the focus, and the actual human suffering is often secondary.

Baudrillard's concept of *hyper reality* suggests that violence, as it appears in the media, is no longer grounded in reality. Instead, it becomes a *simulation*, where representations of violence circulate in a way that detaches them from their original context. This detachment allows for violence to be *repackaged* and *resold* as entertainment, even when it is ostensibly presented as news. The images of violence are endlessly replayed, often stripped of their historical, political, or social context, reducing them to mere *spectacles* that evoke emotional reactions but little deeper understanding.

The Media's Role in Amplifying Violence

The media's role in amplifying violence is central to Baudrillard's critique. He argues that the media does not simply reflect reality but *constructs* it, particularly in the way it presents violence. The portrayal of violent events—whether wars, terrorist attacks, or acts of personal violence—are framed in such a way as to create maximum *emotional impact* and *spectacle*. The selection of images, the framing of narratives, and the repetition of violent scenes all serve to *amplify* the spectacle, making violence appear more pervasive and more dramatic than it often is in reality.

In Baudrillard's view, this amplification of violence is not neutral; it serves specific *cultural* and *political* purposes. The constant portrayal of violence in the media can create a sense of *fear* and *anxiety* among viewers, reinforcing the need for state intervention, surveillance, and control. It can also desensitize individuals to real violence, as the repetition of violent imagery dulls their emotional responses and leads to a form of *compassion fatigue*. Over time, viewers become more interested in the spectacle of violence—the drama and entertainment value it provides—than in the actual human consequences of the violent acts.

The media's portrayal of violence also creates a sense of *distance* between the viewer and the event. By transforming violence into a spectacle, the media allows viewers to observe violence from a safe, detached perspective. This distance turns violence into something that happens *to others* and can be observed without the viewer having to confront the real suffering or moral implications of the act. Baudrillard argues that this detachment is a crucial part of the hyperreal experience of violence, where the spectacle becomes more important than the reality it represents.

The "Aestheticization" of Violence

Baudrillard also explores the *aestheticization* of violence in contemporary culture, particularly through *film*, *television*, and *video games*. In these mediums, violence is often *stylized*, *glamorized*, and *packaged* as entertainment. Action movies, crime dramas, and war films frequently present violence in a way that emphasizes its visual spectacle rather than its moral or emotional consequences. Gunfights, explosions, and acts of destruction are choreographed for maximum visual impact, creating a form of violence that is *beautiful* in its execution but *detached* from its real-world implications.

In Baudrillard's view, this aestheticization of violence further reinforces the illusion that violence is something to be *consumed* rather than something to be confronted. By presenting violence as entertainment, these media forms contribute to the desensitization of audiences, making real acts of violence seem less shocking or morally troubling. The *cinematic* presentation of violence blurs the line between *fiction* and *reality*, as viewers come to associate real acts of violence with the dramatized, stylized versions they see in movies or games.

Video games, in particular, offer an interactive form of violence that Baudrillard might argue deepens the experience of hyper reality. In many popular games, players take on the role of violent characters—soldiers, criminals, or assassins—and engage in simulated acts of violence. These acts, while simulated, offer a sense of *agency* and *participation* in the spectacle of violence, blurring the boundaries between real-life ethics and virtual action. The immersive nature of video games makes the spectacle of violence feel immediate and personal, even though it is entirely mediated by the screen. For Baudrillard, this blurring of boundaries between virtual violence and real violence is emblematic of a world where the *simulation* of violence becomes more significant than the reality of violence itself.

The Reality of Violence in a Hyperreal World

Baudrillard's concept of *hyper reality* raises important questions about the nature of violence in the modern world. If violence is increasingly mediated through images, simulations, and spectacles, what happens to the *reality* of violence? Baudrillard suggests that in a hyperreal world, where the media shapes and constructs reality, the *real* violence is often obscured or replaced by its *representation*. In this context, the reality of violence—the actual harm it causes, the lives it affects, and the political or social causes it represents—becomes secondary to its value as a *spectacle*.

One of Baudrillard's most provocative claims is that in the postmodern world, violence may no longer be experienced as *real* in the traditional sense. The constant mediation and representation of violence create a situation where even the most extreme acts of violence—terrorist attacks, mass shootings, or wars—are experienced through the lens of media. This mediation creates a *buffer* between the viewer and the event, making it difficult to engage with the real suffering and destruction that violence entails. In a hyperreal world, violence becomes a *sign* or *symbol* rather than a material reality, and its meaning is shaped more by the way it is represented than by the act itself.

Baudrillard's analysis of the *Gulf War* in his essay *The Gulf War Did Not Take Place* exemplifies this idea. He argues that the media's portrayal of the Gulf War transformed it into a *virtual war*, where the spectacle of precision bombing and military technology overshadowed the actual human suffering and destruction on the ground. The war, as it was experienced by global audiences, became a *hyperreal event*, where the images of destruction were consumed as a form of *entertainment* rather than as a representation of real violence. Baudrillard's critique suggests that the reality of violence is increasingly lost in a world where the spectacle is all that matters.

Terrorism and the Spectacle of Fear

Baudrillard also addresses the relationship between *terrorism* and the media spectacle, particularly in the aftermath of events like 9/11. He argues that terrorism, in the hyperreal world, functions as a form of *symbolic violence* that is designed to create a spectacle of fear. Terrorist acts are not only acts of physical destruction but also acts of *symbolic disruption*, aimed at destabilizing the established order by exposing its vulnerabilities. In this sense, terrorism operates within the same logic of the spectacle as the media, using violence to create powerful images that circulate through global media networks.

The media plays a crucial role in amplifying the spectacle of terrorism by endlessly replaying images of destruction, chaos, and fear. In this process, the real violence of terrorism becomes secondary to the *symbolic power* it exerts through its representation. The media's portrayal of terrorism transforms it into a *hyperreal event*, where the fear generated by the spectacle often outweighs the actual threat posed by the terrorist act. Baudrillard's critique suggests that in a hyperreal world, the spectacle of fear becomes self-sustaining, as the media's amplification of violence creates a *cycle of fear* that continues long after the actual event has passed.

Conclusion: Violence as a Spectacle in the Hyperreal World

Jean Baudrillard's critique of *violence* within the context of *media* and *hyper reality* reveals how violence, once grounded in immediate, material experience, has been transformed into a *spectacle*—a mediated event designed to shock, entertain, and control. In the hyperreal world, violence is no longer just about physical harm or political conflict; it becomes a *symbolic act*, manipulated and amplified by the media to serve as a form of *entertainment* or *ideological reinforcement*. This shift reduces violence to a set of images and narratives that circulate endlessly, detached from the real suffering and consequences they once represented.

Through his analysis, Baudrillard highlights how the *media* plays a central role in transforming violence into a spectacle. Whether through the news, film, or social media, the portrayal of violence is carefully framed to maximize its *emotional impact*, ensuring it resonates with viewers on a superficial level. This spectacle of violence desensitizes audiences, numbing them to the actual horrors of war, terrorism, or crime, while simultaneously fueling *fear* and *anxiety* that serve political and social agendas.

Baudrillard's notion of *hyper reality* further complicates how violence is understood in modern society. In this state of hyper reality, the representations of violence become more real than the acts themselves. The media's depiction of war, for instance, emphasizes the *spectacle of destruction*—images of bombings, explosions, and suffering that are replayed and consumed—but these images often obscure the *real consequences* of conflict: the human suffering, the social upheaval, and the lasting devastation. In a hyperreal world, violence becomes a *simulation* that serves the purposes of entertainment and manipulation, rather than a direct confrontation with the real.

The *aestheticization* of violence in popular culture, particularly in *film* and *video games*, deepens Baudrillard's critique. Violence is stylized and glamorized, presented as an engaging spectacle that invites participation, whether as a passive viewer or an active player in a virtual world. This blurring of the boundaries between reality and simulation allows audiences to experience violence as something separate from its moral and ethical consequences. Violence becomes a *performance*, a narrative device, rather than a real human experience.

Baudrillard's discussion of *terrorism* as a form of *symbolic violence* further underscores how violence has been transformed in the hyperreal world. Terrorist acts, especially in the context of 9/11, are not only about physical destruction but also about creating powerful symbolic ruptures that challenge global power structures. The media's amplification of terrorism turns these acts into global *spectacles* that generate fear, destabilizing societies far beyond the immediate effects of the violence itself. In this sense, the *spectacle of fear* becomes a self-sustaining cycle, where the representation of violence continually feeds into a sense of vulnerability and anxiety, even as the actual threat diminishes.

In the end, Baudrillard's analysis points to a world where the *reality of violence* is increasingly subsumed by its *representation*. As violence becomes more deeply embedded in the hyperreal system of images, simulations, and spectacles, its meaning shifts. The *symbolic power* of violence grows, but its connection to material reality weakens. In this world, individuals are left to confront the images of violence, mediated and amplified, but they are often detached from the real, human impact that violence once carried. The result is a society where violence becomes both omnipresent and *distant*, a spectacle to be consumed but not deeply felt or understood.

Baudrillard's critique challenges us to rethink the way violence is portrayed and consumed in modern society, urging us to look beyond the spectacle to the *real consequences* that are often hidden beneath the layers of simulation. His work serves as a warning about the dangers of living in a world where violence is no longer real, where its meaning has been transformed into something that can be *watched*, *played*, and *replayed* without ever fully grasping its true impact.

The End of Utopia: Baudrillard's Worldview

Jean Baudrillard's philosophy is deeply rooted in the idea that *utopia*—once a powerful force in shaping human thought, politics, and society—has come to an end. In Baudrillard's worldview, the *postmodern condition* marks the collapse of the traditional concept of utopia, as the distinction between reality and fantasy dissolves and the capacity to imagine alternative futures is engulfed by the *hyperreal* world. Baudrillard argues that the modern age of *simulation* and *media saturation* has not only blurred the line between reality and representation but has also made the concept of utopia obsolete. In a world dominated by *consumerism, technology,* and *hyper reality,* the possibility of envisioning a radically different future is eroded, replaced by an endless repetition of the same signs and symbols.

Utopia and its Historical Role

Historically, the concept of *utopia* has been central to human thought. Utopia represents the dream of an ideal society, a vision of a world that transcends the limitations of the present. From Thomas More's *Utopia* to the revolutionary visions of Marxism, utopia has symbolized the hope for a better future, where human life could be organized according to principles of justice, equality, and harmony. In the modern era, utopian thought was often linked to *political ideologies* that sought to transform society, whether through socialism, communism, or liberal democracy.

For Baudrillard, the problem is not that utopia has failed, but that the conditions for imagining utopia have been fundamentally altered by the rise of *postmodernism* and the hyperreal world. Utopia, in Baudrillard's view, was always an idealized projection, a dream that offered hope for a radically different future. But the hyperreal world—dominated by *simulation* and *media*—has absorbed and neutralized the potential for such dreams. In this new reality, utopia is no longer something that exists as a distant goal or vision; instead, it has been replaced by a *simulated version* of utopia that offers superficial satisfaction while reinforcing the existing order.

The Collapse of Utopia in the Age of Hyper reality

Baudrillard's concept of *hyper reality* is central to his critique of the end of utopia. Hyper reality, for Baudrillard, is a state in which representations and simulations become more real and significant than the actual reality they are supposed to represent. In the hyperreal world, images, signs, and media spectacles dominate, creating a world where the distinction between reality and fantasy collapses. This has profound implications for utopian thinking.

In a hyperreal world, the capacity to imagine *radical alternatives* to the present is undermined. Utopia, which traditionally represented a vision of a different future, is now absorbed into the logic of hyper reality, where it is transformed into a *consumer product* or *media spectacle.* Baudrillard argues that the *simulacra* of utopia—the images of a perfect world promoted through advertising, film, and popular culture—create the illusion that utopia is already here. But this utopia is not the radical, transformative vision that thinkers once imagined; it is a *simulated utopia,* a superficial fantasy that masks the underlying contradictions of the present world.

The rise of *consumerism* plays a key role in this transformation. In the consumer society, individuals are constantly bombarded with images of an ideal life—through advertisements, lifestyle brands, and media representations—that promise happiness, fulfillment, and success. This simulated utopia offers the illusion that by consuming the right products, living in the right neighborhoods, or following the right trends, individuals can achieve a perfect life. However, Baudrillard argues that this is a hollow form of utopia, one that is tied to the logic of consumption and that reinforces the existing social and economic structures rather than challenging them.

The result is a world where the *dream of utopia* has been replaced by the *simulation of utopia*. People are no longer encouraged to imagine radically different futures or to question the structures of power and inequality that shape their lives. Instead, they are offered a hyperreal version of utopia that is designed to keep them complacent, distracted, and content within the confines of the existing system.

The Death of Ideology and the End of Utopian Politics

Baudrillard also links the *end of utopia* to the *death of ideology* in the postmodern world. In the past, utopian visions were often tied to political ideologies that sought to transform society. Marxism, for example, offered a utopian vision of a classless society, while liberalism envisioned a world of individual freedom and equality. These ideologies were grounded in the belief that human society could be radically transformed through political struggle, revolution, or reform.

However, Baudrillard argues that in the postmodern world, ideology has lost its power. The grand narratives of Marxism, liberalism, and other political ideologies have collapsed, replaced by a fragmented, *post-ideological* condition where politics is reduced to a series of media spectacles and superficial debates. The *spectacle* of politics, as Baudrillard describes it, is driven more by *images*, *media performance*, and *public relations* than by any real ideological content or vision for the future.

In this context, the idea of utopia—once central to ideological struggles—becomes increasingly irrelevant. Without the guiding force of ideology, politics becomes a game of *spectacle*, where leaders compete to capture the attention of the media and the public, but where no real change is possible. Baudrillard suggests that this post-ideological condition marks the end of utopian politics. The *future*, once seen as a space of possibility and transformation, is now reduced to a repetition of the present, where the same patterns of power, consumption, and media spectacle continue to dominate.

The Commodification of Utopia

Baudrillard's analysis of *consumer society* also explores how utopia has been commodified in the postmodern world. In the past, utopian visions were often tied to political movements or philosophical ideas. However, in the age of hyper reality, utopia has been transformed into a *commodity* that can be bought and sold. Advertisements, brands, and lifestyle industries all promote images of a perfect life, offering consumers the illusion that they can achieve their own personal utopia through consumption.

This *commodification of utopia* is most evident in the way that the ideal of a perfect life is marketed to individuals through consumer goods. Whether it's through the promise of a luxurious vacation, a new home, or the latest technology, the consumer society constantly offers individuals the illusion of utopian fulfillment. But for Baudrillard, this is a *false utopia*—one that reinforces the structures of power and inequality rather than challenging them. The pursuit of this commodified utopia keeps individuals trapped in a cycle of consumption, where the promise of happiness and fulfillment is always just out of reach.

The commodification of utopia also extends to the world of *entertainment* and *media*. Hollywood films, for example, often present utopian or dystopian futures as spectacles to be consumed by audiences. These films offer a vision of a better (or worse) world, but they do so in a way that is detached from any real political or social engagement. The utopian future becomes just another form of entertainment, something to be watched and consumed rather than something to be actively pursued or realized.

The Loss of Hope for Radical Change

Baudrillard's critique of the end of utopia is ultimately about the *loss of hope* for *radical change* in the postmodern world. In a hyperreal society, where everything is mediated through images and simulations, the capacity to imagine a radically different future is eroded. The collapse of ideology, the commodification of utopia, and the dominance of the spectacle all contribute to a world where people are more focused on maintaining the present than on envisioning or creating a better future.

For Baudrillard, this loss of utopia is not just a political or social issue; it is a deeper *existential crisis*. Without the ability to imagine a different future, individuals are left in a state of *disenchantment*, where the promise of progress and transformation has been replaced by a sense of *stagnation* and *repetition*. The end of utopia, in Baudrillard's view, marks the end of the belief that the future can be different from the present. In a world dominated by hyper reality, the future becomes an extension of the present, endlessly repeating the same patterns of consumption, spectacle, and control.

Conclusion: The End of Utopia in the Postmodern World

Jean Baudrillard's analysis of the *end of utopia* offers a powerful critique of the postmodern condition. In a world dominated by *hyper reality*, *media spectacle*, and *consumerism*, the capacity to imagine radically different futures has been eroded. Utopia, once a source of hope and inspiration for social and political change, has been absorbed into the logic of hyper reality, where it is transformed into a *simulated utopia*—a commodified, superficial version of the ideal world that reinforces the existing order rather than challenging it.

The collapse of ideology and the commodification of utopia leave individuals in a state of existential disillusionment, where the possibility of radical change seems increasingly out of reach. For Baudrillard, the end of utopia is not just a political failure; it is a sign of a deeper crisis in the modern world, where the dream of a better future has been replaced by the endless repetition of the present.

Baudrillard's Legacy in Contemporary Philosophy

Jean Baudrillard's work remains one of the most profound and controversial contributions to contemporary philosophy. His critiques of *hyper reality*, *simulation*, and the *postmodern condition* have had far-reaching implications, influencing a wide range of fields including philosophy, sociology, media studies, political theory, and cultural criticism. Baudrillard's ability to challenge the very foundations of modern thought has secured his legacy as a pivotal figure in the intellectual landscape of the late 20th and early 21st centuries. His exploration of the *simulated* nature of reality, the dissolution of traditional values, and the rise of *media spectacle* continues to resonate in contemporary discussions about the role of technology, media, and consumerism in shaping human experience.

Hyper reality and the Contemporary World

One of Baudrillard's most influential contributions to contemporary philosophy is his concept of *hyper reality*. This idea, which describes a state in which the boundary between reality and simulation collapses, has become a central lens through which many philosophers and theorists interpret the postmodern world. In the age of digital media, virtual reality, and social media, Baudrillard's ideas about hyper reality seem more relevant than ever.

Hyper reality is particularly applicable to the way contemporary society engages with *digital technology* and *social media*. Platforms like Instagram, Facebook, and Twitter allow individuals to construct highly curated and idealized versions of themselves, blurring the line between their real lives and the virtual personas they create. Baudrillard's critique of how media produces simulations that become more real than reality itself anticipates this phenomenon, where users live within *hyperreal* spaces that feel more authentic than their actual experiences. These digital environments have become so immersive that many people's primary interactions, relationships, and even identities are now formed and sustained through these simulations.

Baudrillard's insights into the power of *media representation* also anticipate the rise of *fake news* and *disinformation* in the digital age. His theory that reality is no longer grounded in material truth but in endlessly circulating images and signs has profound implications for understanding the current state of politics and media. Baudrillard's idea that truth has become just another *simulacrum*—a representation detached from any real referent—offers a framework for understanding how false narratives can thrive in a media ecosystem where representations are more powerful than facts.

The Critique of Consumer Society

Baudrillard's analysis of *consumer society* and the role of *commodities* in shaping identity and social relations has had a lasting influence on contemporary thought. His critique of how consumerism transforms objects into *signs*—imbuing them with symbolic meanings that go beyond their functional use—resonates with current discussions about *branding*, *marketing*, and *identity formation* in late capitalism.

Baudrillard's concept of *sign-value*, where commodities are valued for the symbolic meanings they carry rather than for their practical use, is particularly relevant in today's consumer culture, where products are marketed not just as goods but as extensions of lifestyle, identity, and status.

In contemporary philosophy, Baudrillard's critique of consumerism aligns with discussions about the *ethics of consumption*, the environmental impact of consumer culture, and the psychological effects of constant consumption on individuals. His view that consumerism is a form of *social control*, where individuals are conditioned to define themselves through the objects they consume, has been echoed by theorists who explore the links between capitalism, advertising, and personal identity.

Baudrillard's insights into *hyper-consumption* also anticipate current debates about the *digital economy* and the commodification of data. In a world where individuals' personal data is bought and sold, and where digital products like apps and social media platforms dominate daily life, Baudrillard's critique of the commodification of everything—including identity and privacy—offers a critical perspective on how contemporary capitalism operates.

Post-Modernism and the Death of the Real

Baudrillard's work is often seen as a major contribution to *postmodern philosophy*, particularly his exploration of the *death of the real*. His argument that the real no longer exists as something stable or coherent, and that it has been replaced by a system of simulations and representations, is a defining feature of postmodern thought. For Baudrillard, the traditional understanding of reality—as something objective and knowable—has been undermined by the rise of mass media, consumer culture, and technological reproduction.

Baudrillard's critique of the *collapse of meaning* in the postmodern world resonates with other contemporary philosophical movements that question the nature of reality, truth, and knowledge. For instance, his ideas can be seen in alignment with *post-structuralism*, where philosophers like Jacques Derrida and Michel Foucault explore how power and discourse shape our understanding of reality. Baudrillard's assertion that truth is no longer a stable concept but something that is endlessly deferred through signs and simulations reflects post-structuralist concerns with the instability of meaning.

In contemporary philosophy, Baudrillard's concept of the *precession of simulacra*—where representations precede and determine reality—has been influential in shaping how we think about *media*, *technology*, and *culture*. In an age where digital technologies allow for the infinite reproduction of images, ideas, and identities, Baudrillard's work offers a critical lens through which to understand the *virtualization* of reality and the increasing difficulty of distinguishing between the real and the simulated.

Influence on Political Philosophy

Baudrillard's work also has significant implications for *political philosophy*, particularly his critique of the *spectacle* of politics in the postmodern world. His analysis of how politics has been reduced to a media performance, where political figures are valued more for their image and media presence than for their ideas or policies, has influenced contemporary discussions about the nature of democracy and governance in the digital age.

In many ways, Baudrillard's critique of the *mediated nature of politics* anticipates the rise of *populism* and *celebrity politics*. His insights into how media shapes political reality can be seen in the ways modern politicians often function more as *media figures* than as traditional statesmen. The emphasis on *image management*, *social media engagement*, and the spectacle of political rallies and debates reflects Baudrillard's view that politics has become another form of entertainment, consumed by the public in the same way as other media spectacles.

Baudrillard's critique of the *implosion of meaning* in politics—where distinctions between left and right, truth and falsehood, and even power and resistance have become blurred—offers a framework for understanding the current political climate. In a world where political discourse is dominated by *sound bites*, *memes*, and *viral content*,

Baudrillard's ideas provide a lens for interpreting the *degradation of political meaning* and the rise of *symbolic politics*, where gestures and performances replace substantive engagement with policy or governance.

Cultural Criticism and the Arts

Baudrillard's legacy is also evident in the field of *cultural criticism* and the *arts*. His exploration of *simulation* and *hyper reality* has influenced artists, filmmakers, and cultural critics who seek to explore the boundaries between reality and representation. Baudrillard's work has been particularly influential in the development of *postmodern art*, which often engages with themes of *media saturation, consumerism*, and the blurring of reality and fiction.

Films like *The Matrix* draw directly on Baudrillard's ideas about simulation, exploring the notion that reality is a constructed illusion. The concept of living in a simulated world, where the real and the virtual are indistinguishable, is a key theme in contemporary science fiction and speculative fiction. Baudrillard's work has inspired filmmakers and writers to question the nature of reality, often depicting dystopian futures where media and technology have completely overtaken human life.

In the world of *visual art*, Baudrillard's influence can be seen in the works of artists who engage with *consumer culture* and *media imagery*. Artists like Jeff Koons and Damien Hirst create works that reflect the hyperreal nature of contemporary society, where art itself becomes a commodity and images are endlessly reproduced and consumed. Baudrillard's critique of the commodification of culture resonates with these artists, who challenge the traditional boundaries between high and low culture, reality and simulation.

Continuing Relevance in the Digital Age

Baudrillard's legacy remains particularly relevant in the *digital age*, where the proliferation of virtual environments, social media, and digital identities continues to blur the line between the real and the simulated. In an era of *deepfakes*, *virtual influencers*, and *augmented reality*, Baudrillard's critique of how technology mediates and constructs reality has become even more prescient. The question of what is *real*—and whether the real even matters anymore—is central to ongoing philosophical debates about the future of technology and human experience.

Baudrillard's ideas also resonate in contemporary discussions about the *metaverse*, where virtual worlds and digital experiences are becoming an integral part of everyday life. His concept of hyper reality offers a framework for understanding the implications of living in a world where *virtual reality* and *augmented reality* become as significant as, or even more significant than, the physical world. As society continues to move toward an increasingly digital existence, Baudrillard's critique of the simulated nature of reality will remain a vital tool for philosophers and theorists seeking to understand the future of human experience.

Conclusion: Baudrillard's Enduring Influence

Jean Baudrillard's work has left an indelible mark on contemporary philosophy, offering critical insights into the nature of *reality, media, consumerism*, and *politics* in the postmodern world. His concepts of *hyper reality, simulation*, and the *spectacle* continue to shape how we understand the complexities of modern life, particularly in an era where technology, media, and consumption dominate human experience. Baudrillard's *postmodern critique* challenges many of the assumptions that underpinned modern thought, forcing contemporary philosophers, theorists, and cultural critics to rethink their understanding of reality, truth, and meaning in a world saturated with simulations and representations.

Influence on Critical Theory and Philosophy of Technology

In critical theory, Baudrillard's work has had a profound influence on how scholars approach the *philosophy of technology*. His arguments about how *media and technology shape consciousness* have intersected with discussions about how digital technologies mediate human interaction and transform social relations. Baudrillard's critique of hyper reality is particularly relevant in discussions about how social media platforms and algorithms manipulate behavior, creating a reality that is increasingly mediated by digital systems.

Contemporary philosophers and theorists such as *Mark Fisher, Paul Virilio*, and *Franco "Bifo" Berardi* have drawn on Baudrillard's work to explore the implications of living in a world where technology blurs the line between *physical presence* and *virtual reality*. These thinkers further develop Baudrillard's insights to analyze how *speed, information overload*, and *media saturation* affect human perception and political consciousness in the digital age. Baudrillard's concept of *virtualization*—where the real and the digital merge—has become central to discussions on topics ranging from *cybernetics* to *artificial intelligence*.

The Relevance of Baudrillard in Political Theory

Baudrillard's reflections on the *spectacle of politics* continue to be significant in understanding the *mediatisation of politics* and the rise of *political populism*. In the contemporary world, where political discourse is often reduced to *sound bites, viral moments*, and *memetic politics*, Baudrillard's critique of the *emptying of meaning* in political rhetoric is more relevant than ever. The performative nature of modern political campaigns, where image and media presence outweigh substantive policy discussions, reflects Baudrillard's observations about the reduction of politics to spectacle.

Moreover, Baudrillard's analysis of how *power* and *resistance* become entangled in the hyperreal world challenges contemporary political theorists to rethink how political change can occur in a world where everything—including resistance—can be commodified and transformed into a spectacle. This critique has been expanded by scholars analyzing *late capitalism, neoliberalism*, and the role of the media in shaping political reality. The lines between *revolution* and *marketing, dissent* and *performance*, are increasingly blurred, highlighting Baudrillard's foresight in understanding the co-option of political movements by the media and consumer culture.

Baudrillard in Post-Truth and Contemporary Media Studies

In the current era of *post-truth* politics, Baudrillard's notion that *truth* has become just another sign in the marketplace of ideas has proven strikingly prescient. His concept of *simulacra*—the idea that representations no longer reflect any underlying reality but exist only in relation to one another—has helped theorists explore how falsehoods and *disinformation* spread in the digital age. The rise of *fake news* and *deepfake technology* illustrates how Baudrillard's ideas about the collapse of truth in favor of an endless play of signs have materialized in the real world.

In media studies, Baudrillard's theories about the *implosion of meaning* and the creation of a *media-constructed reality* continue to shape critical examinations of how media *frames reality* and *controls public discourse*. His work has laid the foundation for understanding how news media, film, television, and social media shape our perceptions of the world by curating specific images, stories, and narratives that simulate reality. This manipulation of reality—creating a media-driven version of events that can overshadow or replace the real—is one of the core principles in understanding contemporary issues of *media manipulation, propaganda*, and *censorship*.

Baudrillard's Impact on Cultural and Aesthetic Theory

In the world of *cultural theory*, Baudrillard's insights into the *aestheticization of everyday life* and the *commodification of culture* have had lasting effects. His notion that *art, culture*, and even *identity* have been subsumed by the logic of *commodification*—where everything becomes a product for consumption—resonates deeply with contemporary thinkers examining *neoliberalism* and the culture industry. Baudrillard's critique of how art and culture have been reduced to simulacra, with no distinction between high and low culture, is particularly relevant in discussions about how *mass culture* and *branding* shape social values and personal identities.

His work has also influenced the field of *visual culture*, where his concepts are used to explore how *visual media*—from advertising to film—constructs and reproduces social meanings. In an age where images circulate globally and rapidly through platforms like Instagram and TikTok, Baudrillard's ideas help frame the *hyper reality* of cultural production, where images become more real and influential than the subjects they depict. Baudrillard's critique of how culture becomes a *loop of endless reproduction* has helped theorists understand how digital media produces and consumes images in ways that flatten reality into a surface of signs.

Baudrillard and the Future

As we move deeper into the *digital age*, Baudrillard's work continues to serve as a critical framework for understanding the changing nature of reality, identity, and power. The ongoing development of technologies such as *virtual reality, artificial intelligence*, and the *metaverse* makes Baudrillard's theories on *simulation* and *hyper reality* more relevant than ever. The blending of virtual and physical worlds, and the increasing reliance on *digital mediation* in everyday life, reflect the deepening entanglement of the real and the simulated that Baudrillard so powerfully theorized.

Baudrillard's work remains a touchstone for *contemporary philosophers* grappling with the consequences of living in a world where *media, technology*, and *capitalism* increasingly shape human experience. His legacy endures in the ongoing critical examination of how we understand reality, how we navigate identity in a hyperreal world, and how we confront the *ethical and political challenges* of a future where simulations and representations increasingly dictate the terms of existence.

Conclusion: Baudrillard's Enduring Legacy

Jean Baudrillard's legacy in contemporary philosophy is profound and enduring. His concepts of *hyper reality, simulation*, and *the spectacle* continue to influence a wide array of fields, from political theory and media studies to cultural criticism and philosophy of technology. In an era marked by *digital immersion, media saturation*, and the commodification of all aspects of life, Baudrillard's ideas remain central to understanding the nature of reality and power in the postmodern world.

Baudrillard's work offers a critical lens through which to examine the challenges of the modern age, where *truth, identity*, and *meaning* are constantly in flux, mediated through technologies that increasingly blur the boundaries between the real and the virtual. His enduring influence lies in his ability to challenge the very foundations of how we think about reality, providing a philosophical framework that remains vital in an age dominated by simulation and spectacle.

Baudrillard's Critique of Mass Media Culture

Jean Baudrillard's critique of *mass media culture* is one of the most incisive elements of his philosophy, focusing on how mass media shapes and distorts reality, and ultimately contributes to the collapse of meaning in the postmodern world. Baudrillard argues that the *media* has transformed society's understanding of reality by producing a world of *simulations* and *representations* that replace direct experiences of the real. In his view, mass media creates a *hyperreal* environment in which images, signs, and spectacles become more real and influential than actual events. This process of *mediatization* leads to the erosion of truth, the commodification of information, and the creation of a passive society that consumes pre-packaged realities instead of engaging with the real world.

The Media as a Producer of Hyper reality

At the heart of Baudrillard's critique is the idea that mass media is not a neutral transmitter of information but a powerful force that constructs reality itself. In Baudrillard's framework, media does not simply reflect the world; it produces a new kind of reality—one that is dominated by *simulacra* and *hyper reality*. Simulacra, in Baudrillard's philosophy, refer to copies or representations that no longer refer to any original reality. Instead, they generate their own reality, creating a world where the distinction between the real and the simulated is increasingly blurred.

Baudrillard's concept of *hyper reality* describes a state where mediated images and representations become more real than reality itself. Mass media, particularly through television, cinema, and the internet, creates a *continuous flow of images*, narratives, and spectacles that shape people's perceptions of the world. In this environment, people's experiences of reality are mediated through *screens*, and the images they consume come to feel more immediate and powerful than their own lived experiences.

An example of hyper reality in action is how media coverage of events like wars, disasters, or political scandals often becomes more significant than the events themselves. For Baudrillard, the media's representation of an event takes on a life of its own, overshadowing the real event with a *media-constructed narrative* that is consumed as if it were the event itself. The Gulf War, for instance, became a media spectacle where images of precision bombing and military technology were broadcast around the world, creating a hyperreal version of the conflict that obscured the actual human suffering on the ground. Baudrillard famously argued in *The Gulf War Did Not Take Place* that the media's portrayal of the war was so mediated and abstracted that the reality of the conflict was essentially replaced by the images and narratives produced by the media.

The Spectacle and the Commodification of Information

Baudrillard's critique of mass media culture is also tied to his analysis of the *spectacle*, a concept he developed alongside Guy Debord's *The Society of the Spectacle*. In the mass media environment, everything becomes a *spectacle*—a carefully constructed performance designed to capture attention and generate emotional responses. News, entertainment, politics, and even personal identity are all transformed into spectacles that prioritize *image* and *emotion* over truth or substance.

One of Baudrillard's key arguments is that the *commodification of information* has turned the media into a marketplace of signs, where information is packaged and sold like any other commodity. News is not simply a matter of reporting facts or uncovering truth; it is a *product* designed to attract viewers, readers, and clicks. The logic of the market dictates that the most *sensational, dramatic*, or *emotionally charged* stories will receive the most attention, leading to a media environment where *spectacle* takes precedence over critical analysis or nuanced understanding.

In this commodified media landscape, even serious political issues are reduced to *entertainment*, where complex problems are simplified into *digestible sound bites* or *dramatic images*. This transformation of information into spectacle creates a passive society, where citizens are no longer engaged with the realities of the world around them but are instead consumers of a pre-packaged reality that is mediated and manipulated by the media. Baudrillard argues that this process undermines the possibility of genuine political discourse, as the media spectacle replaces meaningful debate with emotionally driven narratives that serve commercial interests.

The Passive Consumer and the Implosion of Meaning

One of the most significant consequences of mass media culture, according to Baudrillard, is the creation of a passive society. In his analysis, individuals in a media-saturated world are no longer *active agents* in shaping their own reality but passive *consumers* of the media spectacle. The media presents a pre-constructed version of reality, and individuals consume this version without questioning its accuracy or considering alternative perspectives.

Baudrillard argues that this passivity is reinforced by the *sheer volume of information* that people are bombarded with on a daily basis. In the mass media environment, individuals are exposed to an overwhelming number of images, stories, and narratives that are constantly competing for their attention. This endless stream of information leads to what Baudrillard calls the *implosion of meaning*. In this state, the constant circulation of images and signs makes it impossible to distinguish between *meaningful* and *meaningless* information. Everything is consumed in the same way, regardless of its importance or connection to reality.

For Baudrillard, the media's role in creating this implosion of meaning is deeply problematic. In a world where images and signs circulate endlessly, meaning itself becomes *fragmented* and *unstable*. The distinction between *truth* and *falsehood*, *reality* and *illusion*, collapses, creating a society where individuals are unable to make sense of the world. In this environment, critical thinking is replaced by *emotional reaction*, and the capacity for *collective action* is eroded, as people are too overwhelmed by the spectacle to engage with the real problems facing society.

The Media's Role in Shaping Politics

Baudrillard's critique of mass media culture extends to the realm of *politics*, where he argues that the media has transformed political life into a *spectacle* that is more concerned with *image* than with substance. In Baudrillard's view, political figures are no longer judged by their policies or ideas but by their ability to perform within the media environment. Political campaigns are increasingly driven by *media strategies*, where the goal is not to engage in serious debate or to propose meaningful solutions but to create the most compelling spectacle.

In this sense, Baudrillard argues that *politics* has been absorbed into the logic of mass media culture, where the line between *entertainment* and *politics* is increasingly blurred. The rise of political figures who are skilled at manipulating the media—whether through *charisma, controversy,* or *image management*—reflects this transformation of politics into spectacle. Baudrillard's analysis can be seen in the contemporary political landscape, where social media, reality television, and viral content play a central role in shaping public opinion and determining the success of political candidates.

Baudrillard also critiques the way the media constructs *political reality*. Just as the media produces hyperreal versions of events like wars or disasters, it also creates a hyperreal version of politics, where *media representation* becomes more important than the reality of governance. In this environment, political debates are often reduced to *sound bites* or *emotionally charged spectacles* that are designed to entertain rather than inform. The result is a political culture where citizens are more likely to engage with *performances* of politics—such as televised debates or social media controversies—than with the actual policy decisions that affect their lives.

The Role of Media in the Production of Terrorism

One of Baudrillard's more controversial arguments is his claim that mass media plays a role in the production of *terrorism* as a spectacle. In Baudrillard's analysis, terrorism in the modern world is not just a political or military tactic but a *symbolic challenge* to the hyperreal system of media and power. Terrorist acts, particularly in the age of global media, are designed to create *spectacles* that disrupt the media-dominated world order. For Baudrillard, the media's amplification of terrorist acts turns them into global events, where the *symbolic power* of the act often outweighs its material impact.

Baudrillard argues that the media's portrayal of terrorist attacks, such as the 9/11 attacks, transforms them into hyperreal spectacles that are consumed by global audiences. The media's constant replaying of images of destruction, chaos, and fear turns terrorism into a *media event*, where the spectacle itself becomes the primary focus. In this sense, terrorism functions within the same logic as the media, using *images* and *spectacle* to create fear, destabilize societies, and challenge the hyperreal world order.

Conclusion: Mass Media and the Loss of the Real

Jean Baudrillard's critique of mass media culture offers a powerful analysis of how the media has transformed society's relationship with reality. In his view, mass media does not simply report on the world; it produces a new kind of *hyper reality*, where representations and simulations replace direct experiences of the real. The media's focus on spectacle, its commodification of information, and its role in shaping political and social life all contribute to the erosion of meaning in the postmodern world.

Baudrillard's work challenges us to critically examine the role of the media in shaping our perceptions of reality, urging us to question the images, narratives, and spectacles that we consume on a daily basis. His analysis of mass media culture highlights the dangers of living in a world where *simulations* become more real than reality itself, where meaning is constantly fragmented and reconstituted in the service of spectacle and *consumerism*. For Baudrillard, the media is not merely an intermediary between individuals and the real world, but rather the force that constructs and dictates the terms of reality itself. As a result, the media's role in society is far more insidious than just reporting or entertainment—it shapes collective consciousness and dictates social behavior, all while eroding the distinctions between truth and falsehood, reality and fiction.

The Media's Creation of a Passive Society

Baudrillard's notion that the mass media produces a *passive society* is particularly relevant to discussions about modern media consumption. In his view, the overwhelming presence of media saturates everyday life to the point where people no longer engage with the world directly but through the *filter of media representation*. Television, social media, and the internet become the primary avenues through which individuals experience reality. This mediated reality creates *spectator-consumers* who are conditioned to passively observe rather than actively participate in shaping their own lives or society.

The passivity that Baudrillard describes manifests in several ways. First, the *endless bombardment* of media content makes critical thinking increasingly difficult. In a world where attention spans are constantly fractured by the rapid influx of images, headlines, and social media posts, the capacity for deep reflection or sustained engagement with complex issues is diminished. Instead, individuals consume fragmented narratives that prioritize *emotion* and *spectacle* over substance.

Furthermore, Baudrillard argues that this passivity is compounded by the media's ability to *recycle* and *reproduce* content in ways that blur the boundaries between reality and entertainment. When serious social issues—such as political conflicts, environmental crises, or social movements—are packaged as *entertainment spectacles*, they lose their urgency and become just another commodity for consumption. As a result, individuals are lulled into a state of *inaction*, where they are constantly exposed to problems but feel powerless to address them.

The Erosion of Public Discourse

Baudrillard's critique of mass media also highlights the *erosion of public discourse* in the age of media spectacle. In the classical sense, public discourse was a space for *rational debate* and *deliberation* on important social and political issues. However, Baudrillard argues that the media has transformed public discourse into a spectacle driven by *emotion* and *manipulation* rather than reasoned argument. Television talk shows, viral social media debates, and sensationalized news reports prioritize *conflict* and *entertainment value* over meaningful discussion.

This erosion of discourse has profound implications for democracy. Baudrillard suggests that in a media-driven world, the ideal of an *informed citizenry*—engaged in thoughtful reflection and debate—has been replaced by a population that is conditioned to respond to *images* and *emotional appeals*. In this environment, political decisions are increasingly based on media performances rather than policy substance, and citizens are encouraged to *consume* politics as a form of entertainment rather than actively participate in shaping their society.

The consequences of this transformation are particularly evident in *electoral politics*. Political campaigns are now media spectacles, where candidates are judged by their ability to deliver sound bites, manage their public image, and capture the attention of viewers through media strategies. Debates become theatrical performances, and elections are increasingly won or lost on the basis of *media management* rather than the depth of the candidate's policies.

Baudrillard's critique suggests that this transformation undermines the foundations of democracy, as the media's control over political representation makes genuine democratic engagement difficult, if not impossible.

The Media and the Spectacle of Catastrophe

Baudrillard also examines how the media's portrayal of *catastrophes*—whether natural disasters, wars, or pandemics—follows the logic of spectacle. In the media, catastrophic events are transformed into *hyperreal spectacles* that are consumed by global audiences. These spectacles are characterized by their focus on *dramatic imagery*, *emotional narratives*, and *sensationalism*, rather than by thoughtful analysis or meaningful engagement with the causes and consequences of the event.

One of Baudrillard's key concerns is that the media's focus on the *spectacle of catastrophe* often *obscures the reality* of the situation. For example, media coverage of war frequently emphasizes the visual drama of destruction—bombings, explosions, and military operations—while neglecting the deeper political, social, and humanitarian dimensions of the conflict.

The result is a media narrative that turns suffering into a consumable product, where viewers are exposed to the spectacle of violence without being encouraged to critically reflect on its causes or consequences.

In addition, Baudrillard argues that the *repetition* of catastrophe in the media creates a form of *desensitization*. Audiences are exposed to so many images of disaster and destruction that they become numb to the real suffering behind the spectacle. This desensitization contributes to the *passive consumption* of catastrophe, where viewers observe but do not act, feel outrage but do not mobilize for change. The spectacle of catastrophe becomes another form of media entertainment, further reinforcing the *passivity* that Baudrillard critiques.

Media and the Disappearance of the Real

At the core of Baudrillard's critique is the idea that the media contributes to the *disappearance of the real*. In a world dominated by media representations, Baudrillard argues that reality itself is increasingly *constructed* by the media rather than experienced directly. This leads to a situation where the *real* becomes indistinguishable from its *representation*, and individuals can no longer tell the difference between what is real and what is simulated.

In Baudrillard's view, the media's ability to *shape perceptions of reality* means that it plays a central role in creating a world of *simulations*. From political campaigns to reality television, the media produces representations that are consumed as reality, even though they are carefully constructed performances. This blurring of the line between reality and simulation creates a *hyperreal* environment in which individuals are no longer sure what is real and what is fabricated.

One of Baudrillard's most striking claims is that this disappearance of the real extends to *individual identity*. In a media-saturated world, people begin to *construct their identities* through the images and narratives that the media provides. Social media platforms, in particular, offer individuals the opportunity to curate their own identities, presenting themselves to the world through carefully crafted images and posts. This process of *self-curation* leads to a situation where individuals are not living authentic lives but are instead performing *simulated versions* of themselves, shaped by the expectations of media and consumer culture.

Conclusion: Baudrillard's Critique and the Future of Media

Jean Baudrillard's critique of mass media culture offers a profound analysis of how media shapes contemporary reality, eroding the distinction between the real and the simulated, and transforming society into a *passive* audience that consumes spectacle rather than engaging with the world. His work challenges us to critically examine the role of the media in shaping our perceptions, our identities, and our understanding of the world.

Baudrillard's insights into the *commodification of information*, the transformation of politics into spectacle, and the media's role in creating *hyper reality* remain highly relevant in the digital age, where new forms of media continue to shape human experience in unprecedented ways. As we move further into a world dominated by *social media*, *virtual reality*, and *algorithm-driven content*, Baudrillard's critique of mass media culture provides a crucial framework for understanding the deeper implications of living in a society where reality is increasingly mediated through screens.

The future of media, in Baudrillard's view, may involve an even deeper entanglement between the real and the simulated, as technologies such as *artificial intelligence, virtual influencers,* and *deepfake videos* push the boundaries of what is real. Baudrillard's legacy lies in his ability to anticipate these developments and to offer a critical perspective on the ways in which media, as a producer of *hyper reality*, shapes not only our understanding of the world but also our very capacity to engage with reality in a meaningful way.

Capitalism, Simulation, and the Consumer Society

Jean Baudrillard's exploration of *capitalism, simulation*, and the *consumer society* offers a profound critique of how contemporary capitalism operates, not through the production of goods but through the production of *signs*, *images*, and *simulations*. His work reveals that in the late stages of capitalism, the economy is no longer based solely on the exchange of material goods or services but on the *circulation of signs and symbols* that shape identity, desire, and social relations. Baudrillard's analysis of the *consumer society* emphasizes how consumption, rather than production, has become the primary driver of capitalist economies and how this shift has transformed the way individuals relate to objects, themselves, and each other.

The Transformation from Production to Consumption

One of Baudrillard's central arguments is that modern capitalist society has undergone a transformation from a *production-based economy* to a *consumption-based economy*. In the early stages of capitalism, wealth was generated through the production of goods, and the value of an object was tied to its *utility* and *labor*. However, Baudrillard argues that in late capitalism, the focus has shifted from the production of goods to the *production of desires*, *images*, and *lifestyles*. Capitalism is no longer concerned primarily with satisfying basic human needs but with generating endless cycles of consumption.

In this *consumer society*, individuals are not simply purchasing goods for their functional use but for their *symbolic value*. Baudrillard introduces the concept of *sign-value*, where objects are consumed not for their practical utility but for the social meanings they carry. In this system, products become *signs* that communicate status, identity, and belonging. For example, purchasing a luxury car is not just about transportation—it's about signaling wealth, success, or membership in a particular social class. Similarly, wearing designer clothing is less about comfort or durability and more about projecting an image of style, sophistication, or social superiority.

Baudrillard's insight into the shift from *use-value* to *sign-value* reveals the deep connection between capitalism and the creation of *simulations*. In a consumer society, goods are no longer valued for what they are but for what they represent. The symbolic meanings attached to commodities become more important than their material existence. This shift is central to Baudrillard's broader critique of *hyper reality*, where the distinction between the real and the simulated collapses, and individuals navigate a world dominated by signs and images rather than direct engagement with reality.

Simulation and the Commodification of Everything

Baudrillard argues that capitalism in its contemporary form is defined by its ability to *commodify everything*. Not only are material goods commodified, but so too are experiences, emotions, identities, and even *reality itself*. The process of *commodification* transforms everything into a product that can be bought, sold, and consumed. This includes not just objects but also abstract concepts such as *love, happiness, adventure*, and *self-expression*—all of which are packaged and sold through advertising, entertainment, and lifestyle branding.

The *advertising industry* plays a central role in this process of commodification by attaching symbolic meanings to products, turning them into *simulacra*. Advertisements do not sell products based on their material properties; they sell *lifestyles, emotions*, and *experiences*. For example, an ad for a vacation package doesn't just sell a trip to a tropical destination—it sells the promise of escape, relaxation, and happiness. Similarly, a perfume ad doesn't just sell a fragrance—it sells the fantasy of love, seduction, and desirability. These symbolic meanings create *simulated experiences* that replace the real, as consumers are drawn into the world of *images and fantasies* promoted by advertising.

Baudrillard's critique of *simulation* extends to the commodification of *identity* itself. In the consumer society, individuals construct their identities through the consumption of goods and experiences, choosing products that reflect their desired image or lifestyle. The process of *self-creation* becomes a matter of selecting from a range of commodified identities offered by the market. This creates a situation where identity is no longer something inherent or authentic but something that is constantly constructed and reconstructed through the consumption of signs and symbols. For Baudrillard, this leads to the *disappearance of the real self* and the rise of *simulated identities* that are shaped by the logic of capitalism.

The Role of Objects in the Consumer Society

Baudrillard's analysis of the role of *objects* in the consumer society reveals the shift from their material function to their symbolic power. He argues that in contemporary capitalism, objects are not simply tools or resources—they are *signs* that convey *social meaning*. The meaning of an object is not tied to its utility but to the social status, lifestyle, or identity it represents. This is why, in a consumer society, the value of an object is determined not by its usefulness but by its ability to signal membership in a particular social group or to express a desired image.

Baudrillard's theory of objects is closely tied to his concept of *fetishism*, where commodities are imbued with an almost magical power to represent and communicate desires. This *commodity fetishism* is not new to capitalism—it was a central feature of Marx's analysis of capitalist society—but Baudrillard takes it further by arguing that in the late capitalist era, the fetishization of commodities has become all-encompassing. Objects are no longer just useful things; they are *fetishized symbols* of power, success, and identity, and their consumption is tied to the pursuit of these symbolic values.

For Baudrillard, this transformation of objects into symbols has profound consequences for how individuals relate to the world. Rather than engaging with objects for their practical value, people become obsessed with *accumulating signs* that enhance their social status or reinforce their identity. This process creates an *endless cycle of consumption*, where the pursuit of new objects is driven not by need but by the desire to keep up with constantly shifting social meanings. In this sense, the consumer society is marked by a kind of *hyper-consumption*, where people are trapped in a cycle of accumulating objects that offer temporary satisfaction but never fulfill deeper desires or needs.

The Myth of Choice and Freedom

Baudrillard's critique of the consumer society also addresses the illusion of *choice* and *freedom* that capitalism promotes. In a consumer-driven world, individuals are presented with an endless array of options—what to buy, where to live, how to dress, how to express themselves. This abundance of choices creates the illusion that individuals have the freedom to shape their own lives and identities. However, Baudrillard argues that this freedom is an illusion because the choices available are determined by the logic of the market and are constrained within the boundaries of the consumer society.

In the consumer society, *freedom* is reduced to the freedom to choose between pre-packaged identities, lifestyles, and experiences. The market dictates what is desirable, fashionable, or valuable, and individuals are guided by advertising and social pressures to make choices that reinforce the existing system. In this sense, Baudrillard argues that *consumer freedom* is not real freedom; it is a form of *social control*, where individuals are conditioned to desire and consume in ways that support the capitalist system. The appearance of freedom masks the deeper reality of *conformity* and *dependence* on the structures of consumption.

This critique is particularly relevant in the context of *digital capitalism*, where platforms like social media and e-commerce sites offer individuals the ability to *curate their lives* through consumption. The algorithms that guide online shopping, content consumption, and social interactions create the illusion of personalized freedom, but Baudrillard would argue that these algorithms are designed to reinforce *patterns of consumption* that benefit corporations and advertisers. The choices that individuals make in the digital world are shaped by the *invisible structures* of capitalism, which guide them toward certain products, experiences, and identities.

Capitalism and the Collapse of Meaning

One of Baudrillard's most radical critiques of capitalism is his argument that it leads to the *collapse of meaning*. In the consumer society, the endless circulation of *signs and symbols* creates a world where meaning becomes *fragmented* and *unstable*. Objects, experiences, and identities are constantly redefined through the logic of consumption, and the meanings attached to them are always shifting in response to changes in fashion, trends, and advertising. This creates a situation where nothing has a stable or inherent meaning; everything is a *floating signifier* that can be transformed and commodified.

Baudrillard's concept of *hyper reality* is central to this critique. In a hyperreal world, the distinction between the real and the simulated disappears, and meaning is produced not by direct experience but by the circulation of images, signs, and representations. The consumer society, with its emphasis on *sign-value* and *symbolic consumption*, contributes to the creation of hyper reality, where meaning is no longer grounded in reality but is constantly *reproduced and manipulated* by the media, advertising, and the market.

In this hyperreal world, Baudrillard argues that the *real* is replaced by *simulacra*—representations that have no connection to any underlying reality. The result is a society where individuals are trapped in a cycle of consuming *simulations of meaning* rather than engaging with any stable or authentic reality. This leads to a deep sense of *alienation*, where people are disconnected from the real world and from themselves, caught in a system that offers endless choices and identities but no real fulfillment or meaning.

Conclusion: Baudrillard's Critique of Capitalism and Consumerism

Jean Baudrillard's analysis of capitalism, simulation, and the consumer society offers a powerful critique of the way late capitalism operates by turning everything into a commodity and reducing human existence to a series of *simulations* and *consumable signs*. His work reveals how contemporary capitalism, through the mechanisms of *advertising*, *media*, and *consumer culture*, shifts focus away from the production of material goods toward the creation of *desires*, *fantasies*, and *lifestyles*. This transformation leads to a world where individuals are no longer primarily defined by their roles as producers but as consumers navigating an endless cycle of sign consumption.

Baudrillard argues that in the *consumer society*, objects, experiences, and even *identities* are commodified and sold as symbols of status, success, or belonging. As consumption becomes the dominant form of social and personal expression, individuals construct their lives through the accumulation of objects and signs, engaging in an endless pursuit of *meaning* that can never be fully satisfied. This constant desire for *the new*, for the *next product* or *trend*, traps people in a cycle of consumption that, instead of liberating them, reinforces the existing structures of capitalism and prevents any deeper form of fulfillment.

The Role of Hyper reality in Consumer Capitalism

Baudrillard's concept of *hyper reality* plays a central role in his critique of consumer capitalism. In a hyperreal world, the boundary between the real and the simulated is dissolved, and individuals live in a reality constructed by *signs, images, and media representations*. The consumer society thrives on this hyper reality, where commodities are imbued with *symbolic meanings* that are more important than their practical uses. Products are marketed not based on their utility but on the lifestyle, emotion, or *social identity* they promise to deliver.

For example, a brand of sneakers is not simply footwear; it becomes a symbol of *youth, rebellion,* or *athleticism,* depending on how it is marketed. This *sign-value* dominates the meaning of the product, and consumers are drawn to it not for what it can do but for what it represents. In this sense, capitalism in the hyperreal world creates an economy of *signs,* where people consume symbols and images rather than real objects or experiences.

Baudrillard's critique extends to how the media reinforces this hyper reality by constantly producing and circulating images that shape desires and expectations. Advertising plays a key role in this process, as it creates simulations of perfect lives, bodies, and identities that people aspire to but can never fully attain. These *simulated desires* drive consumer behavior, keeping individuals locked in a cycle of perpetual consumption, where each new purchase offers only temporary satisfaction before being replaced by a desire for the next simulation.

The Loss of Authenticity and the Rise of Simulated Identities

One of Baudrillard's most poignant critiques is the idea that in the consumer society, *authenticity* has been replaced by *simulation.* Individuals are no longer defined by their intrinsic qualities, but by the *commodities* and *images* they consume. The self, in Baudrillard's view, becomes a *performance* constructed through the consumption of signs, with identity being continually reshaped by the changing symbols of the marketplace.

Social media, in particular, has amplified this phenomenon, where platforms like Instagram and Facebook enable users to construct highly curated versions of themselves, presenting an idealized or simulated identity to the world. Baudrillard's theory of simulation suggests that this process of identity construction is a form of *self-fetishization,* where people turn themselves into *commodities* that are consumed by others through *likes, follows,* and *shares.* The self becomes fragmented, reduced to images and symbols, as individuals increasingly define themselves by how they are perceived rather than who they are.

This loss of *authenticity* creates a world where *simulated identities* become more significant than real experiences or personal truths. People live through representations of themselves, engaging with others through *mediated performances* that reflect the expectations and desires shaped by consumer culture. In this environment, the self is continually *commodified* and *marketed,* reinforcing Baudrillard's critique of how capitalism penetrates even the most personal aspects of human life, transforming them into part of the system of consumption.

Capitalism, Desire, and the Endless Cycle of Consumption

Baudrillard's exploration of the role of *desire* in capitalism is central to understanding how the system perpetuates itself. In traditional economic terms, people consume to satisfy needs, but in Baudrillard's analysis, capitalism generates *endless desires* that can never be fully satisfied. The consumer society does not operate by meeting material needs but by producing new desires that drive consumption in perpetuity. These desires are manufactured by the media, advertising, and cultural narratives that promise fulfillment, happiness, or status through consumption.

This process creates what Baudrillard calls the *myth of satisfaction*. Every commodity promises to fulfill a desire or solve a problem, but once consumed, it fails to deliver the deep satisfaction it promised, leading the individual to seek out another commodity. This cycle of desire and disappointment is essential to the functioning of consumer capitalism, as it ensures the continual flow of consumption without ever providing real satisfaction.

Baudrillard's critique of desire also touches on the deeper *psychological impact* of living in a consumer society. People are conditioned to seek meaning and fulfillment through external commodities rather than through *internal reflection* or personal growth. The consumer society teaches individuals that their worth is tied to the objects they own, the brands they wear, and the experiences they can display, creating a form of *existential alienation* where people are disconnected from their true selves and dependent on external signs for validation.

The Political Implications of Consumer Capitalism

Baudrillard's critique of consumer society also carries important *political implications*. He argues that the focus on consumption and the creation of simulated realities has depoliticized society. In a world dominated by consumerism, individuals are more concerned with the *pursuit of commodities* than with social change or political engagement. The capitalist system, in this view, neutralizes dissent by offering the illusion of freedom through consumption. The ability to choose between products or lifestyles creates the appearance of personal autonomy, but this autonomy is confined within the logic of the marketplace, where deeper forms of freedom or resistance are absent.

In this depoliticized society, *social movements* and *collective action* are often co-opted by the same system they seek to challenge. For instance, countercultural movements that begin as forms of resistance against the capitalist system are quickly commodified and transformed into marketable lifestyles. Baudrillard's analysis suggests that the capitalist system is so pervasive that even attempts to resist it are absorbed into its logic, further reinforcing the structures of consumption and simulation.

Moreover, Baudrillard's critique extends to the *role of media* in shaping political consciousness. In the consumer society, media functions as a tool for reinforcing the status quo by framing political debates and social issues through the lens of spectacle and entertainment. Serious political issues are reduced to sound bites, while public discourse is shaped by *media narratives* that prioritize *emotion* over *substance*.

This creates a political environment where individuals are more likely to engage with the *performances of politics*—such as political scandals, social media controversies, or viral moments—than with the deeper structural issues that affect society.

Conclusion: Baudrillard's Critique of Capitalism, Simulation, and Consumerism

Jean Baudrillard's critique of *capitalism, simulation,* and the *consumer society* provides a profound analysis of how contemporary capitalism operates through the production of *signs, images,* and *simulated desires*. In a world dominated by *hyper reality*, individuals are increasingly defined not by their real experiences or authentic identities but by the *commodities* they consume and the *images* they project. Capitalism, in Baudrillard's view, has transformed society into a space where consumption is the primary mode of existence, and where the pursuit of endless desires drives individuals into a cycle of consumption without fulfillment.

Baudrillard's work challenges us to critically examine the way *consumer capitalism* shapes our lives, identities, and relationships with others. His critique of the *illusion of freedom*, the *commodification of identity*, and the *disappearance of the real* remains highly relevant in a world increasingly dominated by *digital media*, *virtual reality*, and *social media*. Baudrillard's insights offer a powerful lens through which to understand the deeper implications of living in a consumer society, where *simulation*, rather than reality, dictates the terms of existence.

Baudrillard and the Disappearance of the Subject

Jean Baudrillard's concept of the *disappearance of the subject* is central to his critique of *postmodernity*, *hyper reality*, and *consumer culture*. In his analysis, the modern subject—the autonomous individual who possesses agency, self-awareness, and a coherent identity—has been undermined by the rise of *simulacra*, *media saturation*, and the relentless demands of *consumerism*. Baudrillard argues that, in the postmodern world, the subject is no longer the center of experience or meaning but has been *fragmented* and *dispersed* by the forces of *representation* and *simulation* that dominate contemporary life.

The Traditional Subject in Modern Thought

In classical philosophy and modern thought, the concept of the *subject* has been central to discussions of *consciousness*, *agency*, and *identity*. Thinkers from *Descartes* to *Kant* to *Hegel* have emphasized the idea that the individual subject is the foundation of experience, responsible for interpreting the world and making decisions. The subject, in this framework, is seen as *self-aware*, *rational*, and *autonomous*, possessing the ability to act upon the world and shape its course.

In the *modernist* period, particularly during the Enlightenment, the subject was considered the core of human experience, capable of making rational decisions and interpreting the world through reason. Even later, with the rise of *existentialism*, thinkers like *Jean-Paul Sartre* and *Simone de Beauvoir* placed great emphasis on individual *freedom* and *responsibility*, arguing that the subject is defined by its choices and its capacity for *self-creation*.

However, Baudrillard argues that this traditional concept of the subject has been rendered obsolete by the conditions of the *postmodern* world. According to Baudrillard, the subject no longer holds the same central position in relation to reality, truth, or meaning. Instead, the subject has been displaced by the overwhelming power of *media*, *technological systems*, and *consumerism*, which generate a new kind of reality in which the subject is no longer in control.

The Fragmentation of the Subject in Postmodernity

In Baudrillard's analysis, the subject has been *fragmented* by the rise of *media* and *simulation*. With the advent of mass media and digital technology, individuals no longer experience the world directly but through a network of images, signs, and representations. These *mediated experiences* fragment the subject's sense of self, as identity becomes shaped by the constant flow of media content and the endless consumption of images.

Baudrillard argues that in the postmodern world, the subject is no longer a coherent, autonomous entity. Instead, it becomes a *product* of the systems of *representation* that dominate society. Media, advertising, and consumer culture all play a role in constructing the subject's identity, but this identity is not stable or authentic. Instead, it is *fluid* and *performative*, constantly shaped and reshaped by external forces rather than by the individual's inner sense of self.

One key example of this fragmentation is the rise of *social media*, where individuals construct their identities through carefully curated images, posts, and interactions. On platforms like Instagram or Facebook, users often present a version of themselves that is *highly constructed* and mediated by the expectations of the platform and its audience. This self-curation leads to a kind of *simulated identity*, where the subject is no longer grounded in an authentic experience of the self but in the representation of the self to others.

This fragmentation of the subject is deeply tied to Baudrillard's critique of *consumerism*. In a consumer society, individuals are encouraged to define themselves through the products they buy, the lifestyles they emulate, and the images they project. The subject becomes a *consumer of signs*, using objects and commodities to create a version of the self that is always in flux, always contingent upon the shifting trends of the marketplace. This endless consumption of identities erodes any sense of a stable or coherent self, as the subject is constantly being *redefined* by external forces.

Simulation and the Disappearance of the Real Subject

Baudrillard's concept of *simulation* further explains the disappearance of the subject. In the postmodern world, reality itself is increasingly mediated by *simulacra*—copies of reality that have no original referent. This leads to the condition of *hyper reality*, where individuals experience not the real world but an endless circulation of signs and images that stand in for reality. In this hyperreal environment, the subject no longer interacts with the world directly but through simulations that blur the line between the real and the imaginary.

For Baudrillard, this simulation process results in the *disappearance* of the real subject. The individual becomes absorbed into the *system of signs* that constitutes hyper reality, losing any sense of agency or autonomy. In a world where simulations replace direct experience, the subject is reduced to a passive receiver of images, disconnected from any authentic relationship to the world or to itself. Baudrillard argues that this leads to a form of *alienation*, where individuals no longer experience the world as something real or meaningful but as a series of *performances* and *representations*.

In a hyperreal world, the subject's sense of identity becomes increasingly fragile. Because identity is constructed through the consumption of images and signs, it is constantly in flux, shaped by the *simulations* that dominate contemporary life. The subject becomes a *floating signifier*, an entity that is defined not by any intrinsic qualities but by its place within the system of signs. This leads to the disappearance of the subject as a stable, autonomous being and the emergence of the subject as a *simulacrum*—a representation that has no real foundation.

The Death of the Autonomous Subject

Baudrillard's critique of the *disappearance of the subject* also extends to the concept of *autonomy* and *agency*. In modern philosophy, the subject is typically seen as an agent capable of making decisions, taking action, and shaping its own destiny. However, Baudrillard argues that in the postmodern world, the subject's autonomy is undermined by the systems of *control* and *simulation* that define contemporary life.

One of the key forces that undermine the autonomy of the subject is *consumer capitalism*. In a consumer society, individuals are conditioned to believe that their choices define who they are. However, Baudrillard argues that these choices are not truly autonomous because they are determined by the *logic of the market*. The subject's desires, preferences, and actions are shaped by advertising, social norms, and the demands of the consumer economy. This creates an illusion of freedom, where individuals believe they are making independent choices, but in reality, they are simply responding to the *signs* and *images* presented to them by the media and the market.

This loss of autonomy is compounded by the rise of *digital technologies* and *algorithmic systems* that increasingly shape human behavior. In the digital world, individuals are constantly monitored, their data collected and analyzed by algorithms that predict and influence their actions. Baudrillard's concept of *simulation* anticipates this development, as individuals' experiences are mediated and shaped by digital systems that construct their reality. In this environment, the subject's sense of agency is further eroded, as people's choices are guided not by their own desires or intentions but by the *algorithms* that govern their online interactions.

Baudrillard also critiques the ways in which political and social systems contribute to the disappearance of the subject. In his view, modern politics has become a *spectacle*, where individuals are reduced to passive observers of political events rather than active participants. The media transforms political life into a *performance*, where the public is encouraged to consume political images and sound bites rather than engage in meaningful political action. This leads to the erosion of *political agency*, as the subject is no longer an active agent in shaping society but a consumer of political representations.

Identity as a Performance and the Loss of Authenticity

Another dimension of Baudrillard's analysis is the idea that *identity* in the postmodern world has become a form of *performance*. In a society dominated by images and simulations, individuals construct their identities through the *performance of roles* that are dictated by the media, consumer culture, and social expectations. The self is no longer something *authentic* or intrinsic; it is something that is *performed* for an audience, constantly shaped by the gaze of others.

Baudrillard's critique of identity performance resonates with contemporary discussions of *social media*, where individuals carefully curate their online personas to project a particular image. On platforms like Instagram or Twitter, users perform their identities through the selection of images, language, and interactions that are designed to generate *likes*, *follows*, and *social approval*. In this environment, identity becomes a *commodity* that is bought, sold, and traded in the marketplace of attention.

The result, Baudrillard argues, is the disappearance of *authentic identity*. The self is no longer something that emerges from within but something that is constructed through external signs and simulations. This leads to a profound sense of *alienation*, where individuals feel disconnected from their true selves, caught in a cycle of performing identities that are shaped by the expectations of the market and the media. The subject becomes a *simulacrum*—a representation that has no real foundation in reality, only in the system of signs and performances that constitute the hyperreal world.

Conclusion: Baudrillard and the Vanishing Subject

Jean Baudrillard's critique of the disappearance of the subject offers a powerful analysis of how the forces of *media*, *consumerism*, and *simulation* have transformed the nature of identity and agency in the **postmodern world**. Baudrillard's argument that the subject has been fragmented, commodified, and ultimately *displaced* by the logic of *hyper reality* challenges traditional notions of individual autonomy, identity, and selfhood. In a world where signs, images, and simulations dominate, the subject no longer possesses a stable sense of self or meaningful agency. Instead, identity becomes fluid, shaped by external forces that dictate how individuals should *perform* and *consume* their way through life.

The Hyperreal Subject: A Life of Representation

One of Baudrillard's most striking observations is that the subject, in the postmodern condition, lives primarily through *representations*. The modern world is no longer one in which individuals experience reality in a direct, unmediated way. Instead, people engage with the world through *media* and *consumer culture*, which construct and mediate their reality. The subject is bombarded with images and signs from the media, advertising, and social platforms, which dictate how they should feel, behave, and define themselves.

In this hyperreal environment, the subject's experience of life is no longer grounded in *direct encounters* with reality but in interactions with *simulated* versions of reality. For example, consumer culture offers people a series of *pre-packaged experiences*—from vacations to meals to lifestyle choices—that are presented as idealized versions of life.

These experiences are not authentic or spontaneous; they are carefully curated simulations that conform to cultural expectations and media-driven fantasies. The subject, in turn, consumes these simulations in an effort to construct meaning in their life, but this meaning is inherently *empty*, as it is based on the consumption of *signs* rather than genuine experiences.

Baudrillard's analysis of the hyperreal subject also critiques the *loss of depth* in human experience. In a world where images and signs take precedence over reality, people engage with life on a superficial level. They become passive spectators, more concerned with how they are *perceived* by others than with how they truly *experience* the world. The subject's internal life—their emotions, desires, and thoughts—becomes secondary to the *performance* of identity in front of an audience, whether that audience is society at large or a curated group of followers on social media.

Alienation in the Age of Simulation

The *alienation* of the subject is a recurring theme in Baudrillard's critique. In the postmodern world, the subject is alienated not only from reality but also from themselves. This alienation arises because the self is constantly mediated through external signs and simulations, leading to a *disconnection* between the individual's true sense of identity and the identities they perform in the public sphere. The subject is always in the process of *self-construction*, using the tools provided by consumer culture to craft an image of themselves that aligns with social expectations.

This process of constructing a simulated self leads to a form of existential *displacement*. The individual can no longer access a sense of *authentic identity* because their sense of self is fractured by the *hyperreal environment* they inhabit. The subject becomes trapped in a cycle of *performing roles* dictated by the market and media, leading to a profound sense of *detachment* from any real sense of self.

Baudrillard's critique of alienation also ties into his analysis of *consumer capitalism*. The relentless pressure to consume—to buy products, experiences, and identities—leaves the subject in a state of *perpetual dissatisfaction*. In a world where fulfillment is promised but never delivered, individuals are constantly seeking out new signs, new commodities, and new experiences in the hope of achieving a sense of completeness. Yet this search is *endless* and *unattainable*, as the consumption of signs only reinforces the cycle of desire without providing any real satisfaction. As a result, the subject remains *alienated*—from their desires, from society, and from themselves.

Baudrillard's Rejection of the Authentic Subject

Baudrillard takes a provocative stance by arguing that the *authentic subject*—the coherent, autonomous individual who can act meaningfully in the world—may never have existed in the first place. For Baudrillard, the idea of an authentic subject is itself a *simulation*, a construct of modernist thought that has been rendered obsolete by the rise of postmodernity. The notion of the subject as a stable, autonomous individual with a unified identity is an illusion that has been shattered by the proliferation of simulations, signs, and representations.

In Baudrillard's view, the postmodern world does not allow for the possibility of *authenticity*. The subject is always already embedded in a world of representations, where identity is something that is constantly constructed and reconstructed in response to external forces. Authenticity, in this sense, is a *fantasy* that belongs to the *modernist* era—a time when the subject was seen as a rational, self-determined individual. In the postmodern condition, the subject is fragmented and dispersed, lacking any stable foundation on which to build an authentic self.

Baudrillard's rejection of the authentic subject is closely tied to his critique of *nostalgia* for a lost sense of reality. He argues that in the postmodern world, any attempt to recover an authentic sense of self or reality is futile, as these concepts have been rendered meaningless by the dominance of *simulation*. The search for authenticity is just another form of consumption, another desire manufactured by the system of signs that governs modern life. The subject, Baudrillard argues, must come to terms with the fact that they are always already a *product of simulation*, and that any attempt to recover a real, authentic self is an illusion.

Identity as a Commodity

One of Baudrillard's most significant contributions to the critique of contemporary capitalism is his analysis of *identity as a commodity*. In the consumer society, identity itself becomes something that can be bought, sold, and exchanged. People are encouraged to construct their identities through the consumption of *products*, *brands*, and *lifestyles*, each of which carries a specific set of symbolic meanings. These identities are not intrinsic to the individual but are instead part of the *marketplace of signs* that constitutes the modern world.

For Baudrillard, the commodification of identity represents a profound shift in how individuals understand themselves. In the past, identity was something that emerged from within, shaped by personal experience, values, and relationships. In the consumer society, however, identity is something that is *constructed externally*, through the consumption of *signs* and *images* provided by the market. This creates a situation where the individual's sense of self is always contingent upon the commodities they consume, and where identity is constantly in flux, shaped by the demands of consumer culture.

This process of *self-commodification* is particularly evident in the world of *social media*, where individuals curate and present their identities as commodities to be consumed by others. Social media platforms encourage users to present highly idealized versions of themselves, crafting identities that are designed to attract attention, gain followers, and generate *social capital*. In this environment, identity becomes a form of *currency*, exchanged in the marketplace of attention for validation, status, or influence.

The Vanishing Subject and the Future of Identity

As the subject disappears in Baudrillard's hyperreal world, the question arises: What becomes of identity in the future? Baudrillard suggests that identity will continue to fragment and dissolve as the boundaries between the real and the simulated become increasingly blurred. In a world where simulations replace direct experiences, identity will be something that is constantly performed, constantly *constructed* and *deconstructed* in response to the demands of the marketplace and the media.

The future of identity, in Baudrillard's view, may involve a further erosion of the distinction between the self and the *representations* of the self. As digital technologies become more advanced, and as virtual and augmented realities become more integrated into daily life, the self will become even more *immersed* in simulations. The line between the real and the virtual will become increasingly difficult to discern, and the subject will find themselves living in a world where their identity is always a performance, always a simulation, never fully grounded in reality.

Conclusion: The Disappearance of the Subject in a Simulated World

Jean Baudrillard's analysis of the *disappearance of the subject* offers a critical perspective on how the forces of *media, consumerism,* and *hyper reality* have transformed the nature of identity and agency in the postmodern world. The subject, once understood as a coherent, autonomous individual, has been fragmented, commodified, and ultimately dissolved by the endless circulation of signs and images that define contemporary life.

In Baudrillard's hyperreal world, the subject no longer possesses a stable sense of self or meaningful agency. Instead, identity is something that is *performed* and *constructed* through the consumption of commodities, the curation of online personas, and the engagement with simulations. The subject is no longer an agent of meaning but a passive participant in a system of signs that constructs reality for them.

Baudrillard's critique of the disappearance of the subject challenges us to reconsider what it means to be an individual in a world dominated by *representations* and *performances*. As simulations continue to blur the boundaries between the real and the virtual, the future of the subject—and of identity itself—remains uncertain, shaped by the forces of *hyper reality* and the systems of control that govern modern life.

The Role of Desire in a Simulated Society

In Jean Baudrillard's philosophy, *desire* plays a central role in his critique of *consumer culture*, *capitalism*, and *hyper reality*. Baudrillard argues that in the postmodern world, desire is no longer driven by genuine needs or the pursuit of real fulfillment but is instead manipulated, manufactured, and endlessly deferred by the mechanisms of *simulation* and *media*. In a simulated society, desire is not a natural or internal force but a product of the *consumer system*, where individuals are encouraged to desire images, signs, and commodities that ultimately have no connection to reality or satisfaction. Baudrillard's exploration of desire reveals how it fuels the *endless cycle of consumption* and how it is central to the way individuals relate to themselves and the world in the hyperreal age.

The Shift from Real Needs to Simulated Desires

One of Baudrillard's key insights is that in a *consumer society*, desire has been fundamentally transformed. In earlier stages of human history, desire was often linked to *real needs*—the need for food, shelter, security, or social connection. However, Baudrillard argues that under modern capitalism, these basic needs have been replaced by an economy of *simulated desires*. Instead of desiring things for their use or material value, people desire the *symbolic meanings* attached to commodities. These meanings are created and manipulated by the forces of *advertising*, *media*, and *consumer culture*.

In Baudrillard's view, this shift is crucial to understanding the dynamics of consumer society. The consumer is not driven by *rational needs* but by *irrational desires*, which are constantly stimulated and reshaped by the system of signs that permeates everyday life. For instance, people no longer simply buy a car because they need transportation; they buy a specific brand of car because of the *status*, *identity*, and *lifestyle* it symbolizes. This process creates a cycle where desire is perpetually unfulfilled, as the symbolic value of commodities can never fully satisfy the individual's longing.

The key mechanism in this system is *advertising*, which Baudrillard views as a form of *cultural manipulation*. Advertisements do not simply promote products; they create *desires* by attaching *symbolic meanings* to commodities. These meanings tap into deeper emotional and psychological longings, promising happiness, success, beauty, or love through the act of consumption. However, these promises are never fully realized, as the satisfaction offered by commodities is always *illusory* and short-lived. As soon as one desire is temporarily fulfilled, another is created, keeping the individual trapped in an endless cycle of consumption.

Desire as a Function of Sign-Value

Baudrillard's concept of *sign-value* is central to his analysis of desire in a simulated society. In traditional economic terms, objects were valued based on their *use-value* (their practical function) or their *exchange-value* (their market price). However, Baudrillard argues that in the consumer society, objects are primarily valued for their *sign-value*—the symbolic meanings they convey in the system of signs. Sign-value turns commodities into symbols of *status*, *identity*, and *social power*, and it is this symbolic dimension that drives desire in the consumer society.

Desire, in Baudrillard's framework, is no longer directed at the object itself but at the *sign* the object represents. A luxury handbag, for example, is not desired for its practical function or craftsmanship but for the *social status* and *identity* it communicates to others. The act of purchasing and displaying such an object becomes a way of *performing identity* and asserting one's place within a specific social order. This transformation of desire from material to symbolic reflects the broader shift in postmodern society, where the real is replaced by the *simulated*.

The system of sign-value creates a situation where desire is always *deferred*, never fully satisfied. Each object purchased satisfies a desire momentarily, but because the value of the object is tied to its symbolic meaning rather than its utility, the satisfaction it provides is fleeting. The individual is left continually seeking new objects to fulfill their ever-shifting desires, creating an *endless cycle* of consumption where desire is perpetually reignited but never truly quenched.

The Role of Media and Advertising in Shaping Desire

Baudrillard's critique of desire in a simulated society places significant emphasis on the role of *media* and *advertising* in shaping and controlling what individuals desire. In Baudrillard's analysis, media does not simply reflect or report reality; it actively *constructs reality*, including the reality of desire. Through constant exposure to images, narratives, and symbols, the media creates a world where individuals are taught to desire specific *lifestyles*, *products*, and *identities*.

Advertising, in particular, functions as a key mechanism for creating *simulated desires*. Advertisements do not just promote the material qualities of a product; they sell *dreams*, *fantasies*, and *experiences*. The media environment is saturated with idealized images of life, where beauty, success, happiness, and love are all linked to the consumption of certain products. By showing people what they should want—what kind of body they should have, what car they should drive, what kind of house they should live in—advertising creates desires that are based not on reality but on *simulated ideals*.

Baudrillard's analysis reveals how advertising manipulates desire by creating a sense of *lack* or *deficiency* in the consumer. The individual is made to feel incomplete or inadequate without the product being sold, leading them to believe that the act of purchasing the commodity will fill this void. However, because the desire being created is based on a simulation—an image of an ideal life rather than any real need—the satisfaction provided by consumption is never complete. The individual is left continually wanting more, driven by the promises of the media to find fulfillment through the next purchase.

The Hyperreal Nature of Desire

In Baudrillard's theory of *hyper reality*, the line between reality and simulation blurs to the point where simulations become more real than reality itself. In this context, desire takes on a hyperreal quality, where individuals desire not real objects or experiences but the *simulations* of those objects and experiences. The hyperreal nature of desire is evident in how people are drawn to *idealized representations* of life rather than to the reality of their lived experiences.

For example, the desire to travel may be less about the actual experience of visiting new places and more about *performing* the act of travel on social media. People are encouraged to desire the *image* of travel—posting pictures of themselves in exotic locations, participating in the fantasy of the perfect vacation—rather than the reality of the trip itself. In this sense, desire is no longer connected to authentic experiences but to the *representation* of experiences, which exist primarily for others to consume.

This hyperreal desire is also evident in the way people relate to *celebrity culture*, where individuals desire to live the lives of the famous not because of any real understanding of those lives but because of the *media representation* of celebrity. The images of wealth, glamour, and success presented by the media create desires that are entirely detached from the reality of being a celebrity. People desire to participate in the simulation of fame, seeking to emulate the images they see on television or social media, rather than engaging with the actual challenges or complexities of those lives.

The Endless Deferral of Desire

One of Baudrillard's most critical insights into desire is the idea that it is perpetually *deferred* in the consumer society. In traditional terms, desire is something that can be fulfilled—once a person's basic needs are met, they experience satisfaction. However, in Baudrillard's simulated society, desire is never fully satisfied. The system is designed to constantly create new desires as soon as old ones are fulfilled, ensuring that the individual remains caught in a loop of perpetual longing.

This deferral of desire is a crucial component of *capitalism*, which relies on the constant production and consumption of goods. By creating a system in which individuals are never fully satisfied, capitalism ensures the continuation of *economic growth* and *profit*. The market thrives on creating new commodities that promise to satisfy desires, but because these desires are based on *simulated ideals*, they can never be fully realized. As a result, people are left in a state of perpetual *dissatisfaction*, always seeking the next object or experience that will finally bring fulfillment.

Baudrillard argues that this process of deferral has significant *psychological* and *existential* consequences. Individuals in a simulated society are constantly seeking meaning through consumption, but because the objects of their desire are never real or stable, they experience a profound sense of *alienation*. This alienation manifests as a feeling of emptiness or disconnection from the world, as the subject's desires are shaped by external forces that have little to do with their inner reality.

Desire and the Loss of Authenticity

In Baudrillard's critique, desire in the simulated society leads to the *loss of authenticity*. As desire becomes shaped by the consumption of signs and simulations, the individual's connection to their true needs, emotions, and identity is weakened. People are encouraged to desire what society tells them to want, leading to a situation where their desires are no longer a reflection of their genuine selves but a product of external manipulation.

This loss of authenticity is evident in the way individuals perform their identities through consumption. In the consumer society, people define themselves not by who they are but by what they buy, wear, and consume. Baudrillard argues that this commodification of identity leads to a hollow existence, where the self is constantly constructed and reconstructed through the act of consumption. The subject becomes dependent on external objects, images, and experiences to define themselves, losing any sense of a stable, authentic identity. This creates a profound sense of *alienation*, as individuals are no longer grounded in their own experiences or inner desires but are instead shaped by the constantly shifting demands of *consumerism* and *media representation*.

In Baudrillard's view, the *loss of authenticity* is a direct consequence of the way desire is manipulated in a simulated society. Individuals are taught to desire not what is real or meaningful to them, but what the *market* and *media* dictate. This creates a disconnection between the self and its desires, where people pursue superficial symbols of success, happiness, or identity, believing that they will find fulfillment in these simulations. However, because these desires are artificial, they can never lead to true satisfaction, leaving individuals in a constant state of *restlessness* and *longing*.

Desire and the Perpetuation of the Consumer Society

Baudrillard's critique of desire goes hand in hand with his analysis of how the *consumer society* perpetuates itself. The ability of capitalism to continuously generate new desires is what allows the system to sustain itself over time. By keeping individuals in a state of *perpetual dissatisfaction*, capitalism ensures that there is always a market for new products, services, and experiences. Desire, in this context, becomes the *engine of consumption*, driving people to continually seek out new commodities in the hope of finding satisfaction, even though that satisfaction is always out of reach.

The role of desire in sustaining consumerism is particularly evident in the world of *fashion*, *technology*, and *lifestyle products*. These industries thrive on the creation of *ephemeral trends* and *status symbols*, where desire is directed not at the intrinsic value of the product but at the *image* it projects. Fashion, for example, operates on the principle of constant change, where individuals are encouraged to desire the *latest trends*, even though those trends will soon be replaced by new ones. Technology operates in a similar way, where each new device or upgrade promises greater satisfaction but quickly becomes obsolete, leading consumers to desire the next iteration.

This cycle of desire and consumption is what Baudrillard refers to as the *perpetual deferral of meaning*. In a simulated society, individuals are never allowed to rest in their desires or to feel fully satisfied with what they have. Instead, they are kept in a state of *constant anticipation*, always looking toward the next object, the next experience, or the next identity that will finally complete them. However, this completion is never realized, as the consumer society is structured to keep desire alive and unfulfilled.

Desire and the Spectacle

Baudrillard also links the concept of desire to his critique of the *spectacle*, a term he borrowed and expanded from Guy Debord's *The Society of the Spectacle*. In Baudrillard's view, modern society has transformed into a *spectacle* where images and representations dominate every aspect of life, and desire is a key component of this transformation. The spectacle works by producing *fantasies* and *illusions* that captivate the individual, encouraging them to desire the *images* rather than the real.

In the world of the spectacle, desire is constantly directed toward *simulated realities*—whether through advertising, entertainment, or media representation. Individuals are taught to desire the *performance* of a certain lifestyle, the *illusion* of beauty, or the *appearance* of success. These desires are never about real, lived experiences but about the *image* of those experiences as portrayed in the media. For example, people may desire to live like celebrities, not because they understand what that life truly entails, but because the media presents it as the ultimate form of success and happiness.

This desire for the spectacle creates a passive consumer, one who is continually drawn into the world of *media representation* without questioning its authenticity. The spectacle functions by keeping people *entertained*, *distracted*, and *desiring* more, preventing them from engaging with reality or questioning the underlying structures of power and control. Baudrillard argues that desire, in this context, is not a liberating force but a tool of control, used to keep individuals aligned with the interests of the *consumer economy*.

Desire and Alienation

Ultimately, Baudrillard's analysis of desire in a simulated society leads to a deeper understanding of *alienation*. In a world where desire is continually manipulated and deferred, individuals become *alienated* from their true selves, their communities, and their reality. Desire, instead of being a force that connects individuals to what they truly need or want, becomes a means of *disconnection*, as people are driven to pursue simulations that have no grounding in real experience.

This alienation is exacerbated by the *hyperreal environment* in which individuals live. In a world where signs, images, and simulations replace direct engagement with reality, desire becomes a force that pulls people away from authentic experiences and into the world of representation. People become *consumers of signs* rather than active agents in their own lives, constantly seeking meaning through consumption but never finding it.

Baudrillard's critique of desire as a source of alienation is particularly relevant in the context of *digital culture* and *social media*. Platforms like Instagram, Facebook, and TikTok encourage users to perform their desires online, projecting idealized versions of their lives for others to consume. This creates a situation where people are not only alienated from their real desires but are also alienated from each other, as social interactions become mediated by *likes*, *follows*, and *shares*, rather than genuine human connection.

The Radical Potential of Desire

Despite his critique of how desire is manipulated in the consumer society, Baudrillard also hints at the *radical potential* of desire. In certain contexts, desire can be seen as a force that resists the structures of control imposed by consumer capitalism. Baudrillard suggests that desire, if freed from the system of *simulation* and *commodification*, could become a form of *radical disruption*, challenging the social and economic order that seeks to manipulate and contain it.

This potential lies in the idea that desire is fundamentally unpredictable and uncontrollable. While consumer capitalism seeks to channel desire into *safe* and *profitable* avenues—such as the consumption of products and services—there is always the possibility that desire will escape these constraints and manifest in *unexpected* or *revolutionary* ways. Baudrillard's work invites us to imagine what it would mean to reclaim desire from the forces of commodification, to desire not what the market tells us to want, but what we truly need to live meaningful and authentic lives.

Conclusion: Desire in a Simulated Society

Jean Baudrillard's critique of desire in a simulated society offers a powerful analysis of how *consumer culture*, *media*, and *capitalism* shape and manipulate what individuals want. In the postmodern world, desire is no longer directed at real needs or experiences but is instead constructed through the consumption of *signs* and *simulations*. This creates a society in which individuals are trapped in an endless cycle of consumption, constantly desiring new objects, images, and identities that promise fulfillment but never deliver it.

Baudrillard's analysis of desire reveals the deep *alienation* that individuals experience in a consumer society, where their desires are not their own but are imposed by external forces. At the same time, Baudrillard suggests that desire holds the potential for *radical disruption*, offering a way to resist the structures of control that seek to contain it. By understanding the role of desire in a simulated society, we can begin to question the ways in which our own desires are shaped and manipulated, and perhaps imagine new forms of desire that are rooted in *authentic* experience rather than simulation.

Baudrillard's Views on Democracy and Power

Jean Baudrillard's critique of *democracy* and *power* offers a radical and often unsettling perspective on contemporary political systems, particularly in the context of the postmodern condition. Baudrillard argues that modern democracy, rather than being an authentic expression of popular will, has become a *simulation*—a system that operates more as a *media spectacle* and a *performance* of political ideals than as a genuine engagement with governance and decision-making. He suggests that democracy, as it functions today, has been emptied of meaning and reduced to a symbolic ritual that masks the true dynamics of power. Baudrillard's view of power is similarly critical; he sees power as increasingly *diffuse* and *spectacular*, operating through *media manipulation*, *simulation*, and *spectacle* rather than through direct forms of authority or coercion.

Democracy as a Simulation

For Baudrillard, democracy in its current form is a *simulacrum*—a representation of democracy that has lost its connection to any real political engagement or participation. In a simulated democracy, elections, political campaigns, and media debates function as *performances* designed to give the appearance of democratic choice, but they do not offer real agency to citizens. Baudrillard argues that these political rituals serve to maintain the illusion that people have control over their governments and futures, while the actual mechanisms of power operate independently of public will.

Baudrillard's analysis suggests that modern democracy is more concerned with the *representation* of choice than with the substance of governance. The rituals of voting and political debate are highly mediated, with politicians and parties crafting their images and platforms to appeal to a broad electorate through the media. However, this process is less about genuine political engagement and more about the *performance of democracy* as a spectacle. Baudrillard's critique implies that in this mediated democracy, voters are no longer choosing between meaningful alternatives but are instead participating in a *pre-scripted drama*, where the outcomes are largely predetermined by the structures of power that operate behind the scenes.

This view reflects Baudrillard's broader skepticism of *representation* in the postmodern world. Just as *media* and *advertising* produce simulations of reality that replace the real, democratic processes are similarly simulated, offering an illusion of participation without any real impact on the political or economic systems that govern society. Baudrillard argues that democracy, as a *hyperreal construct*, has been hollowed out, becoming a mere representation of itself.

The Spectacle of Politics

Baudrillard's concept of the *spectacle* is central to his critique of democracy and power. He argues that politics, in the postmodern era, has been transformed into a *media spectacle*, where image and performance take precedence over substance. Politicians are no longer primarily concerned with governance or policy but with managing their public image and media presence. Elections, debates, and political campaigns are staged events, designed to entertain and captivate the public rather than to foster meaningful political discourse.

In this spectacle, political figures are reduced to *characters* in a media-driven drama. Their success is measured not by their ability to enact policy or lead effectively but by their skill in *performing* for the cameras, engaging in media-friendly sound bites, and shaping their public personas. The media, in turn, amplifies these performances, turning politics into a form of *entertainment* that blurs the lines between reality and fiction. Baudrillard's critique suggests that the public's engagement with politics is increasingly passive, as citizens consume political content in much the same way they consume entertainment, without critically reflecting on the underlying issues or the real workings of power.

Baudrillard also emphasizes how political debates are *simplified* and *sensationalized* for media consumption. Complex issues are reduced to *sound bites*, and political discourse is framed around emotional appeals rather than substantive analysis. This transformation of politics into spectacle leads to a situation where voters are less concerned with policy details and more focused on the *theater of politics*—the personalities, scandals, and dramatic conflicts that play out on television and social media. This creates a political culture where the *appearance of debate* replaces real debate, and where citizens are encouraged to engage with politics on a superficial level, responding to images and emotions rather than critically analyzing the issues.

The Implosion of Meaning in Democracy

Baudrillard's concept of the *implosion of meaning* is closely related to his critique of democracy. He argues that in the postmodern world, meaning itself has become unstable and fragmented, and this applies as much to politics as it does to other areas of life. In the context of democracy, the implosion of meaning manifests as a collapse of the distinction between *political reality* and *political representation*. Political symbols, rhetoric, and media performances circulate endlessly, but they no longer refer to any coherent political reality. As a result, democracy loses its meaning as a system of governance and becomes a *ritualistic performance* that sustains the illusion of popular sovereignty.

In Baudrillard's view, the collapse of meaning in democracy is tied to the rise of *media saturation*. The constant flow of political images and messages through television, social media, and the internet creates a situation where political discourse is *fragmented* and *diffused*. Citizens are exposed to an overwhelming number of political messages, each competing for attention, but none of these messages offer a clear or coherent narrative. This saturation leads to a sense of *political fatigue*, where individuals become desensitized to political issues and disengage from the democratic process.

Baudrillard's critique of the implosion of meaning also extends to the *structure of elections* and political choices. He argues that the distinction between political parties and ideologies has become increasingly *blurred*, as all parties operate within the same framework of media spectacle and consumer culture. The ideological differences between candidates are reduced to marketing strategies, and the choice between parties becomes a choice between *brands* rather than between fundamentally different visions of society. This collapse of political distinction leads to a form of *political cynicism*, where voters recognize the hollowness of the choices presented to them but continue to participate in the democratic process because there are no alternatives.

The Diffusion of Power

Baudrillard's analysis of power is as complex and radical as his critique of democracy. He argues that in the postmodern world, power has become *diffuse* and *decentered*. Traditional forms of authority—such as the power of the state, corporations, or institutions—still exist, but they no longer function in the same direct, coercive manner as in earlier periods of history. Instead, power operates through *media*, *representation*, and *simulation*, shaping public consciousness and social behavior in more subtle and pervasive ways.

Baudrillard suggests that power in the postmodern world is no longer about *domination* or *control* through direct means but about the ability to *shape reality* through *media manipulation* and *spectacle*. The power of media, advertising, and entertainment lies in their capacity to create a *simulated reality* that defines how people see the world and understand their place within it. This power is diffuse because it does not reside in a single institution or individual but operates through the entire system of signs, images, and representations that constitute modern society.

In this diffuse system of power, individuals are not directly coerced but are subtly conditioned to conform to the norms and expectations produced by the media and consumer culture. Power becomes a matter of *persuasion* and *seduction* rather than force, and individuals are encouraged to internalize the values of the system through their participation in consumerism, media consumption, and the performance of identity. Baudrillard's concept of power is therefore closely linked to his critique of *hyper reality*, where the boundary between the real and the simulated blurs, and individuals become passive participants in a reality constructed by external forces.

The Erosion of Political Resistance

Baudrillard's critique of democracy and power also addresses the problem of *political resistance*. In his view, the diffusion of power and the rise of hyper reality make it increasingly difficult for traditional forms of political resistance to challenge the system. Resistance movements, whether they are based on ideology, protest, or revolution, are quickly *absorbed* and *neutralized* by the very system they seek to oppose.

Baudrillard argues that modern systems of power are highly adaptable and capable of *co-opting* resistance movements by turning them into part of the *media spectacle*. For example, protest movements are often *commodified* and transformed into media events, where their radical potential is diluted by the very process of representation. The media frames protests as spectacles, focusing on the drama of the event rather than the substance of the movement's demands. This leads to a situation where resistance is *performed* for the media but fails to challenge the underlying structures of power.

Moreover, Baudrillard suggests that in a world dominated by simulation, even the idea of political revolution has lost its meaning. In earlier periods of history, revolution was seen as a way to fundamentally transform society, but in the postmodern condition, revolution has become just another *media narrative* or *symbolic act*. The system of power, according to Baudrillard, is no longer vulnerable to direct challenge because it operates through the mechanisms of *simulation* and *spectacle*, which absorb and neutralize any attempt at real change.

Conclusion: Baudrillard's Radical Critique of Democracy and Power

Jean Baudrillard's views on democracy and power present a radical departure from traditional political theory. His critique of democracy as a *simulacrum*—a representation that has lost its connection to real political engagement—challenges the very foundations of modern political systems. For Baudrillard, democracy has become a *media spectacle*, where political choices are reduced to performances, and power is diffused through *media manipulation* and *hyperreal simulations*. In this context, the traditional mechanisms of political participation, such as voting or protest, lose their meaning and become part of the *ritualistic performance* that sustains the illusion of democratic control. Baudrillard's views challenge us to reconsider the nature of power in the postmodern world, where political realities are increasingly constructed and mediated by signs and symbols rather than by genuine engagement or democratic decision-making.

Power as a System of Control Through Simulation

In Baudrillard's view, power no longer operates through direct domination or overt control, as in earlier historical periods. Instead, power in the postmodern world functions through *indirect means*—through the *control of representations*, *images*, and *information*. The media and consumer culture play a pivotal role in maintaining this system of power by continuously creating and circulating simulations of reality that shape how individuals perceive the world, themselves, and their place within society.

This form of power is particularly effective because it operates through *seduction* rather than coercion. Individuals are *encouraged* to participate in the system, often without recognizing the ways in which their thoughts, desires, and actions are being shaped by external forces. The consumption of media and commodities creates a sense of freedom and choice, but Baudrillard argues that this freedom is *illusory*. In reality, individuals are locked into a system of *pre-scripted choices* that keep them aligned with the interests of power structures. The system relies on the ability to *generate desire*—whether for products, lifestyles, or political ideologies—that reinforces the existing order.

The Paradox of Freedom in Democracy

Baudrillard's critique of modern democracy extends to the *paradox of freedom*. He argues that while contemporary democracies claim to offer citizens freedom, this freedom is largely confined to the *realm of consumption* and *media-driven choices*. People are free to choose between various political candidates, products, or lifestyle options, but these choices are shaped by the *media, advertising*, and *consumer culture* in ways that reinforce the status quo. In this sense, freedom in a postmodern democracy becomes a *performance* rather than a substantive political reality.

Baudrillard's concept of *hyper reality* comes into play here. In hyperreal democracies, the *illusion of freedom* is maintained through the spectacle of choice—voters are given the option to choose between candidates or parties, but these options are often devoid of meaningful difference. The differences that do exist are largely symbolic, existing within a narrow framework defined by media narratives and political branding. The act of voting becomes a *symbolic ritual* that reinforces the appearance of democracy without allowing for real political engagement or systemic change.

The Collapse of Political Meaning

Baudrillard's concept of the *implosion of meaning* also applies to his analysis of democracy and power. He suggests that in a society dominated by *media spectacle* and *consumerism*, political language and symbols have lost their meaning. The constant circulation of political images, sound bites, and scandals creates a situation where political discourse becomes fragmented and superficial. In this environment, the public is bombarded with *political signs*—candidates' speeches, media debates, election coverage—but these signs no longer refer to any coherent political reality.

The result is what Baudrillard calls the *implosion of political meaning*, where the boundary between reality and representation collapses, and it becomes increasingly difficult to distinguish between what is real and what is simulated. Political events are staged for the media, and the line between *political action* and *media spectacle* blurs. For example, election campaigns become more about managing *public perception* than about articulating coherent policies or addressing substantive issues. In this sense, democracy, as Baudrillard sees it, becomes a process of *image management* rather than a mechanism for genuine political participation or change.

The Media's Role in Sustaining Power

In Baudrillard's analysis, the media plays a central role in sustaining power by shaping public perceptions of *politics, democracy*, and *reality* itself. The media functions as a *mediator* between the political system and the public, but rather than providing transparency or fostering critical debate, it *creates and controls* the images and narratives that define political reality. News, political coverage, and debates are all framed in ways that reinforce the spectacle of democracy, keeping the public engaged with the performance of politics while obscuring the underlying mechanisms of power.

Baudrillard is particularly critical of how the media *frames political conflict* and *dissent*. In his view, even acts of political resistance are co-opted by the media, which transforms them into part of the spectacle. Protests, uprisings, and social movements are covered by the media not as threats to the political order but as *events* to be consumed by viewers. This process of *mediatization* strips resistance of its radical potential, turning it into just another form of entertainment. In doing so, the media *neutralizes dissent* by reducing it to a spectacle, reinforcing the power structures it purportedly critiques.

This leads to a situation where individuals feel a sense of *political fatigue* or *disengagement*. The overwhelming amount of political content, much of it framed as entertainment or spectacle, leaves people feeling alienated from the political process. Baudrillard's critique implies that the media's role in producing political hyper reality fosters a form of *passive participation*, where individuals consume politics as they would any other form of media content, without the ability to engage meaningfully with the issues or affect real change.

Power and Control in the Digital Age

Baudrillard's critique of power and democracy is especially relevant in the context of the *digital age*. The rise of the internet, social media, and algorithm-driven content has further transformed the ways in which power operates and how individuals interact with political systems. Baudrillard's ideas anticipate the *surveillance capitalism* of the 21st century, where power is exercised not only through traditional political institutions but through the *collection and manipulation of data*.

In the digital world, power is increasingly exercised through *algorithms* that shape what people see, read, and experience online. Social media platforms, for example, control the flow of information by using algorithms to prioritize certain types of content over others. This creates *echo chambers* where individuals are exposed primarily to information that aligns with their existing beliefs, reinforcing *confirmation bias* and deepening political polarization. Baudrillard's critique of simulation and spectacle applies here, as the digital realm becomes a space where reality is increasingly constructed by the *algorithms* that curate individuals' experiences of the world.

Moreover, the digital age has intensified the *commodification of identity*, as individuals participate in creating and consuming political and social identities online. People construct *digital personas* through social media, performing their political beliefs and affiliations in ways that often align with the logic of consumerism. Political engagement in the digital space is often reduced to symbolic acts, such as *liking, sharing*, or *retweeting* content, rather than engaging in substantive political action. In this sense, Baudrillard's concept of the hyperreal subject is expanded to include the ways in which digital platforms mediate political participation and identity.

Jean Baudrillard's critique of *democracy* and *power* offers a radical and often unsettling perspective on the functioning of political systems in the postmodern world. His analysis challenges the very foundations of modern democracy, arguing that it has become a *simulation*—a performance that gives the illusion of popular sovereignty while concealing the real mechanisms of control. Power, in Baudrillard's view, operates through *media manipulation, spectacle*, and *simulation*, shaping public consciousness and controlling individuals through the creation of hyperreal realities.

Baudrillard's views force us to question the nature of political participation, freedom, and resistance in a world dominated by media and consumer culture. His critique of democracy as a spectacle reveals the ways in which political processes have been hollowed out, reduced to *ritualistic performances* that sustain the appearance of democratic choice without offering any real agency to citizens. Similarly, his analysis of the diffusion of power highlights the challenges of confronting systems of control that operate through *images* and *simulations* rather than direct coercion.

In the digital age, Baudrillard's insights are more relevant than ever, as technology and media continue to reshape the nature of political engagement and power. His critique offers a sobering reflection on the *limits of democracy* in a world where reality itself is increasingly mediated and constructed by external forces, leaving individuals in a state of passive consumption rather than active political participation.

Living in a World without Reality: Baudrillard's Vision

Jean Baudrillard's vision of a *world without reality* is one of the most provocative and challenging elements of his philosophy. He argues that in the postmodern world, *reality* as we traditionally understand it has been replaced by a system of *simulations*, *representations*, and *hyper reality*. In this world, the line between the real and the imaginary is blurred to the point where it is no longer possible to distinguish between them. Baudrillard's idea of living in a world without reality explores the implications of this shift, questioning how individuals can understand themselves, their societies, and the world around them when *authentic experience* is continually mediated and replaced by *signs* and *simulacra*.

The Collapse of the Real

At the heart of Baudrillard's philosophy is the claim that the *real* has collapsed under the weight of *simulations*. In earlier stages of history, reality was something that could be experienced directly. Events, objects, and experiences were understood in terms of their *immediacy* and their *material presence*. However, with the rise of *media*, *technology*, and *consumer culture*, reality has been replaced by *representations*—images, signs, and narratives that stand in for the real but ultimately disconnect us from it.

Baudrillard introduces the concept of *simulacra* to explain this transformation. Simulacra are *copies* or *representations* that no longer refer to an original reality. In his view, postmodern society is characterized by the proliferation of simulacra, where representations circulate freely and become more real than the reality they claim to represent. This leads to a condition of *hyper reality*, where simulations dominate experience, and the real is either forgotten or dissolved into the endless play of signs.

For example, consider the way *news media* often frames events. Rather than directly representing an event, the media creates a *narrative* around it, constructing a version of reality that fits its own agenda or satisfies the desires of its audience. In Baudrillard's terms, this narrative becomes more real than the event itself, as people begin to relate to the simulation (the media's version) rather than the real event. The result is a society where individuals live in a world of *representations* that are detached from any underlying reality, yet these representations shape their perceptions, beliefs, and actions.

The Hyperreal World

In a world without reality, *hyper reality* becomes the dominant mode of existence. Hyper reality is the condition in which simulations replace reality to such an extent that the simulations are experienced as more real than reality itself. In this hyperreal world, people no longer interact with the *real* but with *representations* of the real, and these representations shape their experiences and identities.

One of the most obvious examples of hyper reality is found in *theme parks* like Disneyland, which Baudrillard discusses in his work. Disneyland is not a representation of reality; it is a simulated world that creates an experience that feels more real than reality. It is a meticulously constructed environment designed to evoke specific emotions and desires, but its appeal lies in its *artificiality*. Visitors to Disneyland do not expect authenticity; they are drawn to the carefully curated *fantasy* of the place, which offers a hyperreal experience that transcends the limitations of the real world.

This logic of hyper reality extends far beyond theme parks. In everyday life, people experience hyper reality through *media*, *advertising*, *entertainment*, and *consumer products*. Advertisements, for example, do not sell products based on their material qualities but based on the *fantasies* and *experiences* they promise. The image of a happy family enjoying a meal at a fast-food restaurant is more real, in this sense, than the actual experience of eating fast food. The image creates a sense of fulfillment that transcends the mundane reality of the product, turning consumption into a *simulated experience* of happiness and satisfaction.

The Loss of Authenticity

One of the consequences of living in a world without reality, according to Baudrillard, is the *loss of authenticity*. In traditional societies, authenticity was grounded in the *real*, in direct experience, and in the material world. People's identities, relationships, and experiences were rooted in their connection to real objects, events, and emotions. However, in a hyperreal world, authenticity is replaced by *performance* and *simulation*.

Baudrillard argues that in the postmodern world, people no longer live authentic lives but instead *perform roles* that are shaped by media, advertising, and consumer culture. Social media platforms like Instagram and Facebook provide clear examples of this phenomenon. Individuals carefully curate their online personas, presenting idealized versions of themselves that conform to the expectations of their audience. This curated identity becomes a simulation of the self, detached from the individual's real experiences and emotions. In Baudrillard's terms, the online persona becomes more real than the actual person, as the simulation is consumed, liked, and shared by others in ways that the real person cannot be.

This loss of authenticity extends to *relationships*, *work*, and *politics*. People are increasingly encouraged to engage with the world through simulations rather than through direct interaction with others or with the real world. In politics, for example, voters are more likely to engage with the *image* of a candidate—shaped by media narratives and sound bites—than with the candidate's real policies or actions. In this sense, the political sphere becomes another domain of hyper reality, where the *appearance* of governance takes precedence over the actual workings of power.

The Death of the Subject

Baudrillard's vision of a world without reality also includes the *disappearance of the subject*. In modern philosophy, the subject—the individual as a conscious, autonomous being—was seen as the center of experience and meaning. However, in the hyperreal world, the subject is fragmented and dissolved into the system of *signs* and *representations* that dominate contemporary life.

Baudrillard argues that in a world of simulations, the individual's sense of self is no longer grounded in *authentic experience* or *inner consciousness*. Instead, the self becomes a *floating signifier*, constantly shaped and reshaped by the images, narratives, and symbols that circulate in the media. People construct their identities not based on who they are but on the *representations* of identity provided by consumer culture. This leads to a condition in which the self is constantly *performing* and *projecting* an image for others, but this image has no stable or coherent foundation.

The *disappearance of the subject* is particularly evident in the way people engage with *digital technology* and *social media*. Platforms like Instagram, Twitter, and Facebook encourage individuals to present idealized versions of themselves, crafting their identities in ways that are detached from their real lives. The self becomes a commodity, exchanged for *likes*, *follows*, and *shares*, but in the process, the individual's connection to their true self is lost. The subject is dissolved into the endless flow of images and signs, becoming part of the hyperreal system rather than a distinct, autonomous being.

The End of Meaning

In a world without reality, Baudrillard argues, there is also the *end of meaning*. The collapse of the real into simulation creates a situation where meaning itself becomes unstable and fragmented. In earlier societies, meaning was grounded in *material reality*, in the relationship between objects, people, and events. However, in the hyperreal world, meaning is no longer anchored in reality but is constantly produced and reproduced by the system of *signs* and *representations*.

Baudrillard describes this as the *implosion of meaning*. In the hyperreal world, signs no longer refer to any stable reality or meaning. Instead, they circulate endlessly, detached from any referent, creating a situation where meaning becomes *superficial* and *fleeting*. In the realm of politics, for example, political messages, ideologies, and movements are reduced to *symbolic gestures* that are consumed by the public without any real engagement or understanding. Political events are framed as media spectacles, and the deeper meaning of political actions is lost in the endless play of signs.

This implosion of meaning also affects how individuals understand their own lives. In the hyperreal world, people are bombarded with *images* and *narratives* that offer different versions of success, happiness, and identity, but these versions are all simulations. The result is a sense of *disorientation*, as people are unable to find stable meaning in their own experiences. They are left adrift in a sea of simulations, constantly searching for meaning in a world that no longer provides it.

The Radical Potential of the Hyperreal

Despite the bleakness of Baudrillard's vision of a world without reality, he also suggests that the hyperreal world contains a *radical potential*. Baudrillard often emphasizes the idea of *seduction*, the notion that the hyperreal world, with its endless play of signs and simulations, can also be a space of *resistance* and *disruption*. While the hyperreal may dissolve traditional forms of meaning and reality, it also opens up new possibilities for *subversive forms* of play, where the system of signs can be manipulated and overturned.

Baudrillard suggests that the system of hyper reality is inherently unstable, as it depends on the continuous circulation of signs that have no foundation in the real. This creates opportunities for *resistance*, as individuals can exploit the fluidity and ambiguity of hyper reality to challenge the structures of power and control that operate through media and simulation. In this sense, the world without reality becomes a space where traditional forms of resistance are no longer effective, but where *new forms of subversion* can emerge within the system of simulations itself. Baudrillard's vision of the *radical potential* of the hyperreal world lies in its very instability—the endless circulation of signs, images, and representations offers openings for *disruption*, where individuals and groups can play with, distort, or manipulate the system in ways that challenge the status quo.

The Play of Simulation as Resistance

In the hyperreal world, where reality is replaced by simulation, Baudrillard sees a form of *seduction* and *play* that can be used as a strategy of resistance. Traditional forms of resistance—such as political protests, activism, or ideological critique—often fall into the trap of being absorbed by the system they oppose. Protests are *commodified*, *mediatized*, and transformed into spectacles for public consumption, losing their radical edge. In Baudrillard's view, genuine resistance must take place *within* the logic of simulation, using the tools of hyper reality against itself.

This form of resistance is less about directly confronting power and more about *playing with the system* in a way that exposes its absurdities and contradictions. For example, *culture jamming*—a tactic used by artists and activists to subvert corporate advertising and media—reflects this approach. By mimicking and distorting advertisements, slogans, and images, culture jammers reveal the artificiality and manipulation inherent in consumer culture. This form of play undermines the authority of the system by turning its own mechanisms of control into objects of ridicule or critique.

Baudrillard suggests that such playful subversions can disrupt the flow of hyperreal signs, creating moments of *disruption* where the system of simulation momentarily breaks down. These disruptions may not lead to traditional forms of political change, but they challenge the legitimacy of the system by revealing its artificiality. In this sense, the hyperreal world contains within it the seeds of its own undoing, as the very excess of signs and simulations opens up new spaces for resistance.

Hyper reality and the New Aesthetic

Baudrillard also points to the *aesthetic dimension* of living in a world without reality. In the hyperreal world, art, culture, and aesthetics are no longer concerned with representing the real or conveying deeper meanings. Instead, they become part of the *endless play of signs* that circulate in the postmodern condition. Baudrillard's vision of this new aesthetic is one of *pure surface*, where depth, authenticity, and meaning are abandoned in favor of *spectacle* and *simulation*.

This aesthetic can be seen in contemporary culture, particularly in *digital art*, *virtual reality*, and *fashion*. For Baudrillard, the aesthetic of hyper reality is one where the *artificial* becomes celebrated as an end in itself. The goal is not to represent reality but to create *immersive simulations* that are more compelling, exciting, and engaging than reality itself. In this context, the aesthetic of hyper reality blurs the line between *art* and *everyday life*, as individuals become both *producers* and *consumers* of simulated experiences.

This aesthetic shift is not necessarily negative. Baudrillard suggests that living in a hyperreal world allows for new forms of *creative expression* that are liberated from the constraints of realism or authenticity. In the digital realm, for example, artists can create entirely new worlds, identities, and experiences that transcend the limitations of the material world. This offers a form of *freedom*, where individuals can explore new possibilities of self-expression, identity, and existence in a realm that is no longer bound by the rules of the real.

The Paradox of Living without Reality

Baudrillard's vision of a world without reality presents a profound *paradox*. On the one hand, the collapse of the real into hyper reality leads to a sense of *alienation*, *disorientation*, and *loss of meaning*. Individuals find themselves adrift in a sea of signs, unable to anchor their identities or experiences in any stable reality. The traditional markers of truth, authenticity, and meaning are replaced by simulations that offer only fleeting satisfaction. This creates a world where people are constantly *performing* roles, consuming images, and seeking meaning in places where it can never be fully found.

On the other hand, Baudrillard also suggests that living in a hyperreal world offers a form of *freedom* that was not possible in earlier periods of history. The breakdown of reality creates a space where individuals can *play* with their identities, their experiences, and their relationships in ways that were previously unthinkable. In a world where nothing is real, everything becomes *possible*. This includes the possibility of *reinventing oneself, experimenting with new forms of identity*, and *engaging in creative acts of subversion*.

Baudrillard does not romanticize this freedom, however. He acknowledges the *anxieties* and *uncertainties* that come with living in a world without stable meaning. The hyperreal world is one of *constant flux*, where nothing is permanent and everything is subject to change. In this sense, the freedom offered by hyper reality is a double-edged sword—it offers new possibilities for creative expression and resistance, but it also strips away the comforting certainties of a world grounded in reality.

The Future of Reality in a Hyperreal World

As Baudrillard's vision of a world without reality continues to resonate in the digital age, his insights into hyper reality have only become more relevant. With the rise of *virtual reality*, *augmented reality*, and *artificial intelligence*, the boundary between the real and the simulated has become even more blurred. Technologies like *deepfakes, virtual influencers*, and *immersive digital environments* exemplify Baudrillard's concept of hyper reality, where simulations are increasingly indistinguishable from reality and, in many cases, more compelling than the real itself.

In this future, Baudrillard's vision suggests that individuals will continue to navigate a world where *truth* and *meaning* are constantly in question. The digital realm will offer new opportunities for *identity construction, social interaction*, and *artistic creation*, but it will also pose new challenges for understanding what is real, what is simulated, and what matters. As hyper reality becomes more pervasive, the task of making sense of the world becomes more complex, and the role of the individual becomes more fragmented and uncertain.

At the same time, Baudrillard's notion of *seduction* and *play* offers a way of thinking about how individuals might navigate this hyperreal future. Rather than seeking to return to a lost sense of reality, Baudrillard invites us to embrace the instability and fluidity of the hyperreal, finding new ways to live, resist, and create within its framework. In this sense, living in a world without reality is not simply a loss; it is also an opportunity to explore new forms of existence that are unbound by the traditional limits of truth, meaning, and authenticity.

Conclusion: Baudrillard's Vision of a World without Reality

Jean Baudrillard's vision of a world without reality is both a critique of the *postmodern condition* and an exploration of its *radical potential*. In the hyperreal world, where simulations replace the real, individuals find themselves living in a world of *surface, performance*, and *representation*. The collapse of the real leads to a loss of authenticity, meaning, and stable identity, as people become immersed in a system of signs that shape their perceptions, desires, and actions.

Yet Baudrillard's vision is not entirely pessimistic. He suggests that the hyperreal world also opens up new possibilities for *play, creativity*, and *subversion*. The very instability of hyper reality allows individuals to engage in new forms of *resistance* and *self-expression* that were not possible in a more rigid, reality-bound world. Baudrillard's vision challenges us to rethink how we understand reality, identity, and meaning in the context of a world dominated by simulations, and it invites us to explore new ways of living in a world where the real no longer holds sway.

About the Author

Andrew Parry is a writer whose fascination with the great thinkers, philosophers, and the nature of reality deeply influences his work. His writing is shaped by an enduring curiosity about the fundamental questions of existence—what it means to be human, how we understand the world around us, and the intricate relationships between thought, perception, and reality. Through his exploration of these themes, Andrew seeks to provoke thoughtful reflection and open new pathways of understanding for his readers.

Read more at https://lonetrail.blog.

www.ingramcontent.com/pod-product-compliance
Lightning Source LLC
Chambersburg PA
CBHW081144130726
47996CB00009B/2974